LEGENDARY LOCALS

OF

BOISE

IDAHO

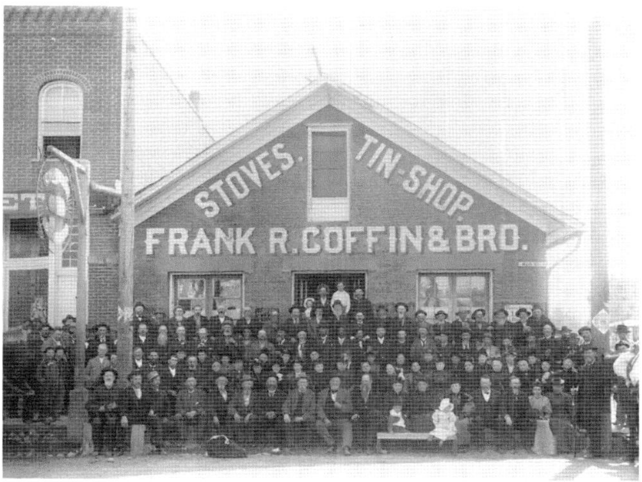

I0806113

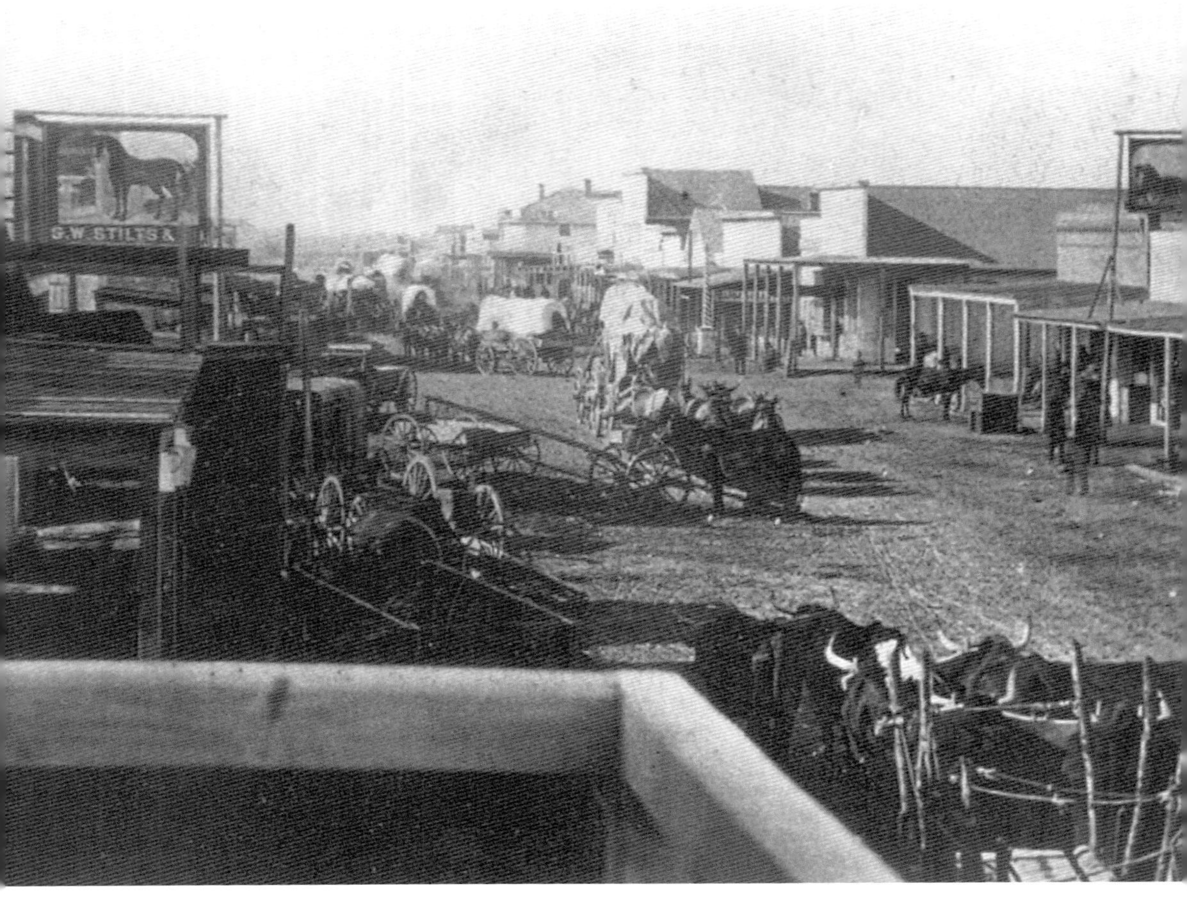

Boise
This is one of the earliest known views of Boise's Main Street, dating to around 1866. (Courtesy of the Idaho State Historical Society.)

Page 1: Pioneers
Boise pioneers gather at Frank Coffin's tin shop near the corner of Eighth and Main Streets in April 1894. The building was demolished not long after this photograph was taken. (Courtesy of the Idaho State Historical Society.)

LEGENDARY LOCALS OF

BOISE

IDAHO

BARBARA PERRY BAUER AND ELIZABETH JACOX

LEGENDARY LOCALS

ISBN 978-1-4671-0166-0

Legendary Locals is an imprint of Arcadia Publishing
Charleston, South Carolina

Printed in the United States of America

Library of Congress Control Number: 2014933472

For all general information, please contact Arcadia Publishing:
Telephone 843-853-2070
Fax 843-853-0044
E-mail sales@arcadiapublishing.com
For customer service and orders:
Toll-Free 1-888-313-2665

Visit us on the Internet at www.arcadiapublishing.com

Dedication
We dedicate our book to all the individuals of the past and present who have created and sustained our beautiful city.

On the Front Cover: Clockwise from top left:
Will Gillet (right) and Kent Collins, Flying M Coffeehouse (courtesy of Melanie Folwell; see page 104), Walter E. Pierce, businessman (courtesy of the Idaho State Historical Society; see page 93), James Pinney, business owner and politician (courtesy of the Idaho State Historical Society; see page 75), Mary Elizabeth Collister, society woman and philanthropist (courtesy of the Idaho State Historical Society; see page 40), Juan (left) and Jimmy Jausoro, musicians (courtesy of the Basque Museum and Cultural Center; see page 82), Elvina Moulton, pioneer and businesswoman (courtesy of the Idaho State Historical Society; see page 18), Cecil Andrus, politician (courtesy of Cecil Andrus; see page 48), William Ridenbaugh, businessman (courtesy of the Idaho State Historical Society; see page 19), James Hawley, pioneer, attorney, and statesman (courtesy of the Idaho State Historical Society; see page 44).

On the Back Cover: From left to right:
Harlan P. Ustick (in top hat) (courtesy of the Idaho State Historical Society; see page 56), J.R. Simplot, businessman and philanthropist (courtesy of the Idaho State Historical Society; see page 103).

CONTENTS

Acknowledgments 6

Introduction 7

CHAPTER ONE They Built the City 9

CHAPTER TWO Bankers, Builders, Editors, and Scallywags 25

CHAPTER THREE Movers and Shakers 43

CHAPTER FOUR Learning from the Best 65

CHAPTER FIVE The Arts from A to Z 71

CHAPTER SIX Keeping Boise Beautiful 91

CHAPTER SEVEN Mom & Pop and Then Some 101

CHAPTER EIGHT Home Runs, Touchdowns, and Olympic Gold 111

CHAPTER NINE Out of the Ordinary 119

Bibliography 126

Index 127

ACKNOWLEDGMENTS

Boise's history has been well documented. Merle Wells, Arthur Hart, Todd Shallat, J.M. Neil, and Faith Turner are only a few of the outstanding historians who provided a foundation for us. The photographs in this book have come from many sources, and we gratefully acknowledge the assistance of Brandi Burns and Karen Bubb of the Boise City Department of Arts and History; Patty Miller of the Basque Museum and Cultural Center; Julia Stringfellow and Jim Duran of the Special Collections Department, Albertson Library, Boise State University; Marcia Franklin, Bruce Reichert, and Jeff Tucker of Idaho Public Television; Jenaleigh Kiebert of the Idaho State Archives Research Library; and Joe Jaszewski of the *Idaho Statesman*. Photographs and information were provided to us by Cecil Andrus, Mark Baltes, Robynn Browne, Kim Coe, Kent Collins, Dan Everhart, Melanie Flitton Folwell, Maureen Ingram, Rebecca Kelada, Margaret Lundy, Theresa McLeod, Sally Mitchell, Alison Perry, Marjorie Rabdau, David Nels Reese, Angie Stevens, and Jon Swarthout. Invaluable support was provided by our assistant Jennifer Lee, intern Kyle McCormick, and Larry Burke, who knows a lot more about sports than we do. We wish to thank our editor, Erin Vosgien, for her patience and assistance as we slowly developed this book.

Any list is subjective, and the legendary locals we selected for this book will not be the same as a list created by someone else. We based our choices on our own experience doing research over the past 20-some years and on conversations we have had during that time with others about Boise history. Readers will no doubt find names missing or included in the book that would not match their own selections. We cheerfully acknowledge that we do not know everything, but we hope that our book will prove enjoyable and informative, and perhaps spark some friendly debates.

INTRODUCTION

Through Boise's 150-year history, a parade of actors have played central roles in the story of the city. Initially, the area was home to the Shoshone, Bannock, and Paiute tribes, who inhabited the area for generations. Until the 1860s, the area that became Idaho was passed through by Euro-American settlers on their way to Oregon and California. The dry climate and desert terrain held little charm for people headed for the green fields of the Willamette Valley or the glittering gold of California. But when gold was discovered in north Idaho in 1860 and in the Boise Basin in 1862, people began to stream to the rivers, plains, and mountains of Idaho. When Fort Boise was established by the US Army in 1863 to protect miners and travelers on the Oregon Trail, Boise's founders platted a new town within shouting distance of the fort. A few years later, rail lines and irrigation projects fostered Boise's growth as a service center in largely rural southwest Idaho. In the 21st century, the city's economy is based on its role as the state capital and county seat of Ada County, along with technology and agriculture.

Legendary Locals of Boise begins with the people who settled here in the 1860s and continues through to entrepreneurs, inventors, artists, and athletes of the 21st century. Boise's history is built on the stories of the people who platted the town and established the fort—Maj. Pinckney Lugenbeel, Thomas and Julia Davis, Cyrus Jacobs, William Ridenbaugh, and others. Within 20 years, Boise was a leading center for business, with banks, schools, churches, a daily newspaper, and electricity. Among the residents who helped make the city a success were Moses Alexander, the Falk brothers, and John Lemp. Writer/artist Mary Hallock Foote, known for her illustrations and stories in magazines like *Century* and *Frank Leslie's Illustrated Weekly*, came to Boise with her husband, Arthur DeWint Foote. He was intent on developing a large-scale irrigation project. She became involved in local society and continued to write and draw, inspired by her experiences in southwest Idaho.

In the 1890s, despite a national economic panic, Boise experienced prosperity. Developers brought in streetcar lines for transportation and established an innovative system using geothermal water to provide hot water to heat homes. Boise was the first city in the world to make use of this natural resource. Walter E. Pierce, Harland Ustick, and C.W. Moore were a few of the players who brought these changes to town. Architect John Tourtellotte helped a modern city of fine buildings and substantial business blocks emerge from the Western frontier town of hastily constructed wood-frame buildings and tents.

State government, federal irrigation projects, regional wholesale and distribution of products, and financial services all contributed to Boise's economic base. Between 1900 and 1910, the city's population almost tripled. Following the assassination of former governor Frank Steunenberg, Boise saw the "Trial of the Century" in the spring and summer of 1907. The eyes of the world were focused on the city as Boise attorneys James H. Hawley and William E. Borah faced attorney Clarence Darrow to argue the case of William "Big Bill" Haywood and others charged with conspiring to murder the governor. In the 1910s and 1920s, Boise began to evolve as a modern city, as architects and engineers designed multistory buildings that changed the skyline. During the Depression, leaders created a local junior college. Under the leadership of Eugene Chaffee, the college grew into a high-quality institution, the foundation of Boise State University.

World War II brought an expansion of Gowen Field and created the need for housing for military families. This led to the development of roads and neighborhoods on Boise's Bench, located near the airfield. Postwar industrial expansion strengthened the city's economy, and businessmen like Harry Morrison, J.R. Simplot, and Joe Albertson became community leaders.

Urban renewal in the 1970s destroyed much of the city's charm and divided Boiseans over questions on how to manage the city's growth. New opportunities were realized in the 1970s and 1980s, when high-tech companies like Micron Technology and Hewlett-Packard chose Boise as the location for major manufacturing plants. In the 1990s, Steve Appleton's leadership made Micron a powerhouse in the microchip field. And in the early years of the 21st century, Olympic gold medalist Kristin Armstrong Savola and the Fiesta Bowl champion Boise State Broncos focused international attention on their hometown. Musicians such as Gene Harris and Curtis Stigers, and artist Surel Mitchell, have enriched the cultural life of Boise.

Today, Boise is often touted as one of the best places to live because of its beautiful surroundings, outdoor activities, affordable living, and environmental awareness. This reflects the broad spectrum of the contributions of the many individuals who have helped make Boise a vibrant, livable place to call home for 150 years.

CHAPTER ONE

They Built the City

Boise was born in 1863 at the crossroads of the Oregon Trail and the Boise Basin gold mines. The town was established to serve the needs of the military stationed at Fort Boise and the hundreds of miners seeking wealth in the surrounding mountains.

Idaho was settled from the west to the east. The first emigrants passed through the arid Snake River Plain, following the Oregon Trail beginning in the 1840s to the fertile valleys of Oregon and Washington. The discovery of gold in California in 1849 spurred interest in developing mining areas in other regions of the West. Gold discoveries in Montana, British Columbia, and then in north Idaho brought miners to the future territory of Idaho. It was not long before hopeful prospectors moved down through the central mountains and continued farther south, finding themselves in the Boise Basin.

In 1863, Maj. Pinckney Lugenbeel led the military from Walla Walla, Washington, to a location near the intersection of the road to the Boise Basin mines (in the vicinity of present-day Idaho City) and the Oregon Trail. He established a fort to provide protection for those traveling the two routes. Brothers Tom and Frank Davis had already established a small farm in the valley when the troops arrived. The brothers tried their luck at mining, but found more success raising cattle and crops to sell to the miners. Within days of the official establishment of the fort, the Davis brothers and a few other enterprising former miners were instrumental in platting a new city adjacent to the fort. Tom planted the first orchards in the area, and with his wife, Julia, raised a family of six children. Julia, known for her kindness and hospitality, was revered in the town. Julia Davis Park, a jewel of the Boise park system in the 21st century, is their legacy.

Merchant Cyrus Jacobs arrived with Major Lugenbeel and set up a tent store near the fort. He built a fine adobe brick house for his wife, Mary Ellen, and their three small children. The family grew up with Boise, and Cyrus invested in the community as a merchant, mill owner, and philanthropist. Along with the other early arrivals, Cyrus and Mary Ellen helped create the underpinnings of a successful town.

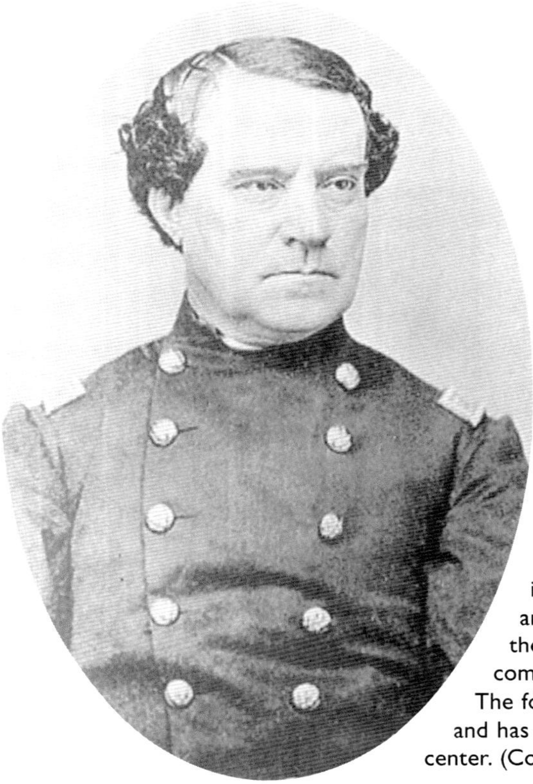

Pinckney Lugenbeel

Maj. Pinckney Lugenbeel (left) and four companies of infantry from Fort Walla Walla arrived in the Boise Valley on a hot June day in 1863. The major selected a site for Fort Boise at the foot of the hills, with fresh water nearby. He led a large force of skilled civilian workmen, including bricklayers, stonemasons, carpenters, and plasterers, during the initial construction of the fort. A career military man, Major Lugenbeel completed his assignment at Boise in October 1863. The fort he helped establish (below) remains standing and has transitioned from a military facility to a medical center. (Courtesy of the Idaho State Historical Society.)

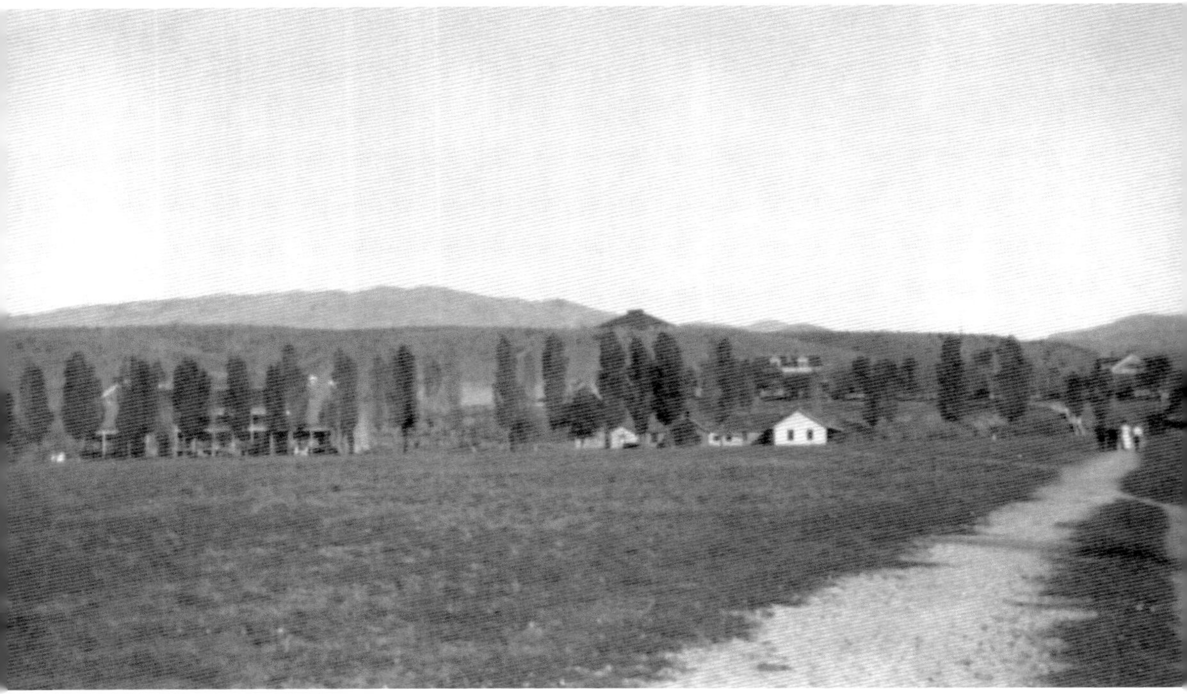

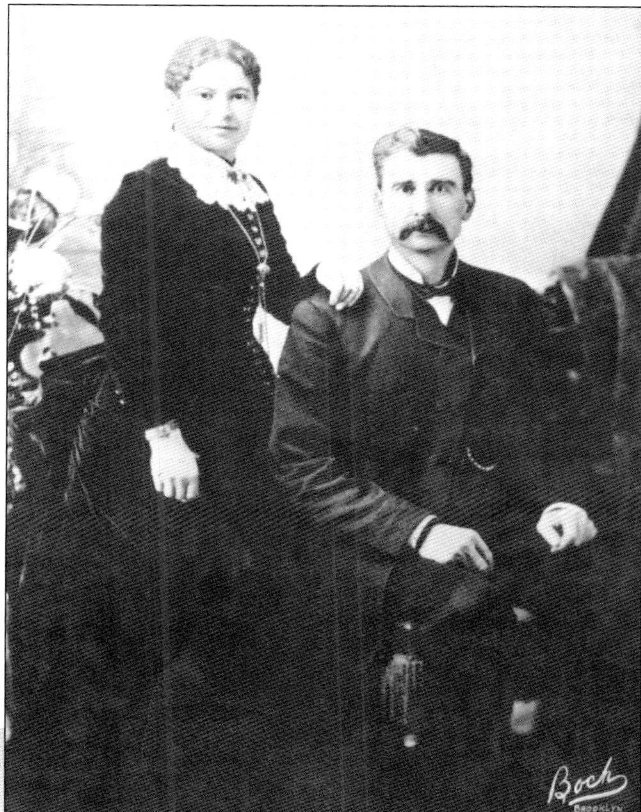

Tom and Julia Davis

Tom and Julia Davis, two of Boise's best-known pioneers, lived on a farm near present-day downtown Boise. Tom homesteaded land along the Boise River just a few months before Major Lugenbeel selected the site for Fort Boise. Tom Davis, one of the city founders, planted an orchard and sold fruit to city residents and miners. He married Julia McCrum in April 1871. In 1899, Tom and Julia offered a section of their orchard lands to the city for a park. The city did not accept the offer. In 1907, after Julia's death, Tom deeded 40 acres of land to the city in her memory, asking that "always and forever" it be known as Julia Davis Park (below). (Right, courtesy of the Idaho State Historical Society; below, courtesy of Mark Baltes.)

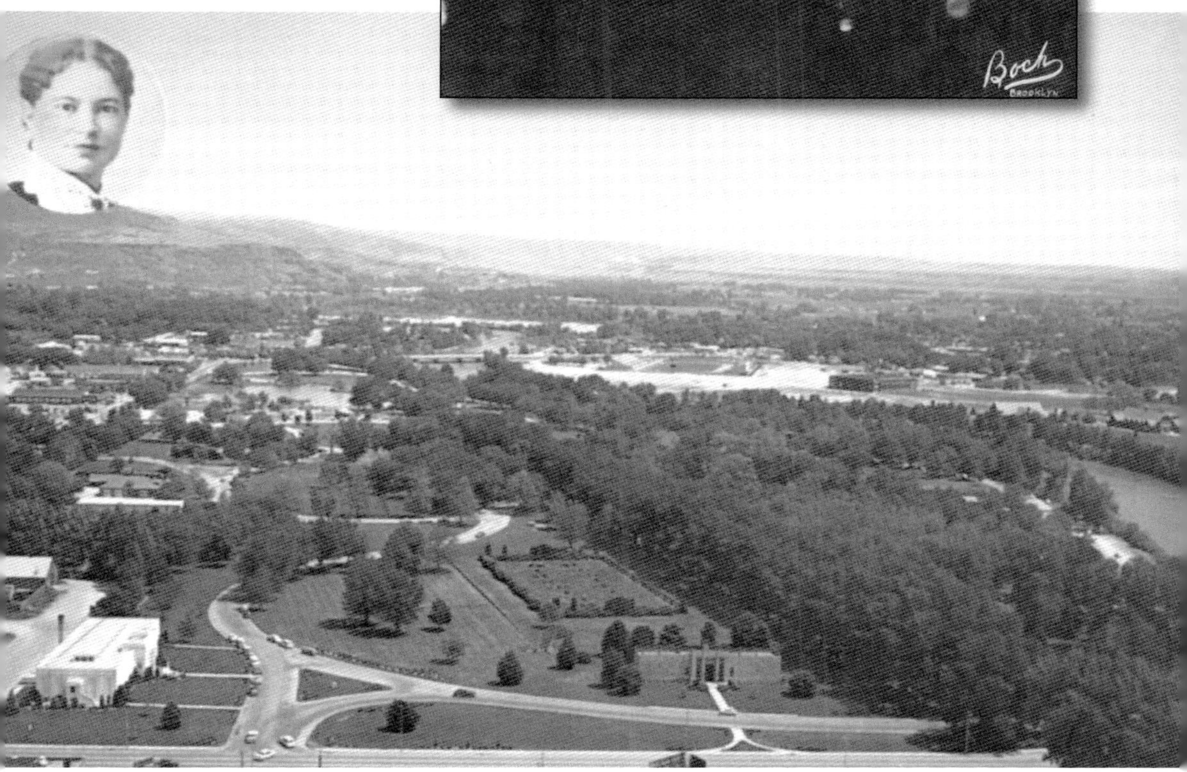

Cyrus Jacobs

Hundreds of miners entered the region looking to strike it rich in the mines surrounding Boise. The rough new town offered opportunities for merchants, who provided the miners with food and supplies. Jacobs, shown here with his wife, Mary Ellen, arrived with Major Lugenbeel from Walla Walla, Washington. He sold his wares from a tent pitched at the corner of Seventh and Main Streets. He later constructed a brick store. (Courtesy of the Idaho State Historical Society.)

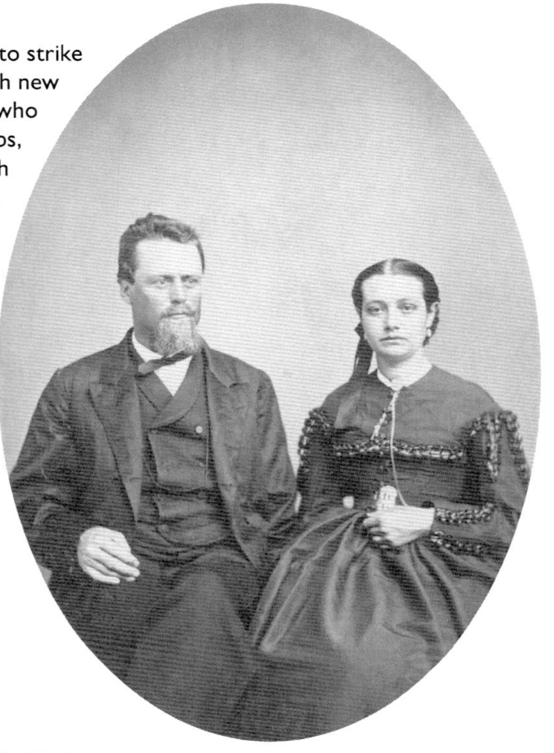

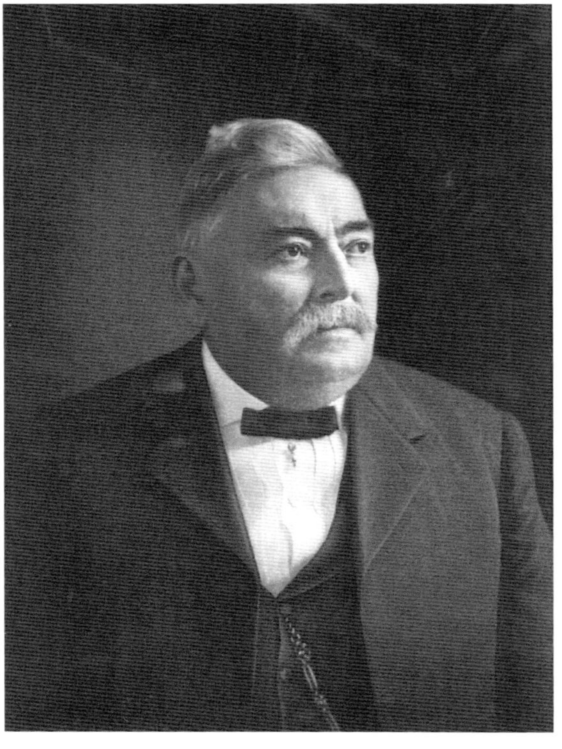

John Lemp

German-born "Beer King" John Lemp made Boise his home in 1863. A miner and prospector, Lemp, according to legend, bought a brewery at the east end of Main Street for a "teacup full of gold dust." Miners, farmers, and speculators swarmed to the bustling and growing community, which Lemp supplied with a rich beer to quench their thirst in the dry, dusty desert town. (Courtesy of the Idaho State Historical Society.)

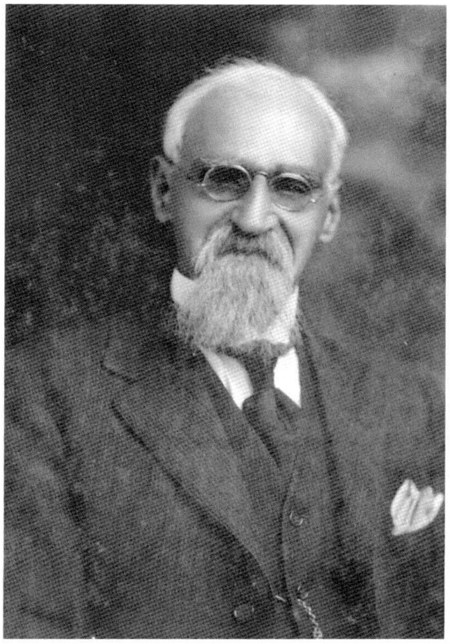

Jesus Urquides

Gold discoveries in the Idaho Territory attracted Mexican immigrants. They worked as miners, *vaqueros* (cowboys), and mule packers. Mexican packers learned their trade in their home country, the Southwest, and California. They also worked as Army packers and began packing supplies to the mining camps in Idaho in the 1860s. Jesus Urquides came to Boise in 1863. He established a successful packing business and created Urquides Village near the intersection of Broadway and Main Street as a place to house the Mexican packers who worked for him. The Jesus Urquides Memorial, a public art piece, was installed at 115 Main Street in 2013. (Left, courtesy of the Idaho State Historical Society; below, authors' collection.)

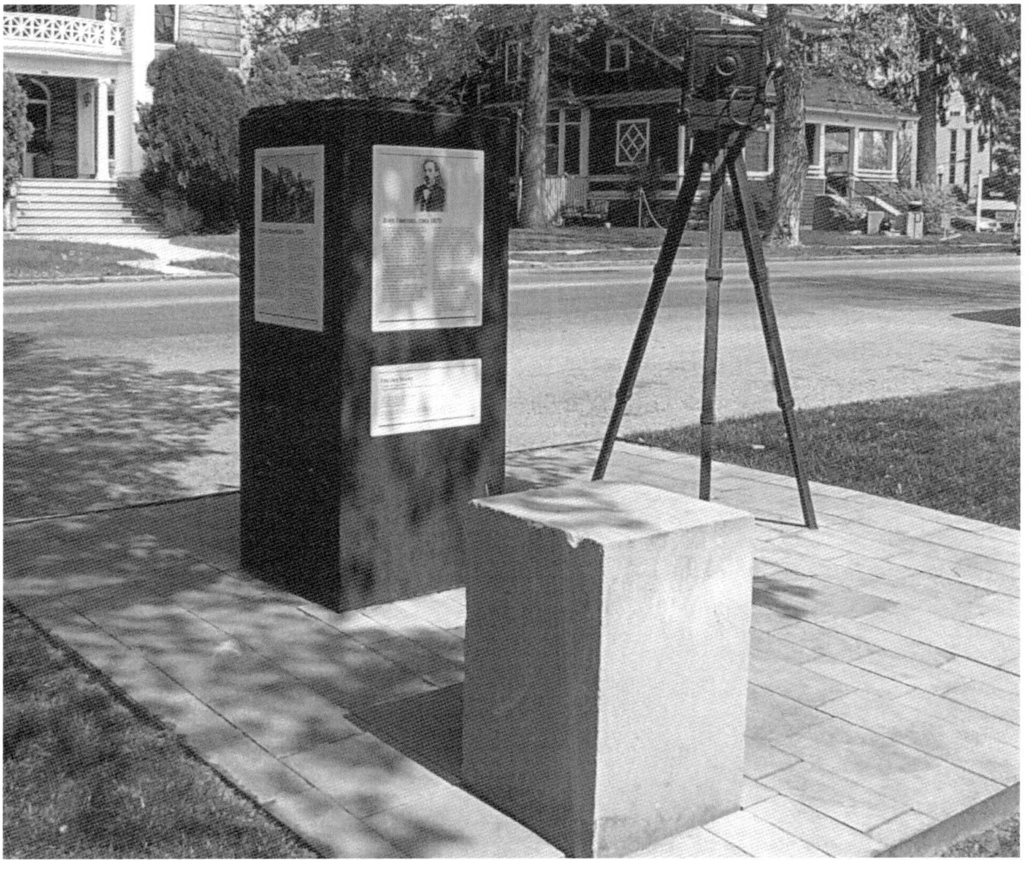

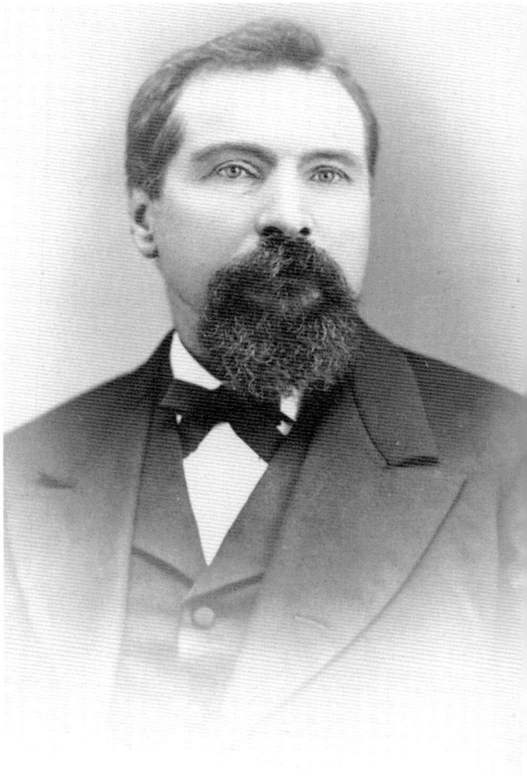

Joseph Bown

Bown, an English immigrant, came to Boise Basin in 1865 for the same reason as many other early arrivals—gold. Like others, he quickly realized that his fortune lay in supplying horses and hay to the Army and other miners. In 1879, he started construction on a two-story stone house, hauling rocks from a quarry across the river. The Bown family lived in the house until the late 1890s. The house and surrounding land were purchased by the Independent School District of Boise in 1987. A new elementary school was planned for the Bown House site, and the historic home was slated for demolition. The building (below) was saved through the efforts of Preservation Idaho, a statewide nonprofit group dedicated to the protection of Idaho's and Boise's heritage. (Right, courtesy of the Idaho State Historical Society; below, authors' collection.)

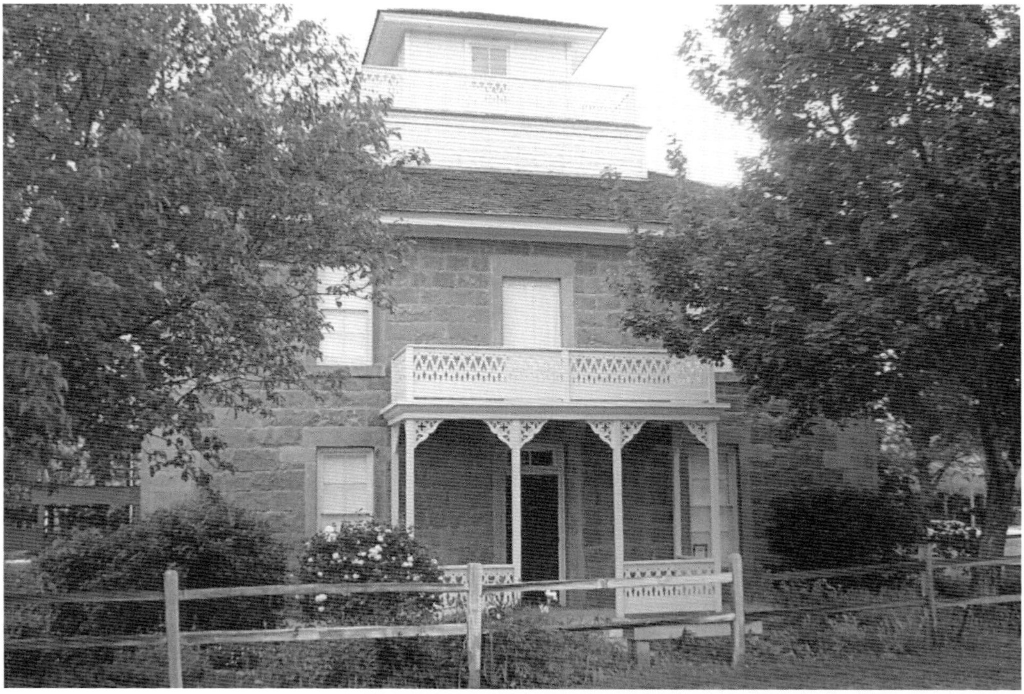

Lafayette Cartee

Early visitors to Boise often commented that the city was an oasis in the midst of the surrounding arid desert. The Western town boasted many varieties of fruits, including apples, plums, apricots, and grapes. Lafayette Cartee is credited with helping the desert bloom. He was born in Tioga, New York, in 1823 to John and Seclendia Cartee. When Lafayette was about two, his parents moved to Coudersport, Pennyslvania. Cartee made his way west in 1848, traveling first to California and then Oregon before making Boise his permanent home in 1863. Cartee settled on Grove Street (originally called Market Street) with his family. Although he was employed as a surveyor and cartographer, Cartee's passion was for horticulture. For 20 years, he helped create "Boise the Beautiful." (Courtesy of the Idaho State Historical Society.)

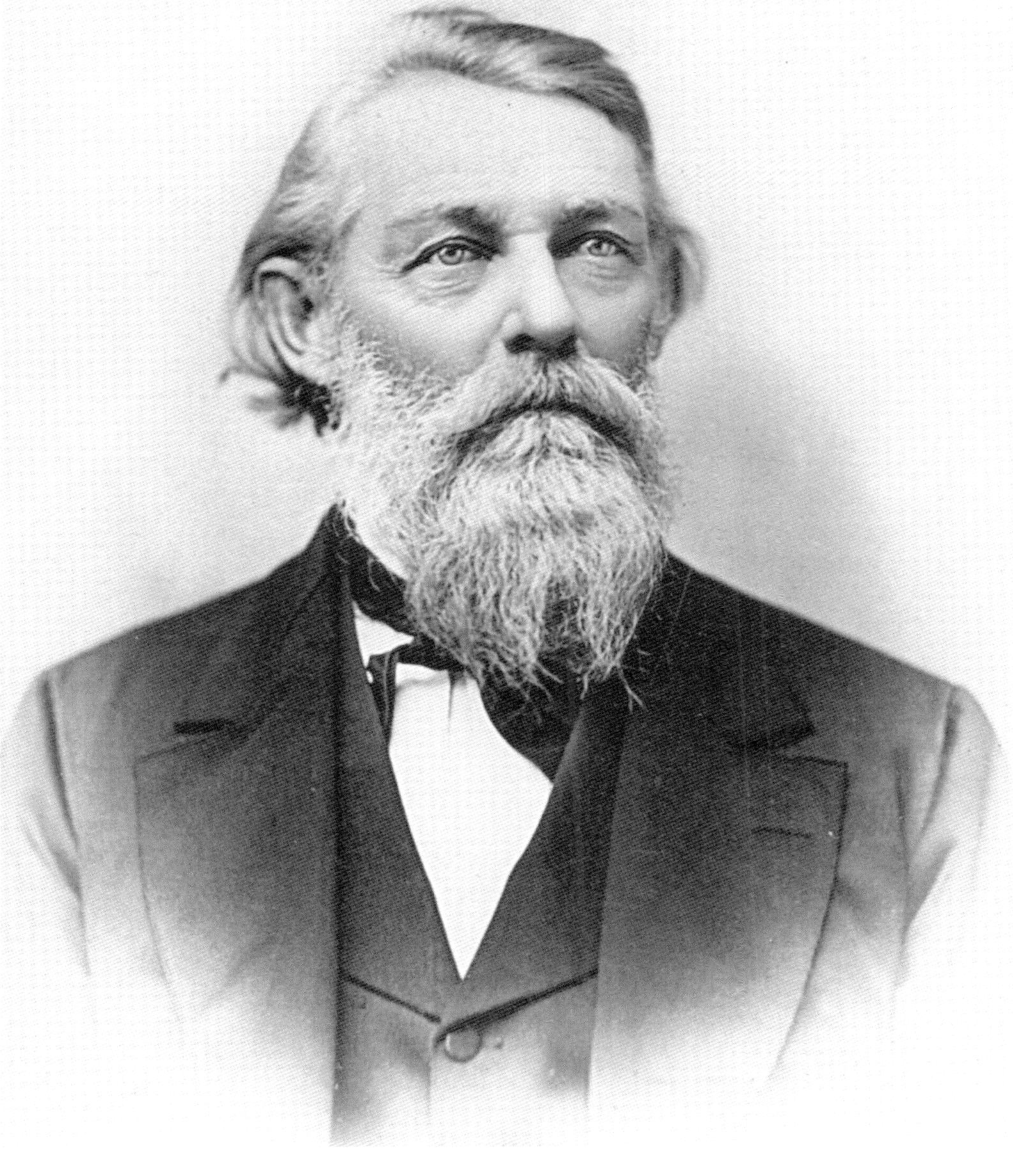

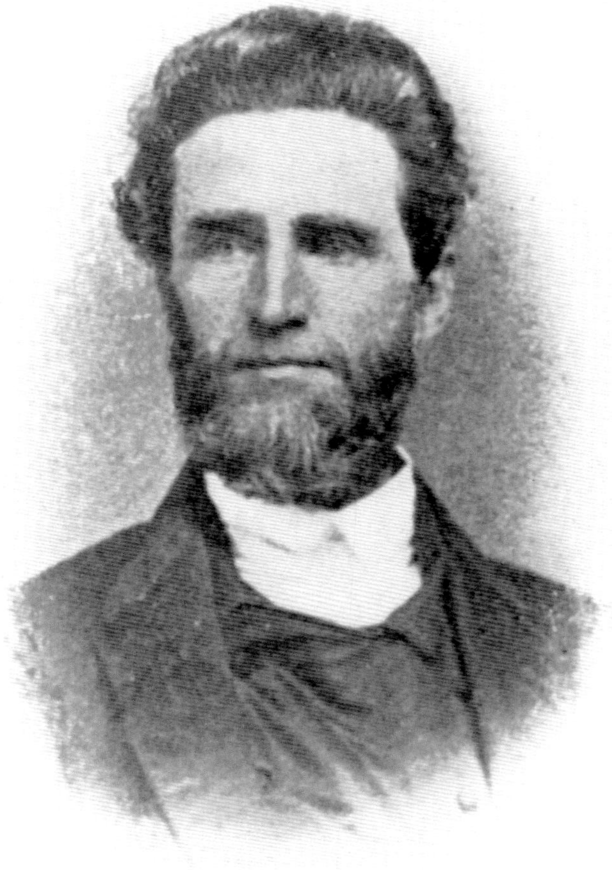

St. Michael Fackler

Rev. St. Michael Fackler was the first Episcopal clergyman to come to the Pacific Northwest. Born and educated in Virginia, after his graduation from seminary in 1840, he began a westward movement that led him first to Missouri, then Wyoming, then Oregon, and finally Boise. Reverend Fackler presided over Boise's first Episcopal service, which was held in the home of A.G. Redway in August 1864, a little more than a year after Boise was founded. Services were held in seven different buildings until 1866, when Reverend Fackler delivered a sermon in a new church. Funds for the new building were raised by church women, who held ice-cream socials, bazaars, and talent shows, raising $1,500 for construction. It was the first Episcopal church built in the territory that now comprises the states of Idaho, Utah, and Montana. A few months later, Reverend Fackler left Boise in the fall of 1866 for New York, traveling first to California to board a ship. His voyage took him east via Central America and Key West, Florida. During the voyage, there was an outbreak of cholera on the ship. Reverend Fackler helped to treat the sick and contracted the disease himself. He died before the ship arrived in Key West and was buried there. His congregation in Boise honored his memory by naming the newly constructed church St. Michael's Church of Boise City. When the original church building was replaced, the name was carried over to the new church, now St. Michael's Episcopal Cathedral. (Courtesy of the Idaho State Historical Society.)

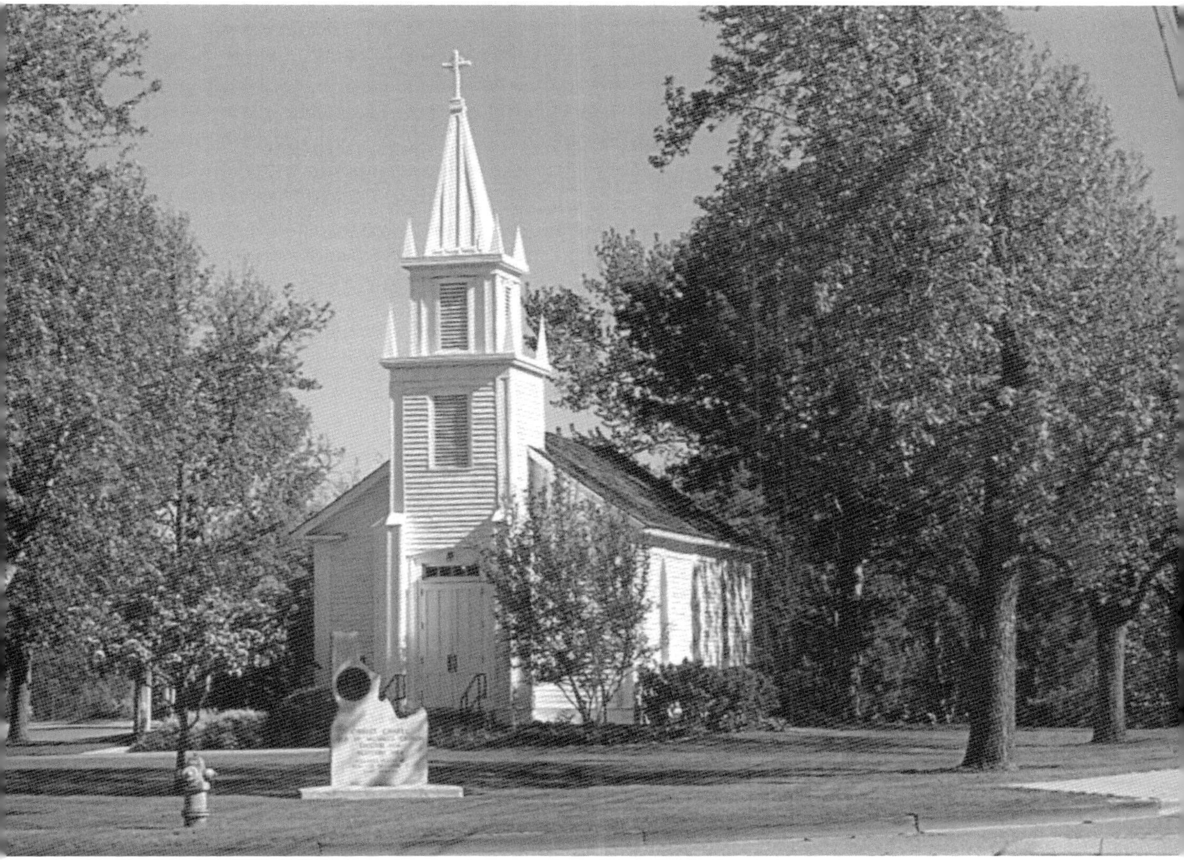

Christ Chapel
Originally named to honor Rev. St. Michael Fackler, this church is located in downtown Boise on the corner of Seventh and Bannock Streets. It served the Episcopal congregation as a church until 1902, when St. Michael's Cathedral was built. The church building was moved to Fifteenth and Ridenbaugh Streets and repurposed for use as a mission. Renamed Christ Church, it was used as a chapel until 1963. It was moved again, to the campus of Boise State University. The church was deconsecrated, then rededicated on May 17, 1964. It is primarily used for weddings. (Authors' collection.)

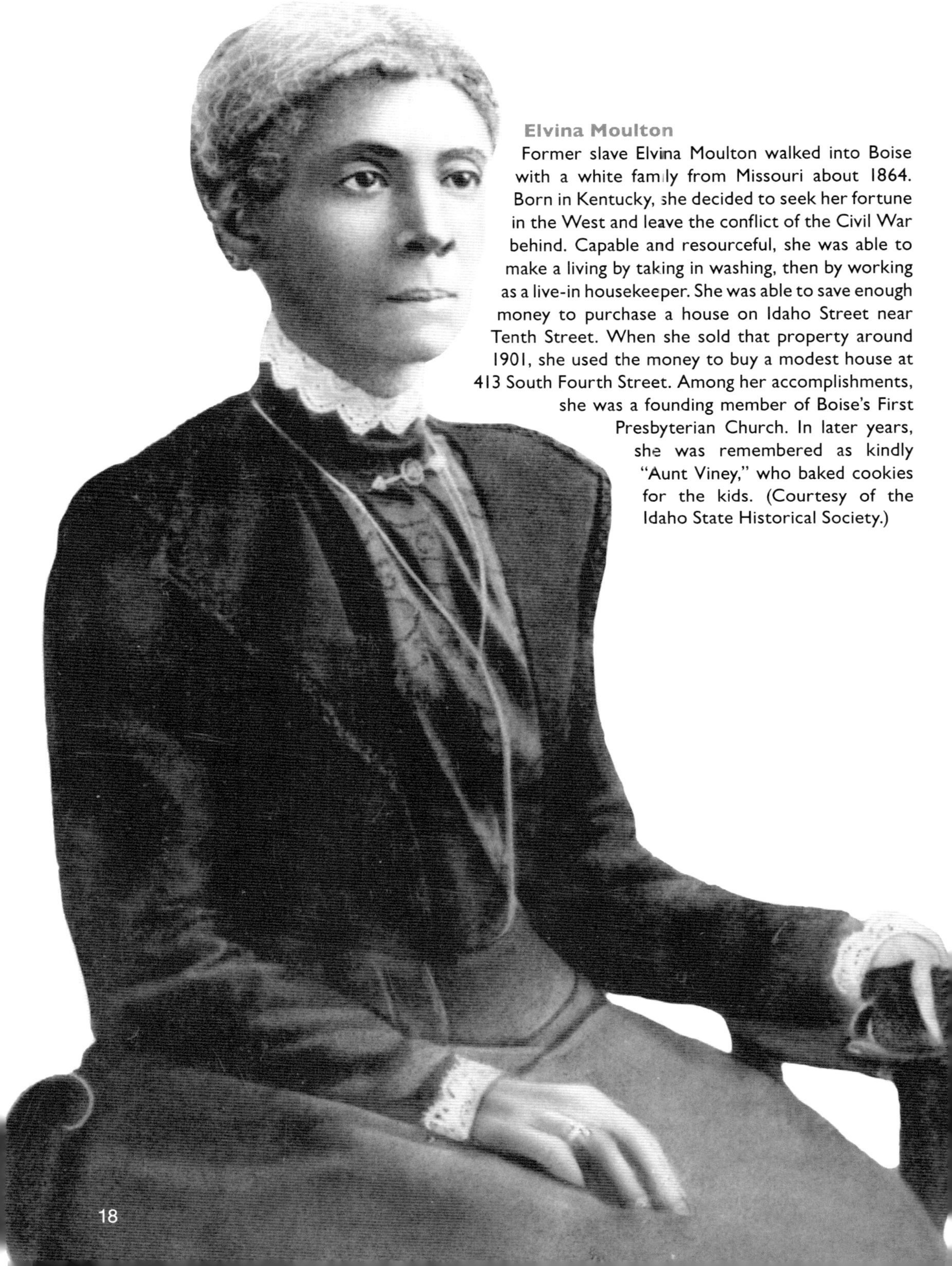

Elvina Moulton

Former slave Elvina Moulton walked into Boise with a white family from Missouri about 1864. Born in Kentucky, she decided to seek her fortune in the West and leave the conflict of the Civil War behind. Capable and resourceful, she was able to make a living by taking in washing, then by working as a live-in housekeeper. She was able to save enough money to purchase a house on Idaho Street near Tenth Street. When she sold that property around 1901, she used the money to buy a modest house at 413 South Fourth Street. Among her accomplishments, she was a founding member of Boise's First Presbyterian Church. In later years, she was remembered as kindly "Aunt Viney," who baked cookies for the kids. (Courtesy of the Idaho State Historical Society.)

William Ridenbaugh

The Ridenbaugh Canal is an extensive irrigation canal that makes its way from its headgates on the Boise River near Barber Park west to Canyon County. The canal is named for William Ridenbaugh, one of Boise's 19th-century businessmen. Ridenbaugh came to Boise in 1872 to work for his uncle William B. Morris, who was the superintendent of the Northwestern State Company. Young Ridenbaugh worked several different jobs for his uncle, eventually becoming his uncle's right-hand man as assistant superintendent. Morris owned a large tract of land south of the city and promoted an irrigation ditch, known as the Morris Ditch, to water the land. Morris died in 1878, and his nephew extended the ditch, renamed the Ridenbaugh Canal, seven miles to the desert. Ridenbaugh had extensive business interests, including railroad investments, geothermal heat, and a lumber company. (Courtesy of the Idaho State Historical Society.)

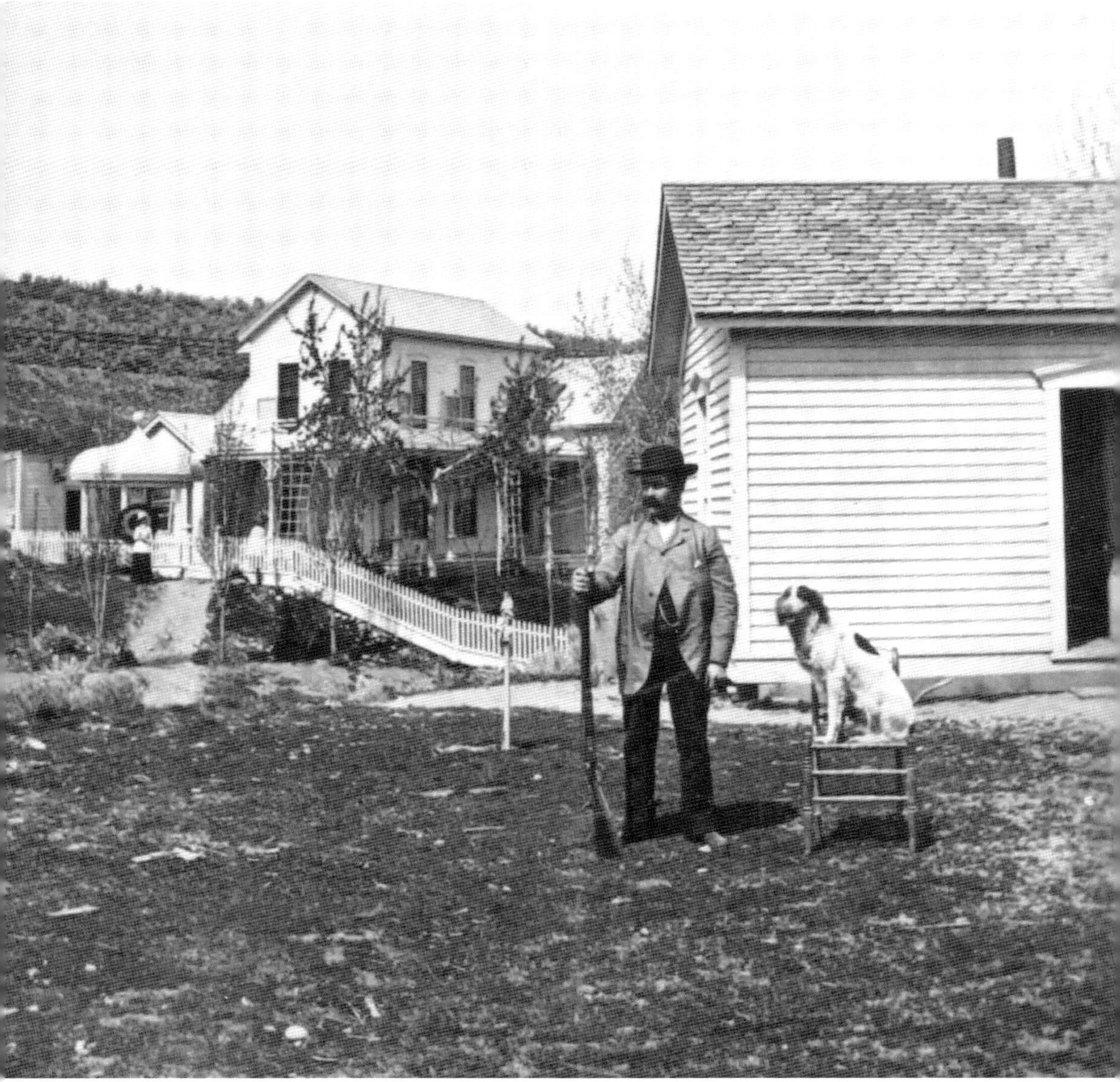

Mary Black Ridenbaugh

Mary Elizabeth Black Ridenbaugh was active in politics, education, and social circles. The daughter of Charles and Anne Black, who ran a stage station, Mary attended St. Michael's School in Boise as a young girl and received her higher education at Walla Walla, Washington, and Sacred Heart Academy at Oakland, California. After graduating, she taught school before marrying William H. Ridenbaugh in 1878. After her marriage, Mary was active in Boise society and numerous philanthropic efforts. She was a charter member of the Columbian Club (see page 22), helped establish Boise's Carnegie library, and served as a regent of the University of Idaho under three governors. (Courtesy of the Idaho State Historical Society.)

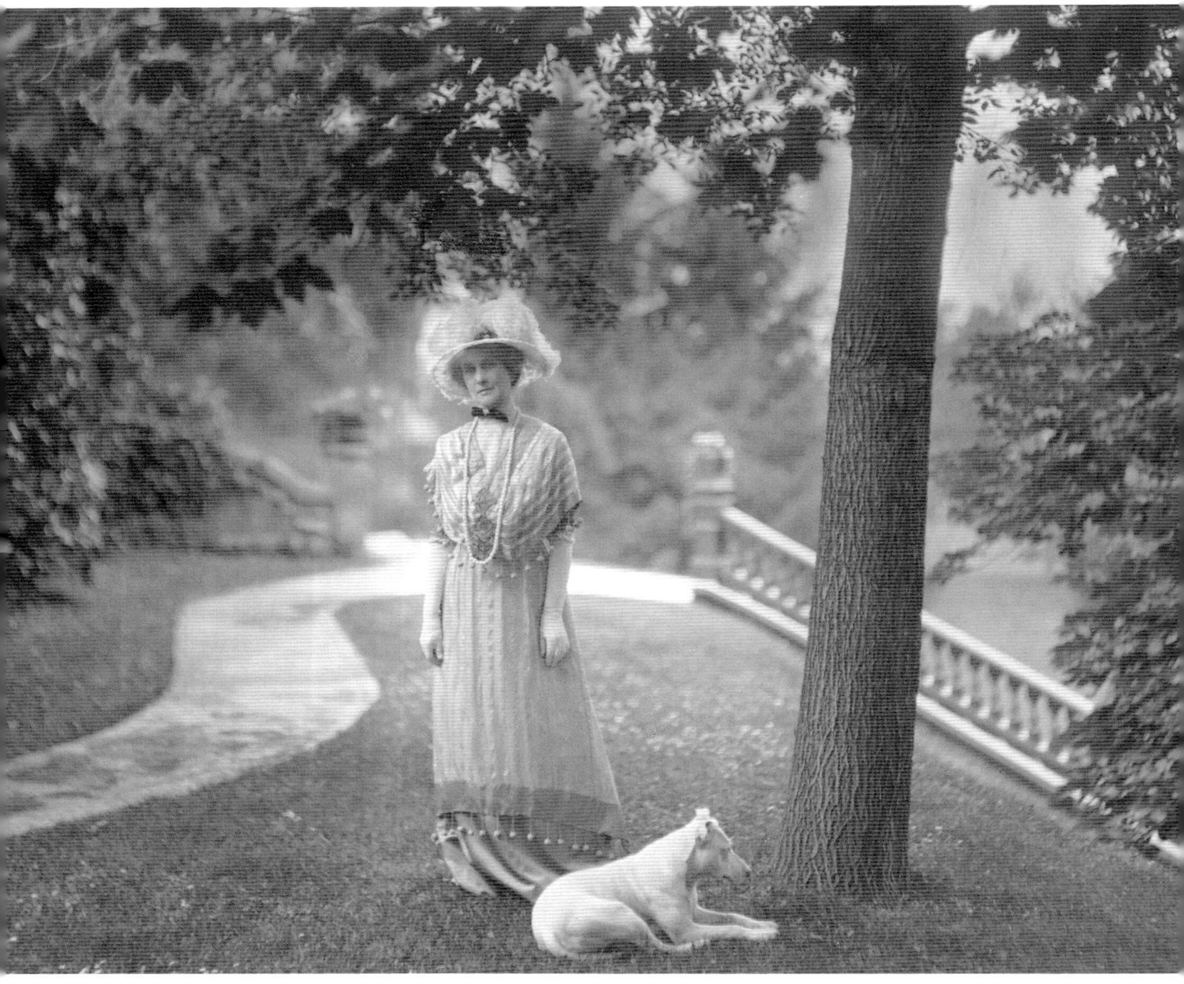

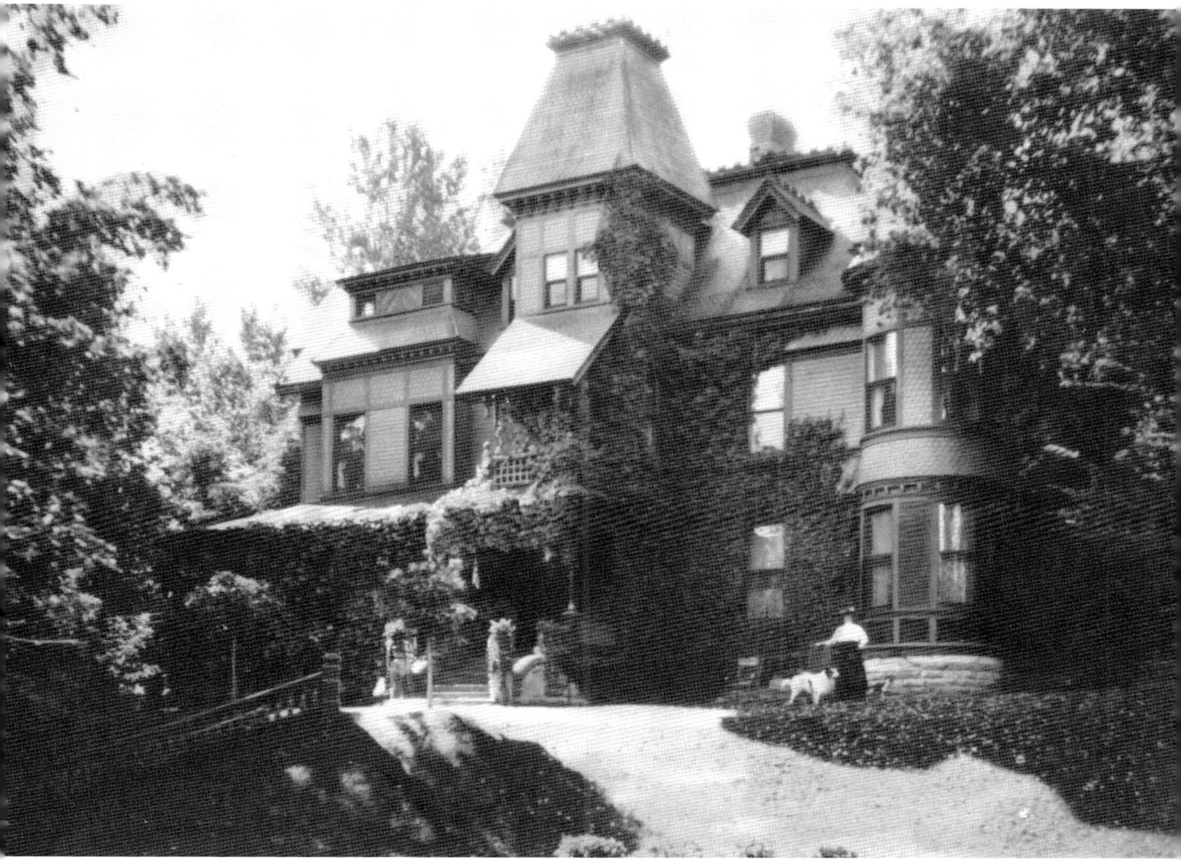

Ridenbaugh Mansion
William and Mary Ridenbaugh's home, The Mills, was built in South Boise in 1890. The two-story mansion was designed by architect James King in the Queen Anne style. It featured a cut stone foundation, and the many rooms were outfitted in a variety of wood finishes. The surrounding ground featured ornamental bushes, shrubs, and trees. Following the deaths of Mr. and Mrs. Ridenbaugh, the house was sold and razed in 1926. (Courtesy of the Idaho State Historical Society.)

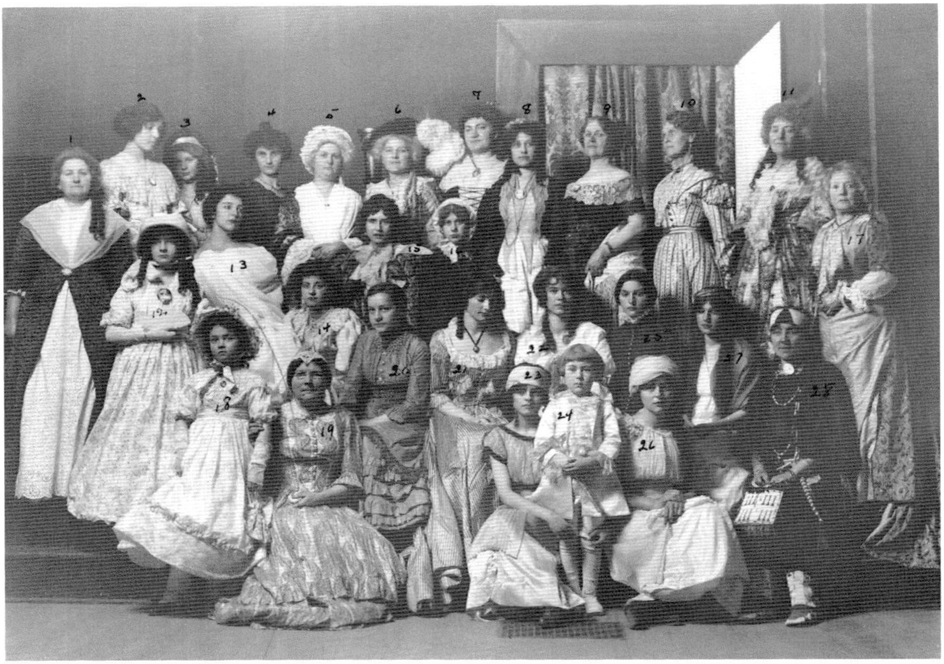

The Columbian Club

The Columbian Club, a leading women's organization, was commissioned by Gov. Norman Willey in 1892 to help provide Idaho's exhibit for the World's Columbian Exposition in 1893 (also known as the Chicago World's Fair). After the fair, the club continued to be active, establishing a permanent public library for Boise in 1894, and lobbying the legislature to create a state library, an effort that succeeded in 1901. The Columbian Club is Boise's oldest service organization. (Above, courtesy of the Idaho State Historical Society; below, courtesy of the Columbian Club.)

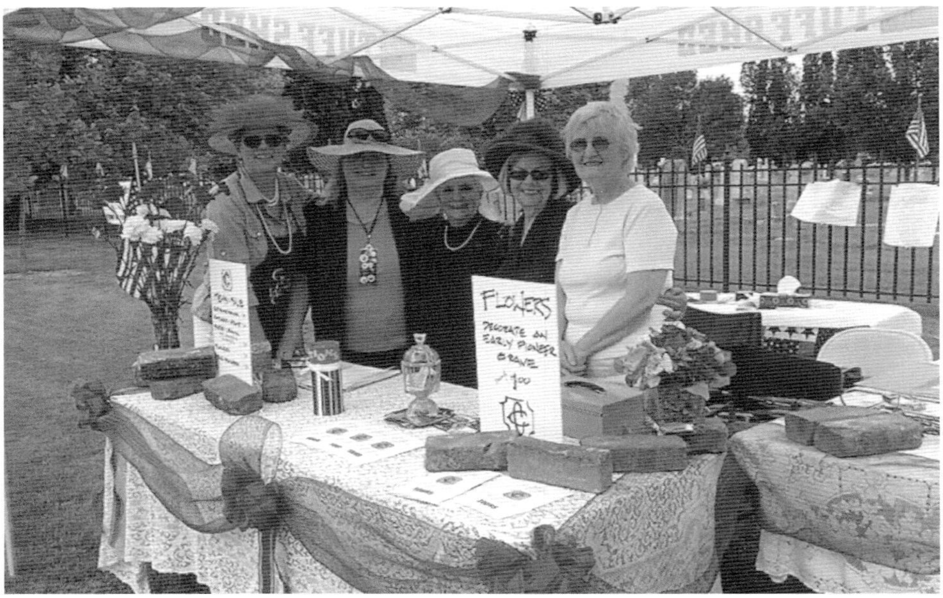

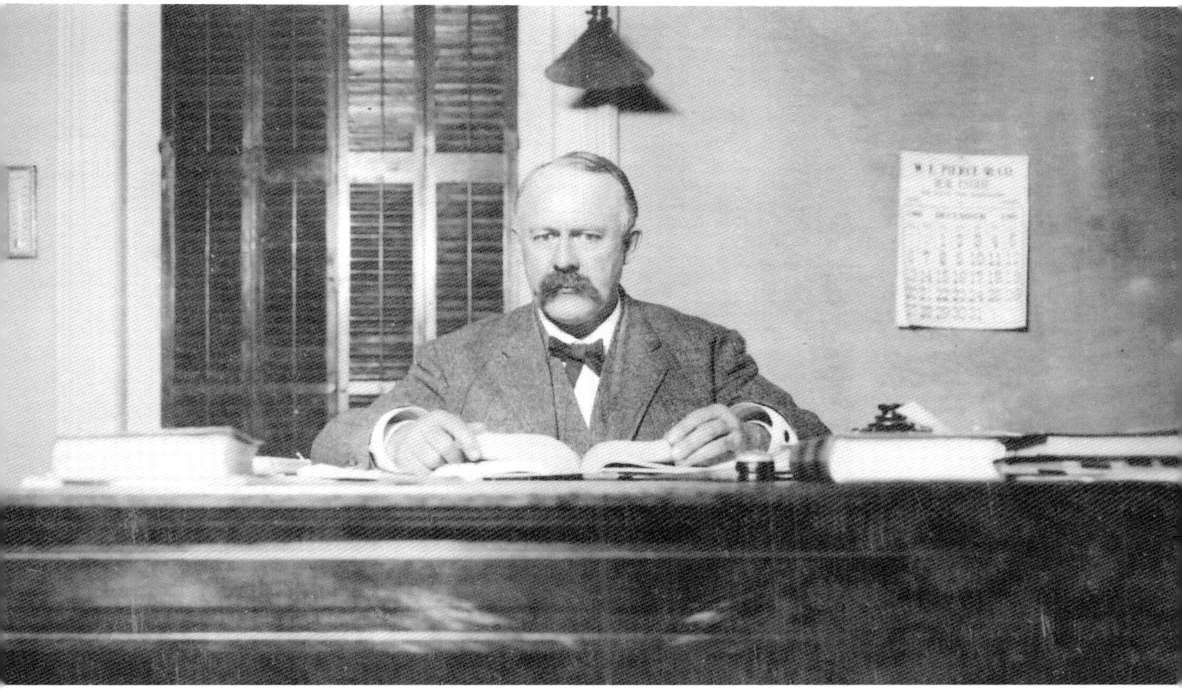

Fremont Wood

Wood, a native of Winthrop, Maine, arrived in Boise in 1881 with W.R. White, the newly appointed territorial attorney for Idaho. He was appointed US attorney in 1889, and in November 1906, was elected judge for the Third Judicial District (Ada and Boise Counties). Wood presided over the sensational trial of William "Big Bill" Haywood. (Courtesy of the Idaho State Historical Society.)

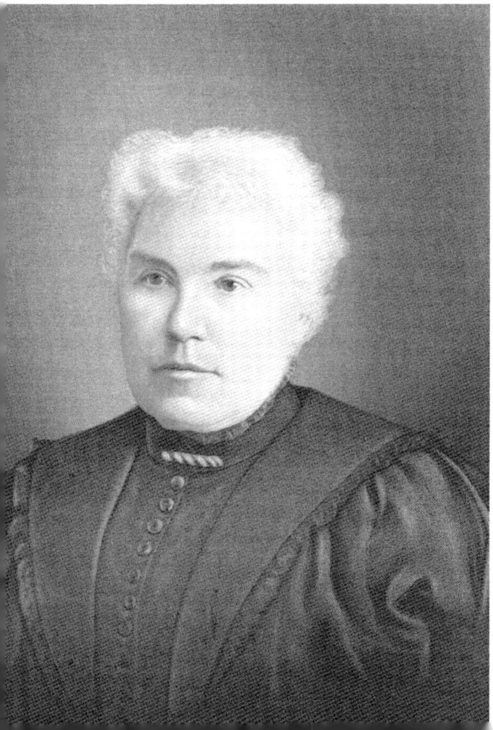

Hester Davis

Her obituary noted that Hester Davis was "the last of her line—A Pioneer Woman." Hester Cory was born in Ohio and arrived in Boise in 1864. She married Frank Davis, and together they ran a dairy farm on the south side of present-day State Street near its intersection with Twenty-sixth Street. Widowed at age 49, Hester managed the farm alone. Later, she subdivided the farm to take advantage of the streetcar system that was laid west from downtown Boise. She moved to California to live with her daughter in 1927, where she died 10 years later. (Courtesy of the Idaho State Historical Society.)

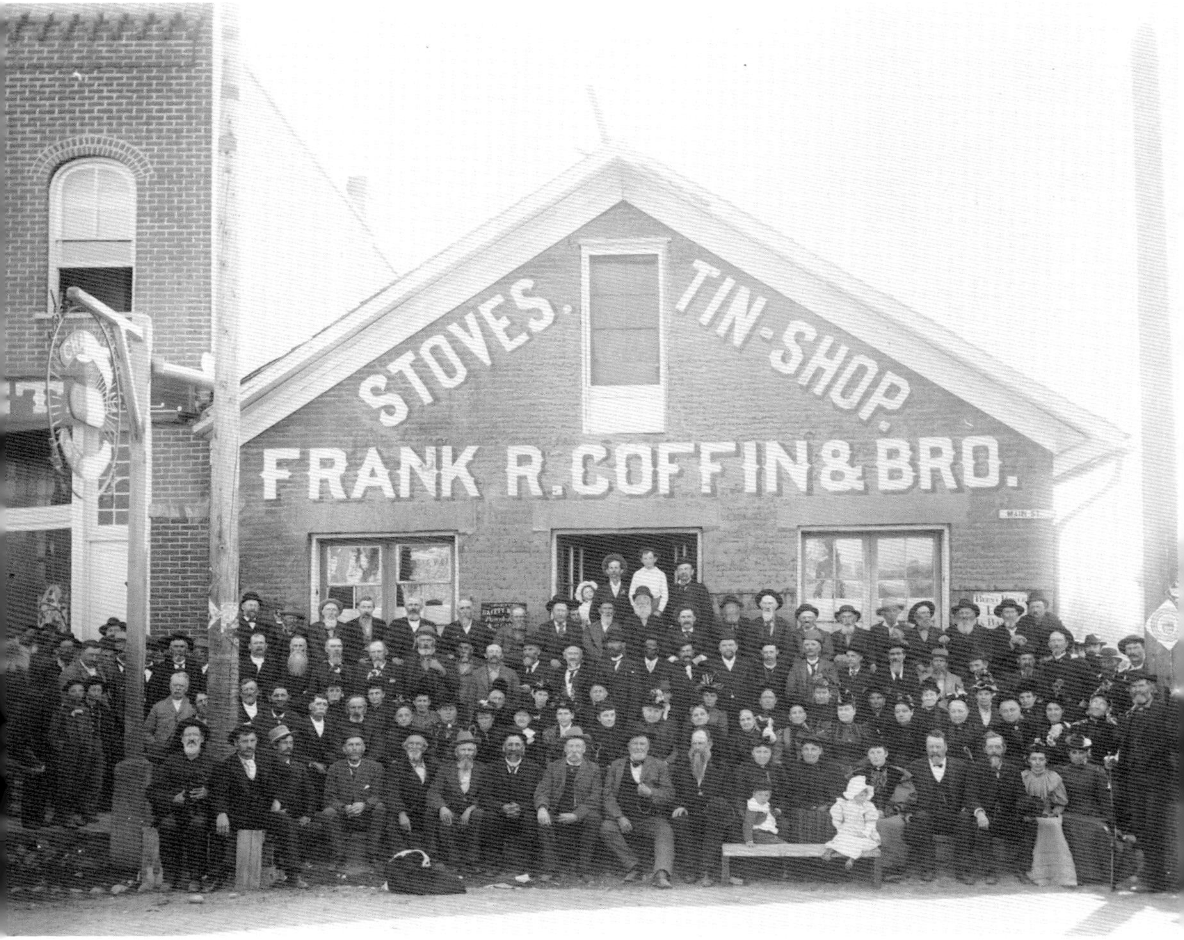

John West

The settlement of Idaho Territory coincided with the Civil War and Reconstruction. Passed between 1865 and 1870, the 13th, 14th, and 15th Amendments to the US Constitution abolished slavery, granted citizenship to African Americans, and protected their right to vote. The struggle from slavery to freedom represents one of the major themes in the history of African Americans, and many individuals played vital roles in the work toward freedom, equality, and justice. Their contributions have helped shape society today. Boise pioneer John West was one of these individuals. Considered to be the first civil-rights activist in Boise, he was born a free man in Pennsylvania in 1834 and moved west to Washington in 1858 as the servant of an officer on staff with Gen. Winfield Scott. By 1864, West had worked his way to the Idaho Territory, arriving in the new town of Boise. He worked as a general laborer and also as a cloakroom attendant during the legislative season. He was a trailblazer for other African Americans and fought for his right to vote. Officials presiding over an election in 1870 refused his vote. West was persistent and overcame obstacles to vote in city and county elections. Following his death in 1903, his obituary noted that he was "Dean of Colored Pioneers in Idaho." In this photograph, John West is in the second row from the top, 11th from the right. (Courtesy of the Idaho State Historical Society.)

CHAPTER TWO

Bankers, Builders, Editors, and Scallywags

In 150 years, a community will ebb and flow. Opportunities for success will come to some, and what seem to be insurmountable obstacles will hinder others. Through the years, some of the people who were known to Boiseans of the past are remembered. But the stories of other residents fade over time, even though people may walk by their legacies every day.

Mining activity brought people to Idaho Territory. Many of them had already followed gold discoveries to other locations in the West, and they had learned that, sometimes, the most success came from supplying miners with food, clothing, and a place to stay. Some of those early entrepreneurs became successful and were soon investing in other enterprises, including mining, land speculation, and irrigation projects. Even those who were successful had their moments of struggle and teetered on the brink of failure. In the 21st century, residents have experienced firsthand the recent ups and downs of the national economy. This cycle has occurred countless times before. From those earliest days to now, it takes people from many backgrounds and experiences to build a city.

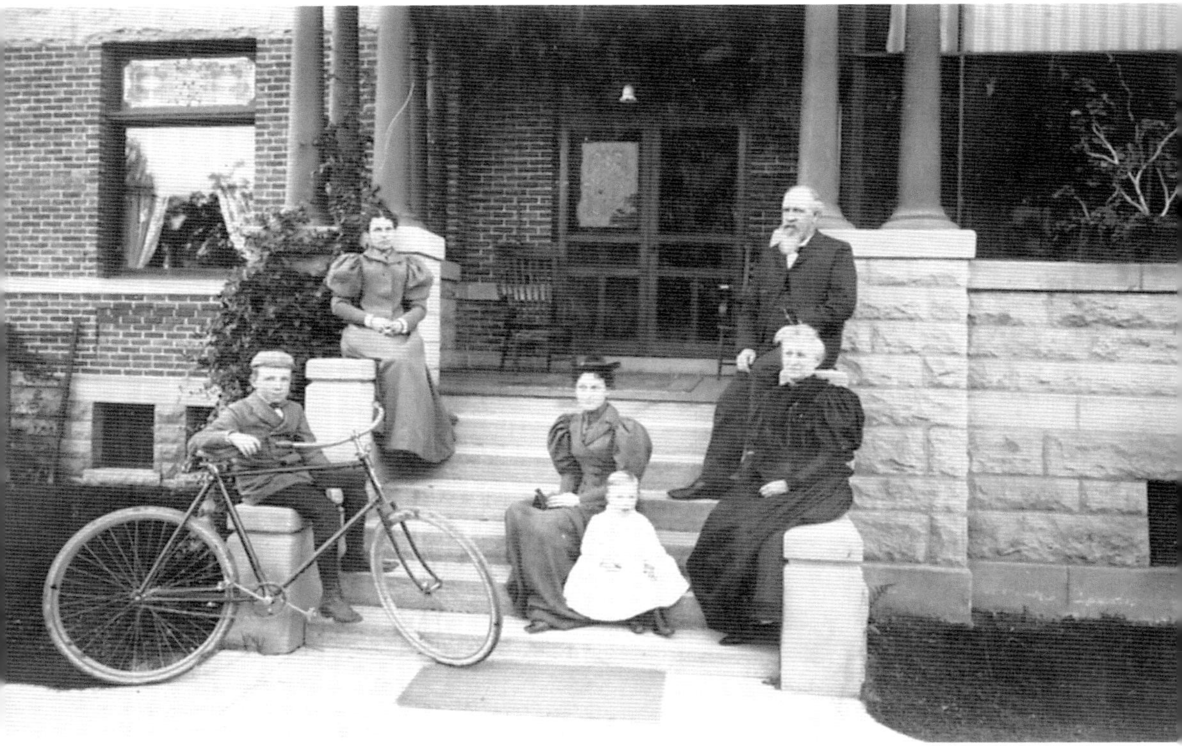

C.W. Moore

Banker Christopher Wilkinson Moore made Boise his home in 1867. Born in Toronto, Canada, he left home at the age of 17. Over the next 10 years, he sold livestock and mined in the goldfields of California, Oregon, and finally, Idaho. Mining was not his destiny—he eventually formed a partnership with Benjamin M. DuRell to supply miners with food and equipment. Locating in the Boise Basin, the partners used a string of 42 mules to supply workers in the mining towns of the Owyhees, including Booneville, Delamar, Ruby City, and Silver City. Moore and DuRell eventually opened stores at Ruby City and Silver City. At the time, merchants also acted as bankers, keeping valuables for the miners, establishing credit accounts, and receiving payments in gold dust.

C.W. met his future wife, Catherine, in Ruby City, where she had traveled from West Virginia to visit her brother, a quartz miner. They married in 1865, moving to Boise two years later, where they reared six children. In March 1867, Moore and DuRell established the First National Bank of Idaho. DuRell was bank president, and Moore served as cashier. National banks were a new development in the United States, established during the Civil War as a way to stabilize currency, regulate banks, and help finance the war. Few financial institutions in the West held national bank charters at the time; for Boise to have a national bank only four years after the town was established was a remarkable achievement. C.W. and Catherine Moore are pictured here (at right) on the front steps of their Warm Springs Avenue home around 1895. (Courtesy of the Idaho State Historical Society.)

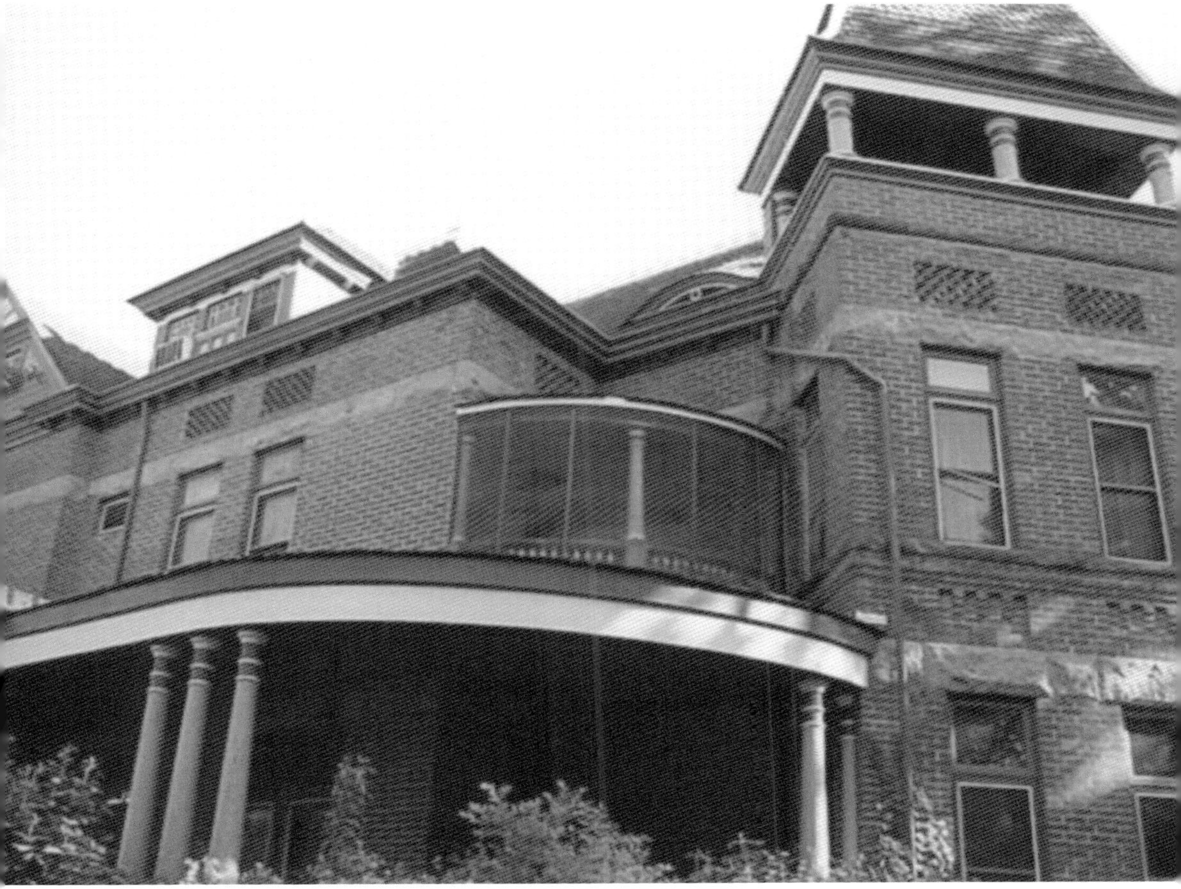

Cunningham-Moore Mansion

C.W. Moore was involved in other businesses, including the Artesian Hot and Cold Water Company. The company was founded in 1891 to pipe geothermal water to heat homes in town. Moore became the first customer when hot water was piped into his new mansion on what is now Warm Springs Avenue. Designed by architect James King, the house was a novelty, not only for its size and design, but also because it was the first residence in the nation heated by hot water. Moore's daughter Laura, who later inherited the house, married banker J.W. Cunningham in 1894. Laura lived in the house until her death in 1963. (Courtesy of the Boise Architecture Project.)

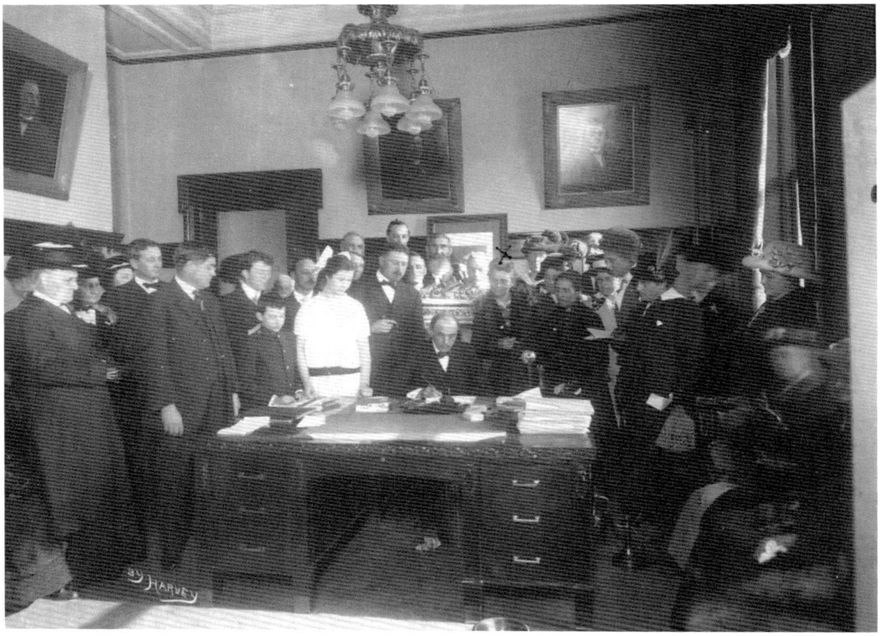

Moses Alexander

Alexander, a successful merchant, was born in Bavaria in 1853 and immigrated to the United States at age 14. He was a partner in a clothing store in Missouri before deciding to move his family to Alaska in 1891. Along the way, however, the family stopped in Boise. Impressed by the city's business opportunities, Alexander and his family settled in Boise and opened a clothing store, which remained in business until the late 1980s. He was instrumental in organizing the first Jewish synagogue in Idaho, Congregation Beth Israel (below). Alexander served two terms as mayor of Boise and two terms as governor of Idaho. He was the first elected Jewish governor in the nation who actively practiced his faith. (Above, courtesy of the Idaho State Historical Society; below, authors' collection.)

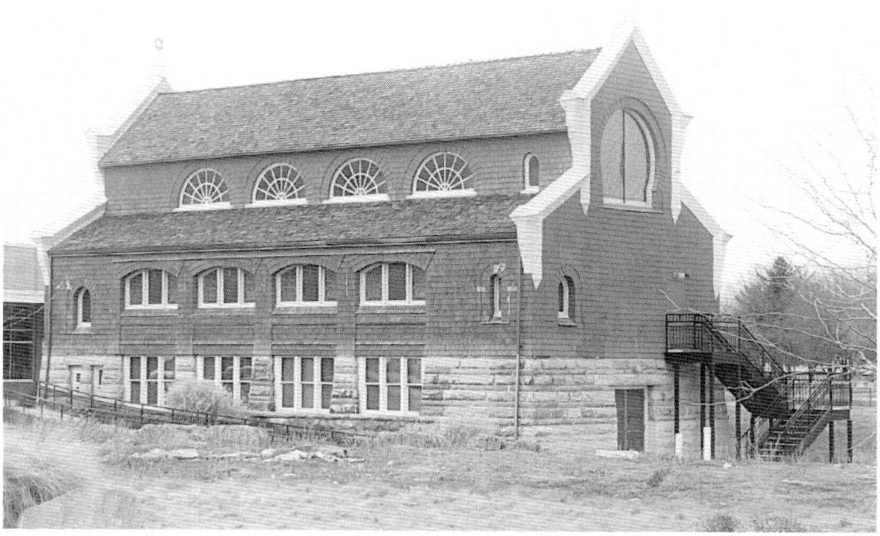

Milton Kelly

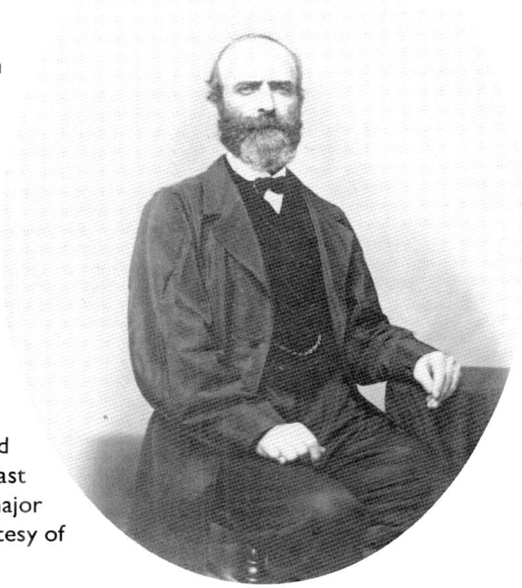

Attorney, politician, and newspaper editor Milton Kelly (right) arrived in Boise from Lewiston in 1871. Kelly was born in New England and made his way to Wisconsin, where he studied law and was admitted to the bar in 1845. The lure of gold attracted him first to California and then to Oregon, where he operated a stage to mines in Idaho. He settled in Placerville in 1863. A Republican, he was elected to the first session of the Idaho territorial legislature. In addition, he was an associate justice of the Idaho Supreme Court from 1865 to 1870. In 1871, he purchased the *Idaho Tri-Weekly Statesman* and edited the paper for 20 years. When he retired in 1892, he developed a resort, Kelly's Hot Springs (below), at a location east of Boise. Kelly did not live to see it develop into a major resort; he died in April that same year. (Both, courtesy of the Idaho State Historical Society.)

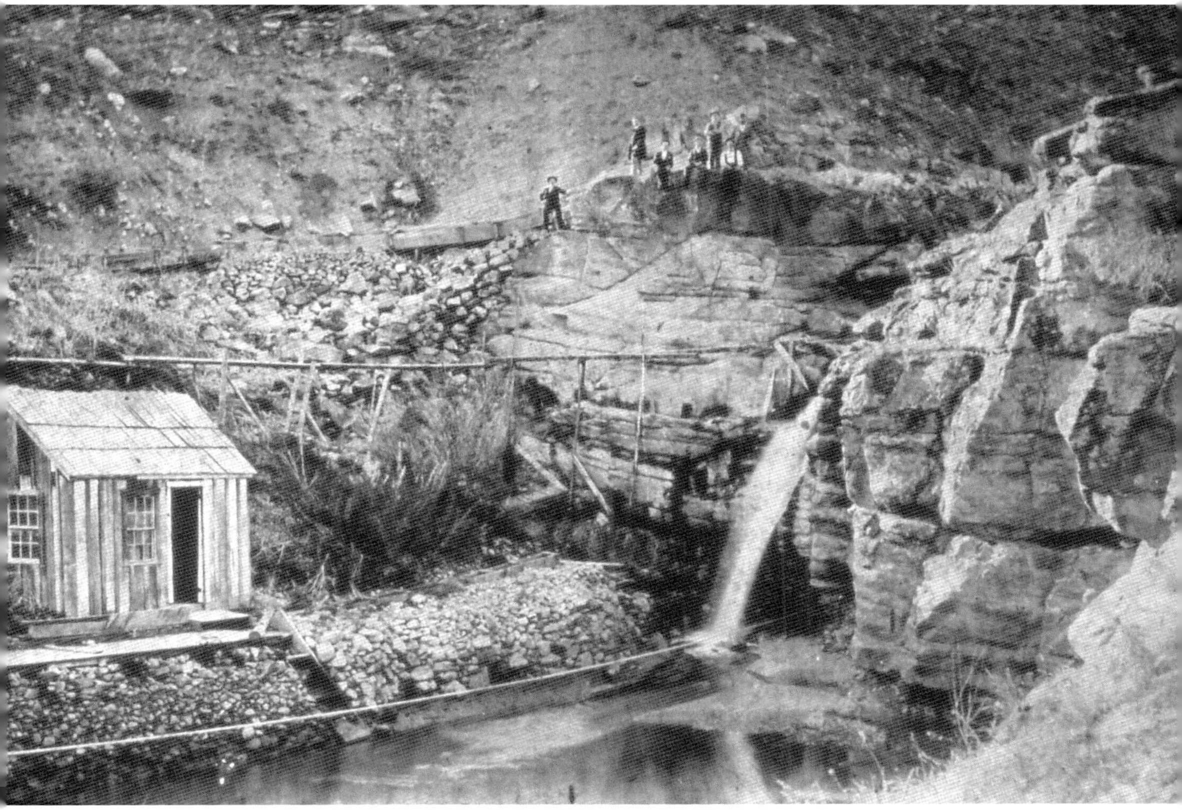

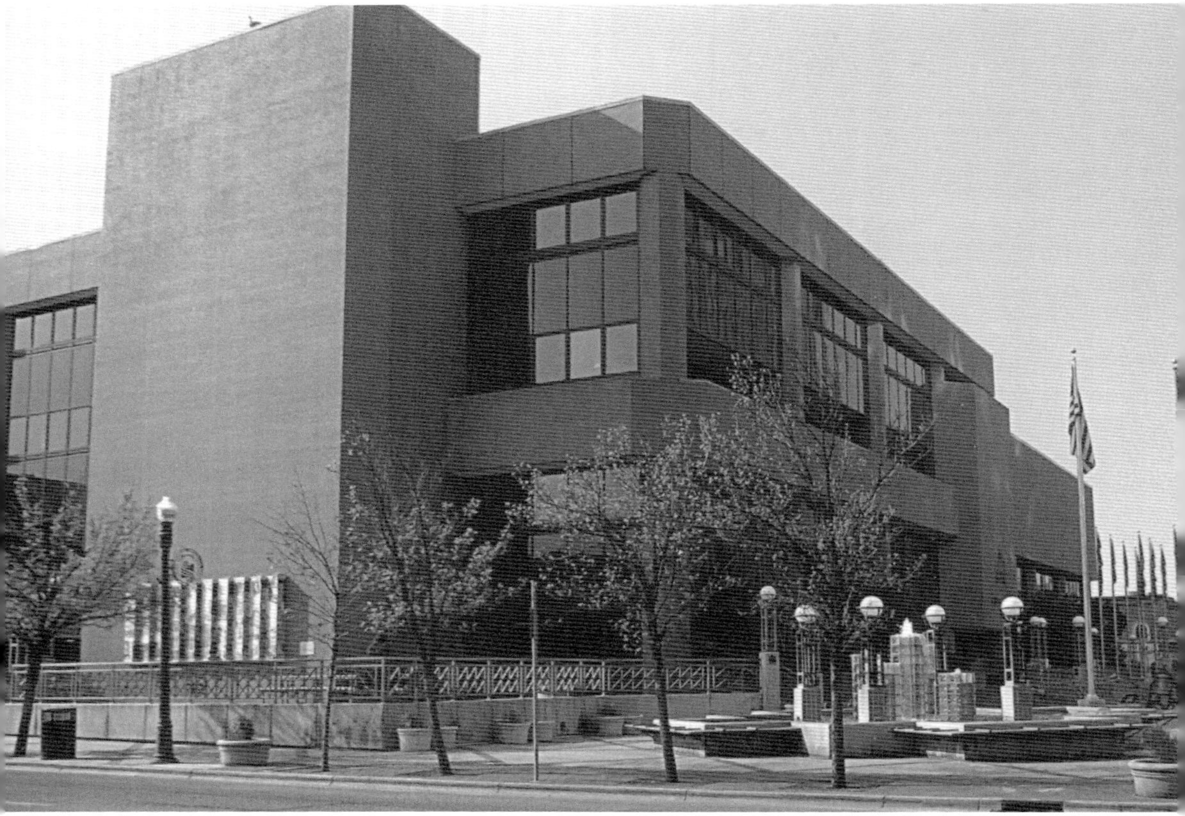

Davis Levy

Although no photograph has been located of Davis Levy, his name is legendary. In the late 1970s, a popular restaurant at 620 West Idaho Street was called Levy's Alley. The name harked back to Boise's bad old days, when the blocks from Sixth to Eighth Streets between Main and Idaho Streets were the center of the vice district. Here, gambling, prostitution, and drugs were available. Since many of the buildings were owned by businessman Davis Levy, the bad part of town took on his name. Today, Boise City Hall (pictured), constructed in 1976, stands on the site of his buildings.

Levy was an early arrival to Boise, setting up a bakery business in 1867. He was successful, and through the years, acquired more property. By 1872, the *Idaho Statesman* reported that he was operating "a grocery and a saloon, a lunch house and candy shop, has a vegetable depot and does a commission business, and may shortly be expected to have a tannery and sawmill connected with his establishment." But things slowly began to go badly for him—he lost buildings and businesses to fire on several occasions, and was the frequent victim of robberies. Over time, the enthusiastic young businessman had become, whether because of bad luck or unrecognized mental issues, an angry, bitter, and paranoid man with a reputation as a miser. His business was centered on prostitution. Rumors abounded that he kept large sums of money hidden in his home. When the city felt the need to run a cleanup campaign, his property became the target of raids.

Davis Levy was murdered, his body discovered in his room in a building at 612-1/2 Main Street. He had been strangled while eating his dinner, and his body was moved to a bed and his face covered with a towel. Recent events in Levy's life had included a conflict with a man named George Levy (not related), and the police eventually arrested him. George Levy was tried and convicted of the crime. Originally sentenced to death, on appeal, his sentence was commuted to life. Later appeals to the pardon board resulted in George Levy's release after serving nine years of his sentence. (Authors' collection.)

Hortense Adams

Adams lived in Boise for more than 30 years, making a living through her investments in local real estate and mining properties. Soon after arriving in Boise in 1894, she purchased a large tract of land from local businessman Jeramiah Brumback, which she subdivided into the Locust Grove Addition. As business partners, she and Brumback invested in mines that were being developed in the Black Hornet District, located in the foothills east of Boise. Adams was successful in her business pursuits, one of few women working in such a capacity in the early 20th century, based on articles published about her and other female mine owners and managers in the *Salt Lake Herald* and the *Weekly Miner Herald* (Prescott, Arizona) in 1902. (Authors' collection.)

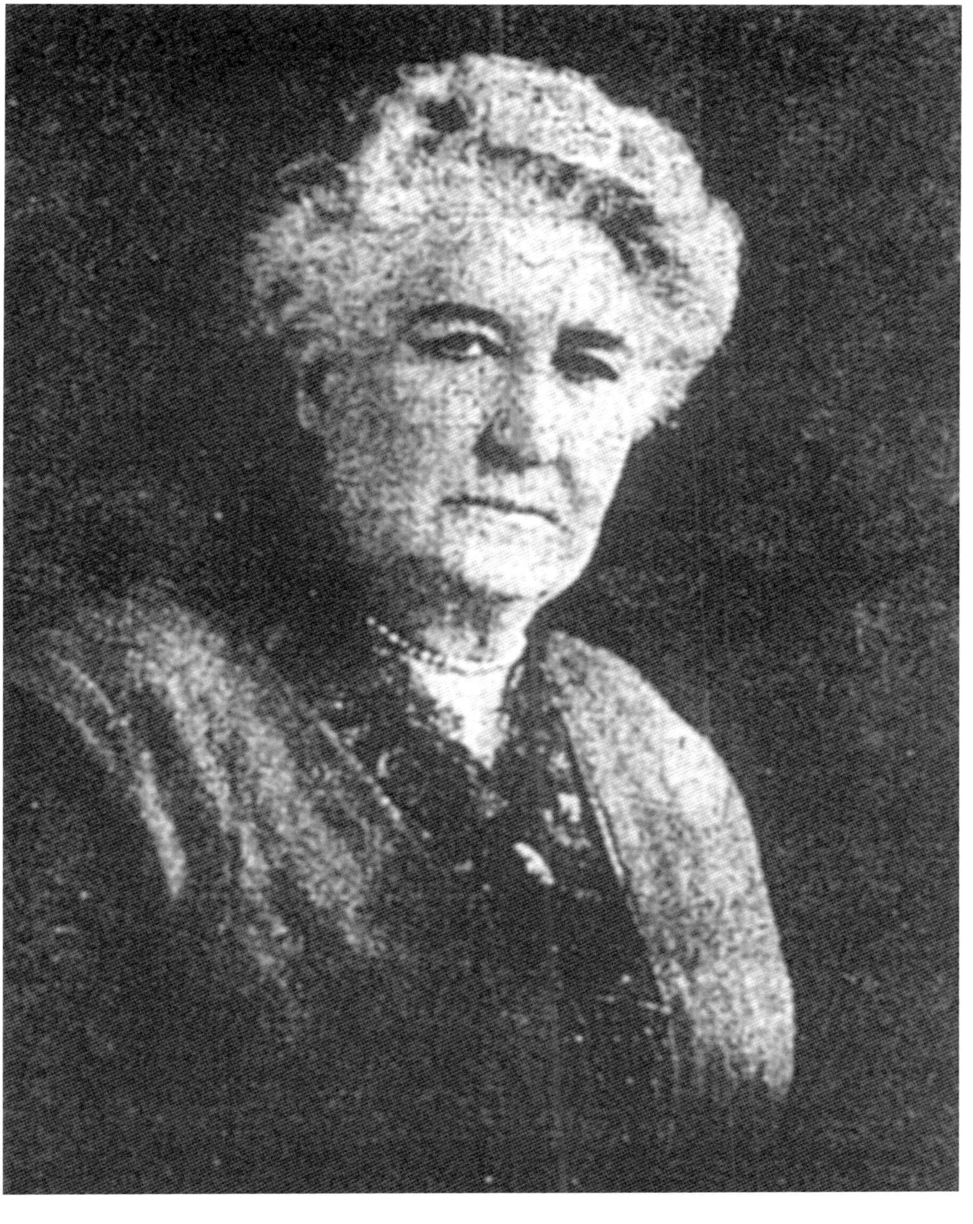

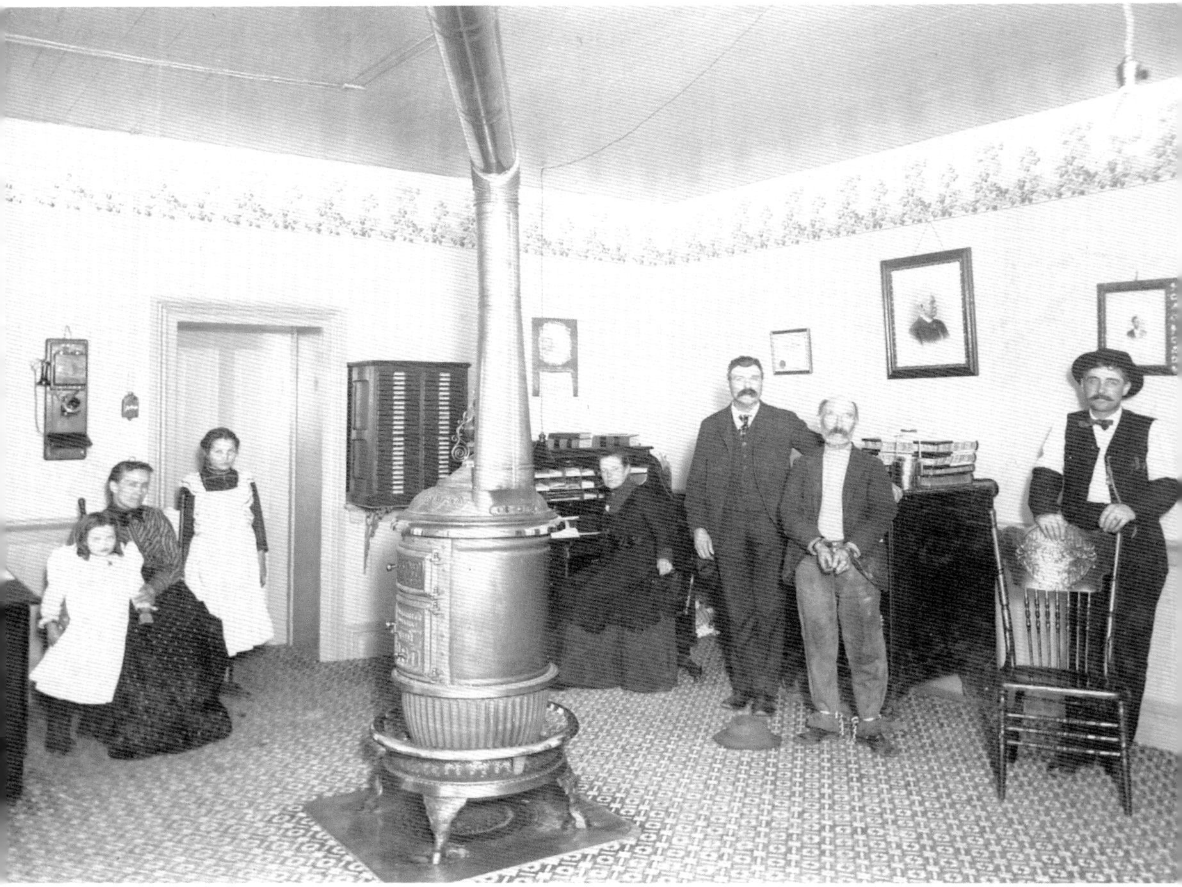

James Hogan

"Jimmy, just plain Jimmy," was the name that James Hogan begged a reporter to use when writing a story of his sentence for vagrancy and public drunkenness on August 30, 1904. Hogan never owned property, filed a homestead or mining claim, or ran for office. In the 1880s, he gained notoriety in Boise because of his inability to stay out of jail. He was identified in the newspapers as "Hogan the Stiff," a cruel reference to the alcoholism that had shaped his life.

Hogan lived a cycle of drinking and sobriety, worked when he could, and relied on the kindness of his jailers and court officers to survive. When he died in October 1907, members of the community who had known him for years chipped in to pay for flowers, a funeral service, and a plot in Morris Hill Cemetery. Pictured here from left to right are Alberta, Rebecca, and Zelma Daly; unidentified; Sheriff Joe Daly; James Hogan; and Deputy Andy Robinson. (Courtesy of the Idaho State Historical Society.)

Calvin Cobb

Born in Cleveland, Ohio, in 1853, Calvin Cobb was raised in Chicago and worked for his father, who owned a private circulating library, until the mid-1880s, when Calvin engaged in the livestock business. In 1887, he traveled to Boise with a group representing the Union Pacific Railroad and decided to move his family west. In 1889, Cobb and two partners purchased the *Idaho Statesman* from Milton Kelly. Cobb remained in charge of the newspaper until his death in 1928, bringing national notice to Boise through his promotion of the city and his staunch Republican politics, as well as the professionalism of the newspaper itself. He supported Theodore Roosevelt until 1912, when Roosevelt left the Republican Party. Cobb's editorial headline in response was "Teddy, you stink!" Pictured here from left to right are Fannie, Margaret, Lyon, and Calvin Cobb. (Courtesy of the Idaho State Historical Society.)

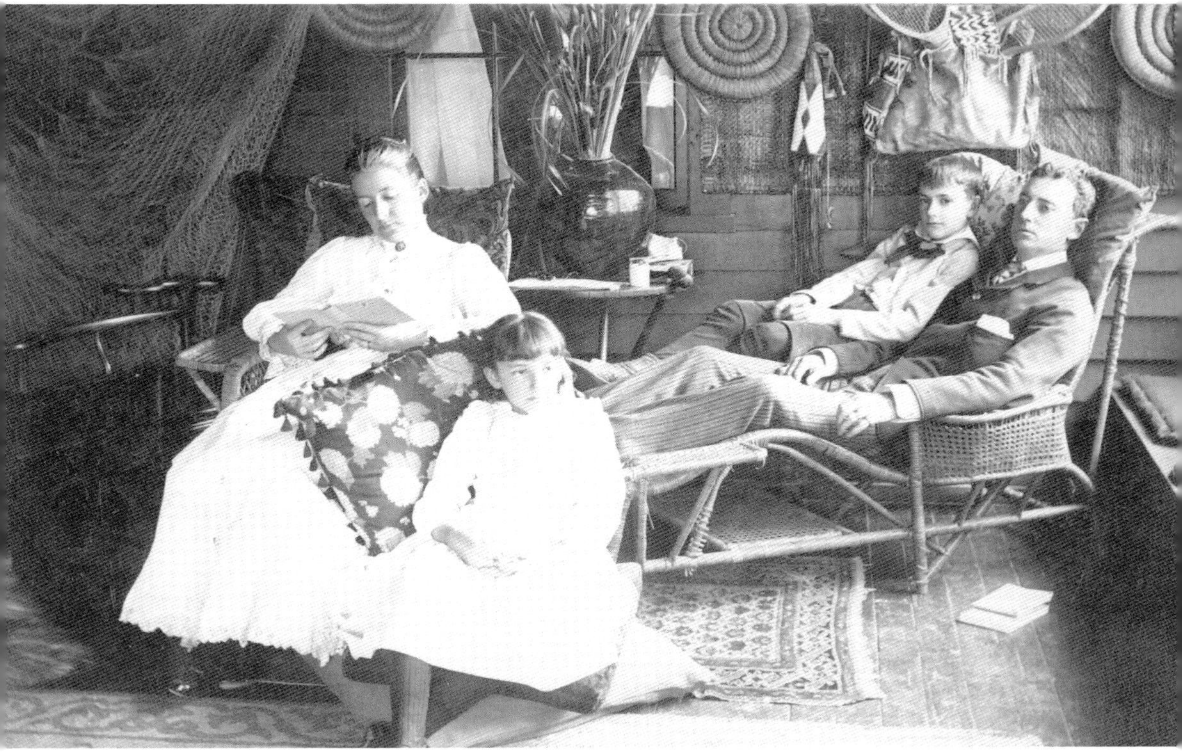

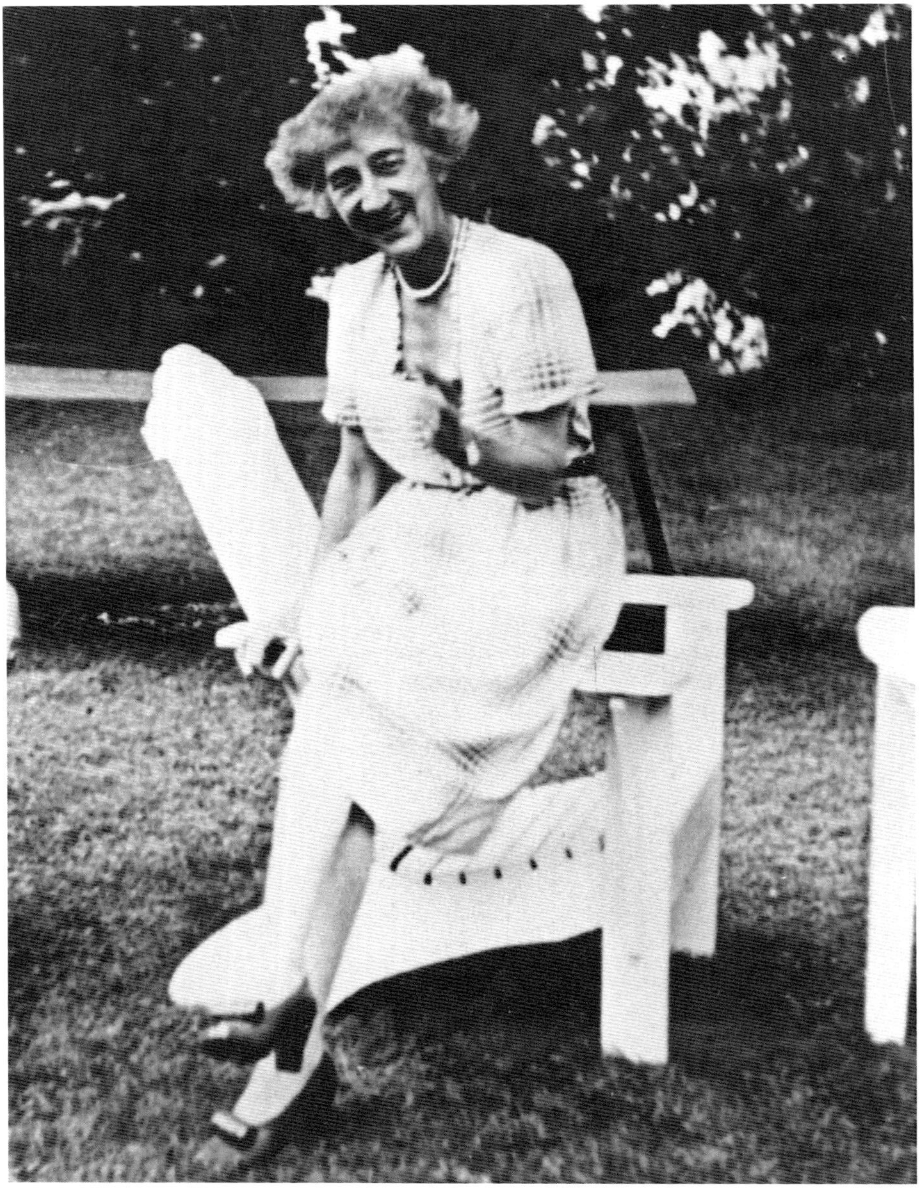

Margaret Cobb Ailshie

When *Idaho Statesman* publisher Calvin Cobb died in 1928, no one expected that his daughter Margaret would take on the job. She was raised to enter the upper reaches of society, to join clubs, make afternoon calls, and go to dances—but she had also been exposed to the idea of social responsibility. When World War I began, she joined the Red Cross and worked in canteens and hospitals in New York and France. Returning to Boise in 1919, she remained active in the Red Cross, serving as the local chapter president. She married James Ailshie Jr. in 1924, but was widowed only five years later. After taking over at the newspaper, Ailshie increased its circulation and started an evening edition, having purchased and absorbed the rival *Evening Capital News*. When Ailshie died in 1959, the Cobb family's era at the *Statesman* ended after 70 years. (Courtesy of the Idaho State Historical Society.)

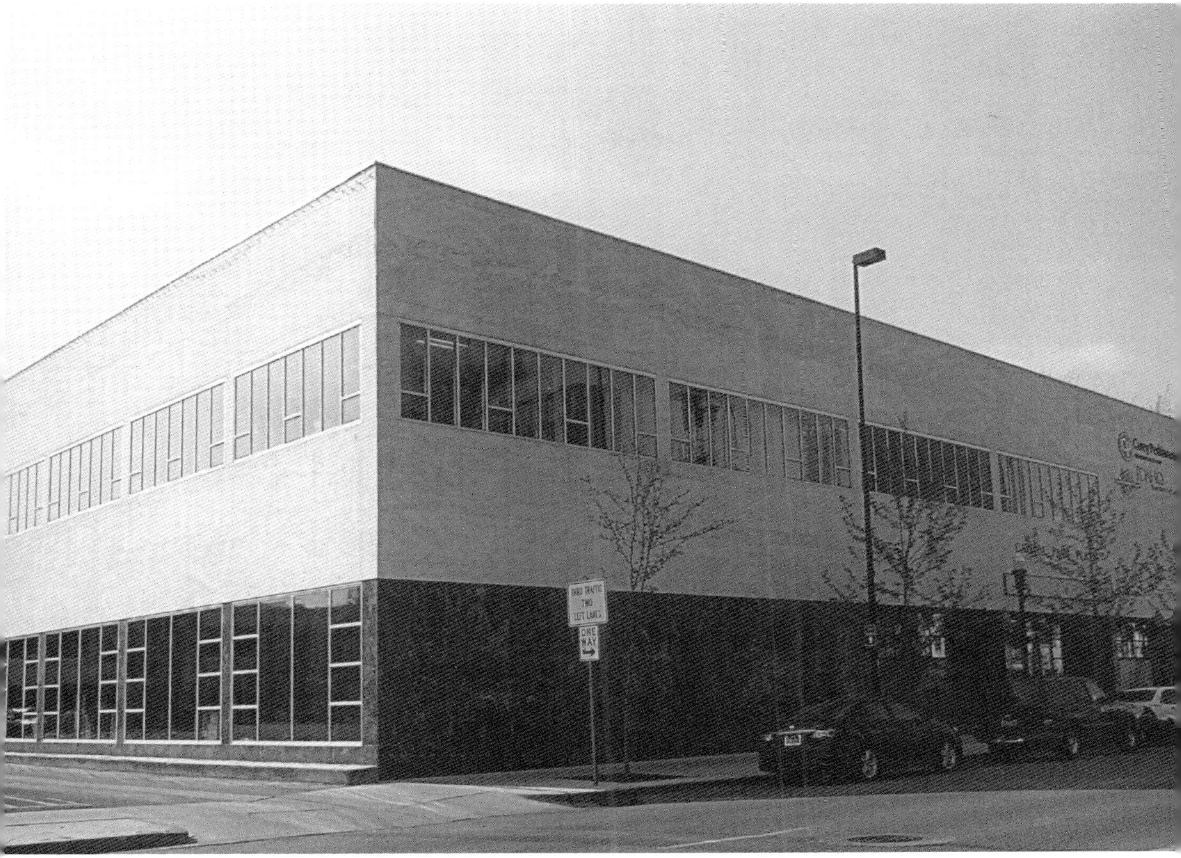

Idaho Statesman Building

Boise's premier newspaper has been located in several buildings over the course of its 150-year history. The paper was first printed in a log building with a dirt floor on Main Street. The log building was replaced by a two-story wood frame building on the northwest corner of Sixth and Main Streets. In 1909, the architectural firm of Wayland and Fennell was commissioned to design a new building, which would be home to the paper until 1952. A new building designed by architect Pietro Belluschi was built on the corner of Sixth and Bannock Streets. The building is a smaller version of the *Oregonian's* building in Portland, which Margaret Cobb Ailshie had visited. This Mid-century Modern building served as headquarters for the newspaper until the 1970s, when a much larger office building and printing plant was constructed west of Boise on Curtis Road. (Authors' collection.)

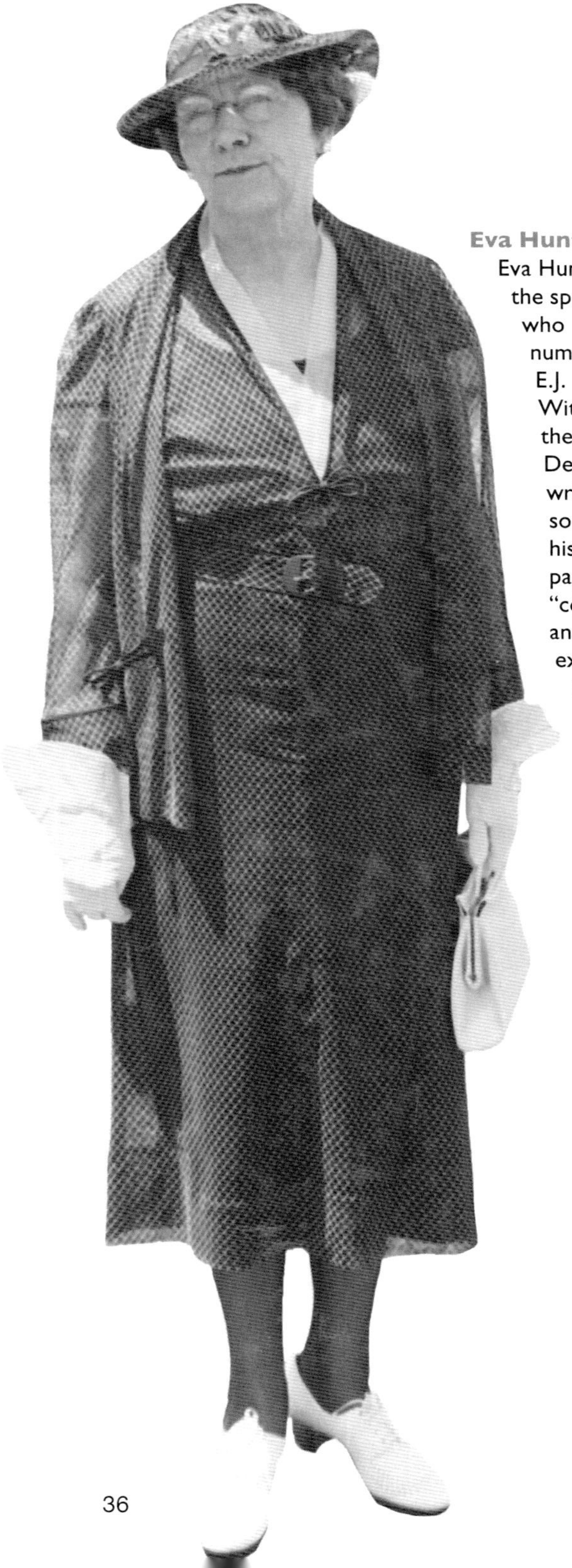

Eva Hunt Dockery

Eva Hunt Dockery, shown here leaving for a European tour in the spring of 1937, was a tireless volunteer and club member who championed women's rights, public libraries, and numerous charitable causes. She and her husband, attorney E.J. Dockery, moved to Boise from Wisconsin in 1900. Within a short time, she was working as a reporter for the *Idaho Daily Statesman*. By the time of her death on December 24, 1937, she was known as "the dean of Idaho writers" and had become the editor of the *Statesman*'s society page and the pioneer page, which covered local history. Dockery reported that working for a small-town paper had afforded her a wide variety of experiences, "covering police and Supreme Courts, hotel interviews and celebrities—everything at one time or another except the legislature." (Courtesy of the Idaho State Historical Society.)

Betty Penson-Ward

Reporter, author, women's rights advocate, and historian Betty Penson-Ward was a Boise native who contributed to the *Idaho Statesman* for over 50 years. When she passed away on September 4, 2002, the top headline of the *Statesman* declared, "Writer personified *Idaho Statesman* for half a century." Born Betty Butler to H.B. and Maybelle Tingley Butler, she taught herself to read at age four, which she claimed in 1990 was "probably the most magnificent thing I've ever done." She attended St. Theresa's Academy and Boise High School and excelled at spelling. This led Penson-Ward to her first job at age 19 as a proofreader for the *Boise Capital News* in 1934. Working there, she also gained newspaper experience when she served as church editor, weather editor, society editor, and editor of country correspondence. She left the *Capital News* three years later to become a rookie police reporter for the *Idaho Statesman*. Taken under the wing of her mentor and *Idaho Statesman* publisher, Margaret Ailshie, she traveled to New York to cover fashion openings and was named editor of the women's department, eventually becoming the travel editor and conducting interviews from all over the globe. Ward also used her weekly column to support local issues, including Music Week, the public library, the Morrison Center, and women's organizations. (Courtesy of the Idaho State Historical Society.)

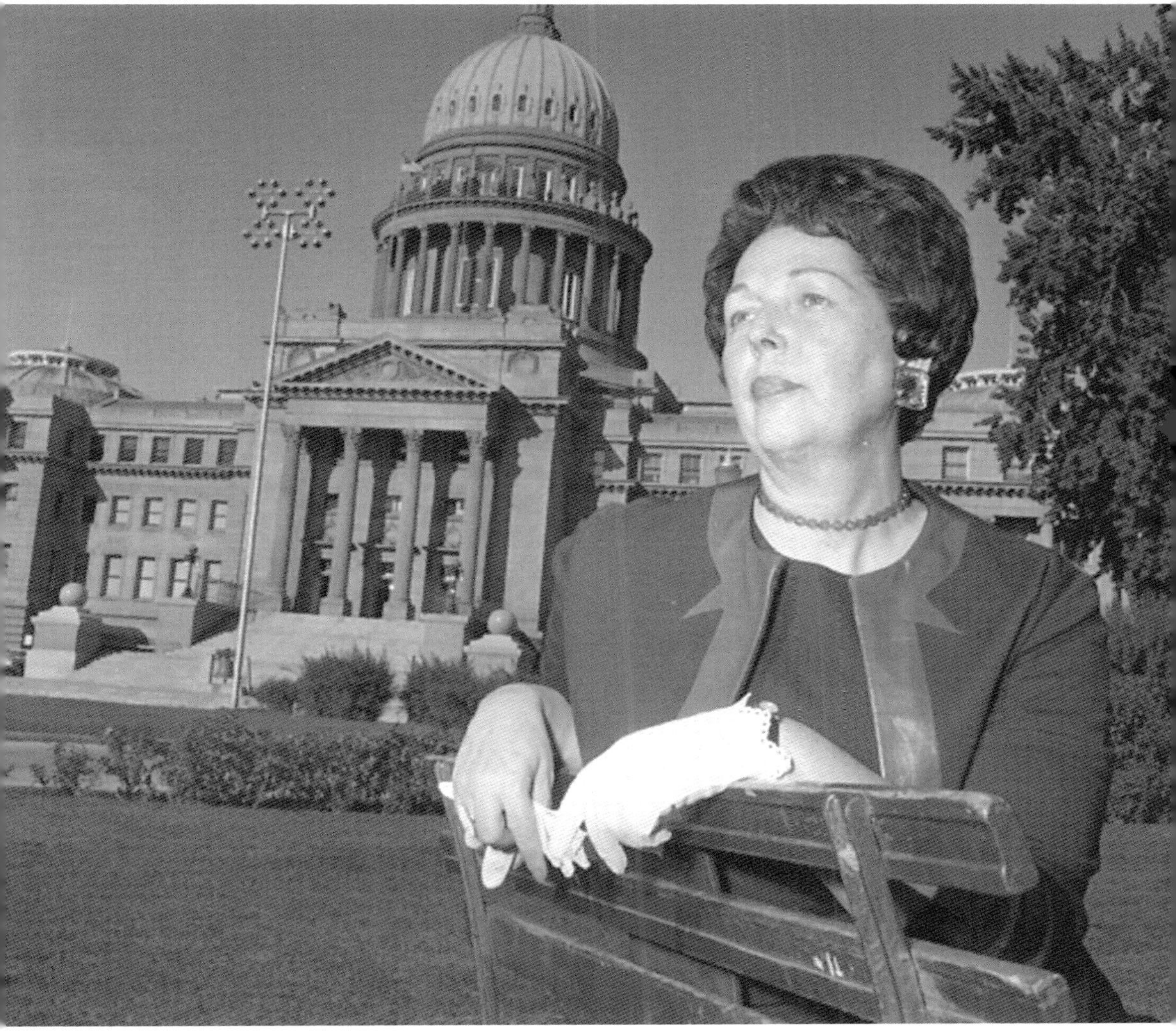

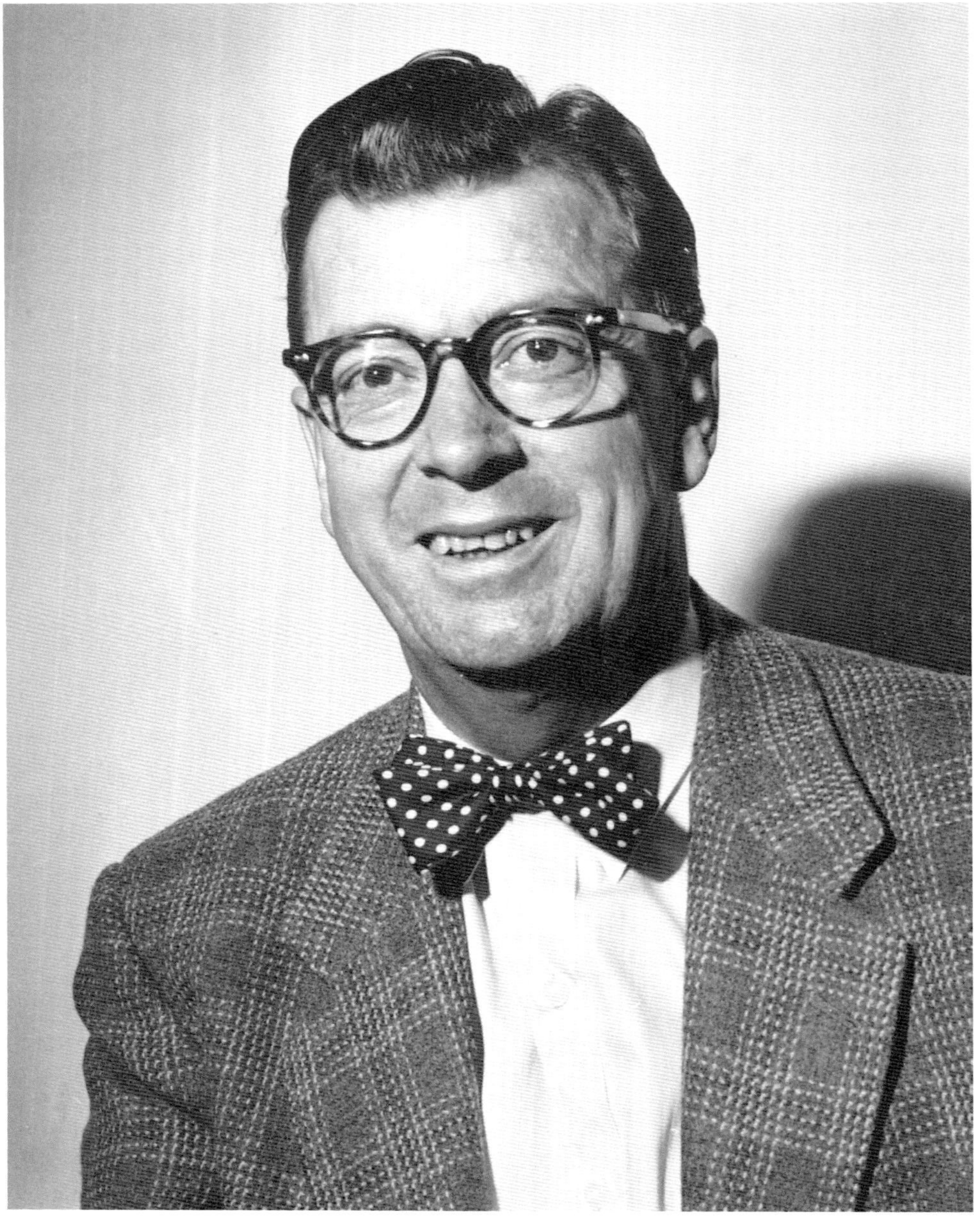

John Corlett

Idaho Statesman political editor John Corlett was known as the dean of Idaho political writers. In over 40 years of reporting, he established a reputation as a fair, hard-hitting, knowledgeable journalist who was committed to providing readers with information about their local and state government. In his long tenure with the *Statesman*, he covered the politics and administrations of 11 governors, 7 presidents, 12 senators, and 15 congressmen. When he retired in 1975, the *Statesman* noted: "He was accurate when it sacrificed impact, dull when it avoided pedantry, and candid when he was wrong. He is also not afraid to think. These things have made him the most influential journalist in Idaho political history." (Courtesy of the Idaho State Historical Society.)

Dr. George Collister

At the time of his death at the age of 79 in 1935, Dr. Collister had practiced medicine in Boise for 54 years. He was born in Willoughby, Ohio, in 1856. After completing medical school, he made his way west to Boise in 1881, where his sister Francis lived. The Collister siblings were joined by one more sister, Julia, who moved to Boise by 1886. Dr. Collister was not only a physician, he was also one of the leading fruit growers in Ada County. He owned a 113-acre orchard approximately six miles from downtown Boise. Here, he raised prize-winning prunes, apples, pears, and peaches. His orchard was located on Valley Road, today known as State Street. His property's intersection with Valley Road was known as "Collister Corner," and the area surrounding his farm became known as Collister. He invested in the electric railway system, the Boise & Interurban, which ran between Boise and Caldwell. (Courtesy of the Idaho State Historical Society.)

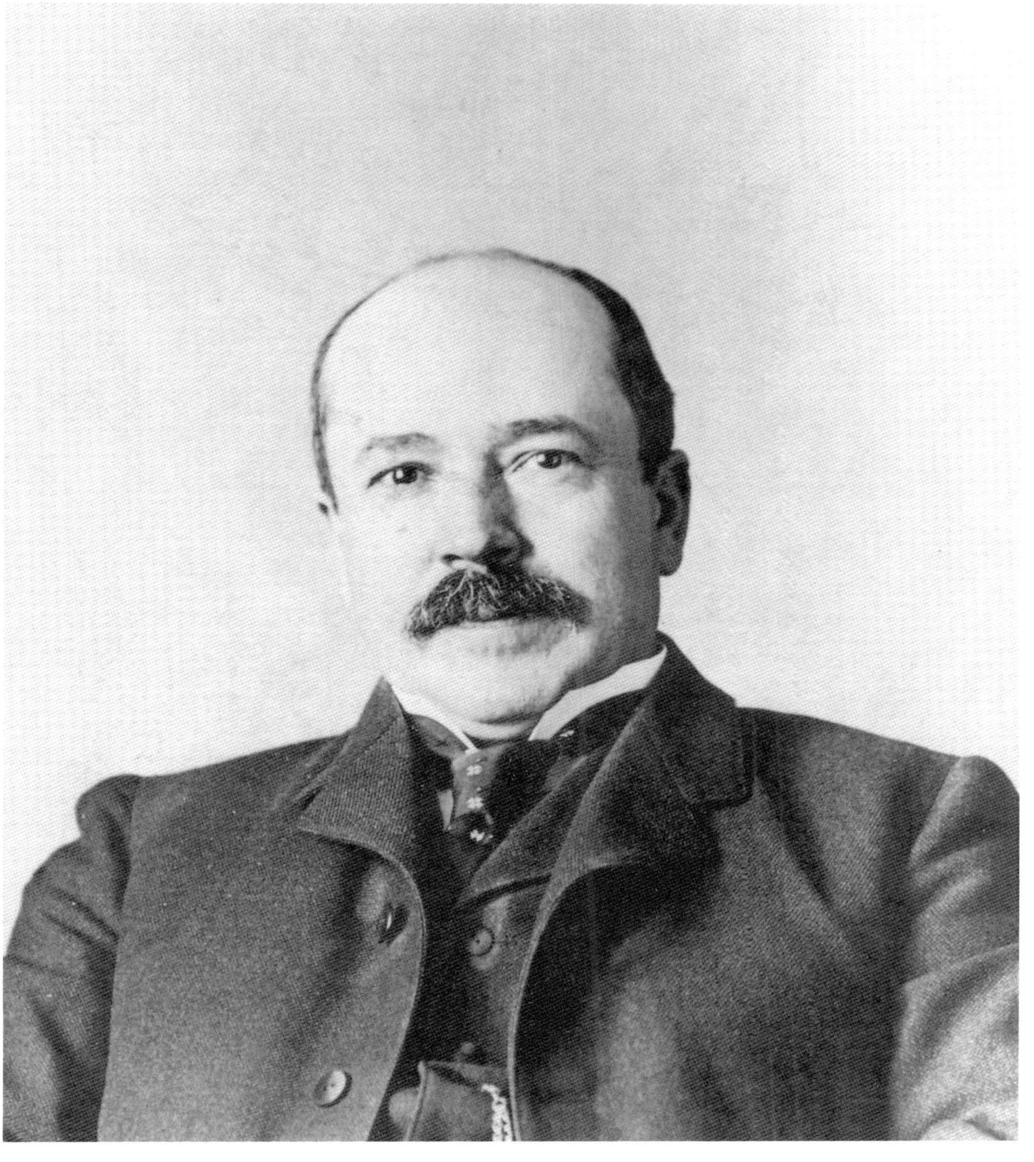

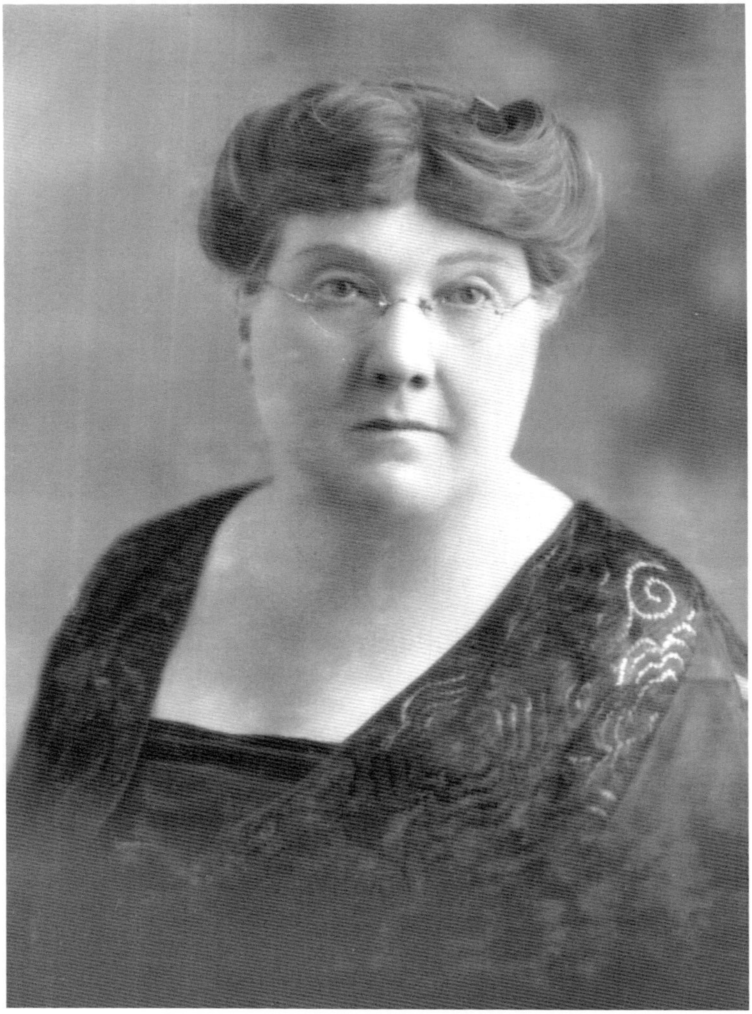

Mary Elizabeth Collister

Today, Mary Collister is best known for her philanthropic and charitable donations while she was married to Dr. George Collister. A lifelong Methodist, she was instrumental, along with George, in donating land from their farm for both a school and two churches. Mary was a successful businesswoman prior to her marriage to Dr. Collister. Born Mary Elizabeth Cook, she moved west from Illinois and married her first husband, a miner, John Morden, in 1875 in Kernville, California. By 1885, Mary (at that time called Lizzie) moved to Boise with her husband and son Thomas. In 1866, she opened the Capital Restaurant at the corner of Main and Seventh Streets (now Capitol Boulevard). The restaurant was a success, and newspaper articles regularly reported on the fine fare she served. She owned and operated several different restaurants, even after the death of her first husband in 1892. After her marriage to Dr. Collister, Mary sold her restaurant business, devoting her time to numerous social and community organizations. She was active in the Methodist church, the Columbian Club, and other groups. In 1911, Mary and George moved to a three-story house designed by the local architecture firm Tourtellotte & Hummel. Named Mountain View, it was a landmark in Collister for many years. In the mid-1940s, it was remodeled into the Elks Convalescent Home for Children. (Courtesy of the Idaho State Historical Society.)

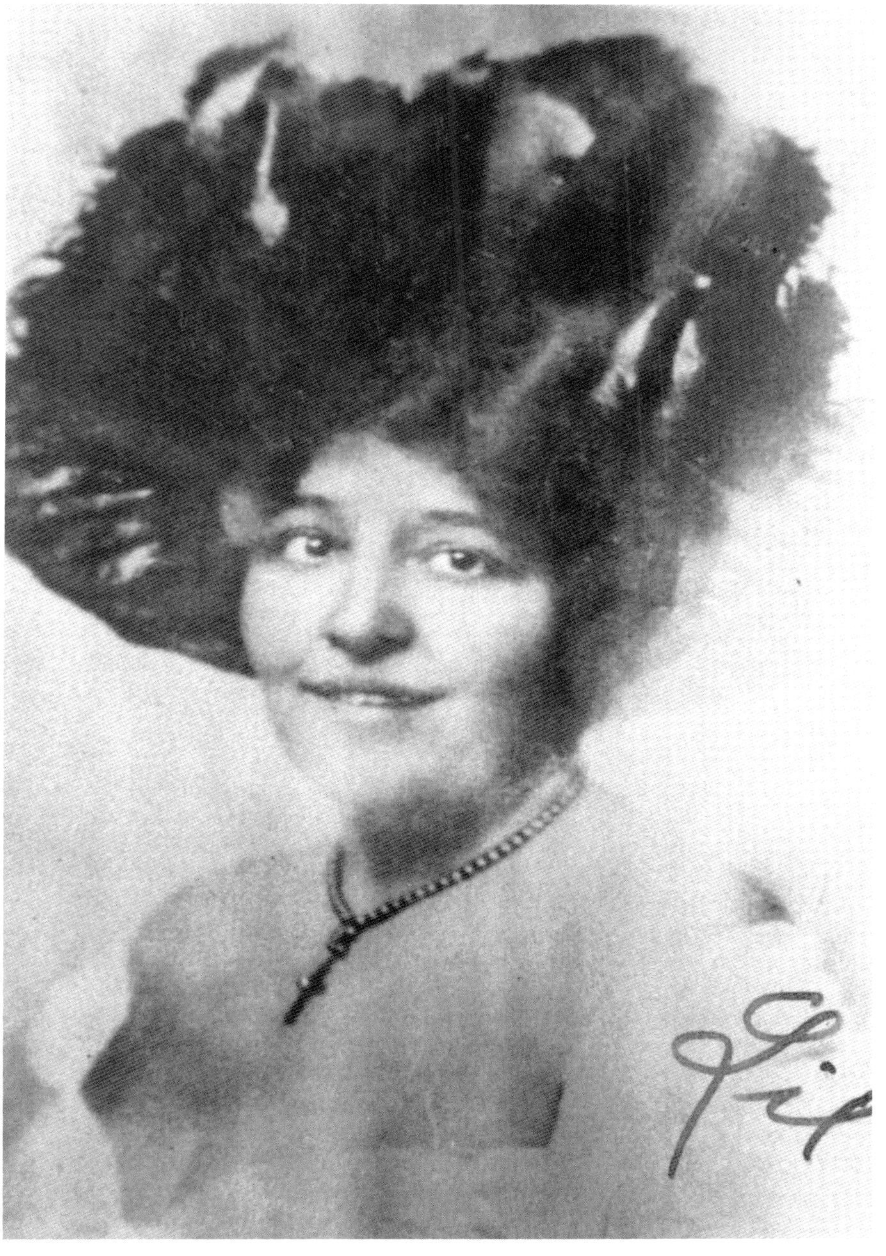

Diamond Tooth Lil

In the early 1940s, the legendary Diamond Tooth Lil resided in Boise, where she managed a tourist court. She put Boise in the national news when she announced that she was going to leave the diamond embedded in her tooth to the Idaho Children's Home when she died. An entertainer, dancer and reputed madam, she was born Evelyn Failla in Austria in 1887. Her family immigrated to Ohio when she was a child. By 13, she had left her family, dancing her way across the country to San Francisco. Her nickname stemmed from the diamond she had embedded in a gold tooth in 1907. She claimed that she won it after winning a bet on a horse race from a Reno, Nevada, dentist. (Courtesy of the Idaho State Historical Society.)

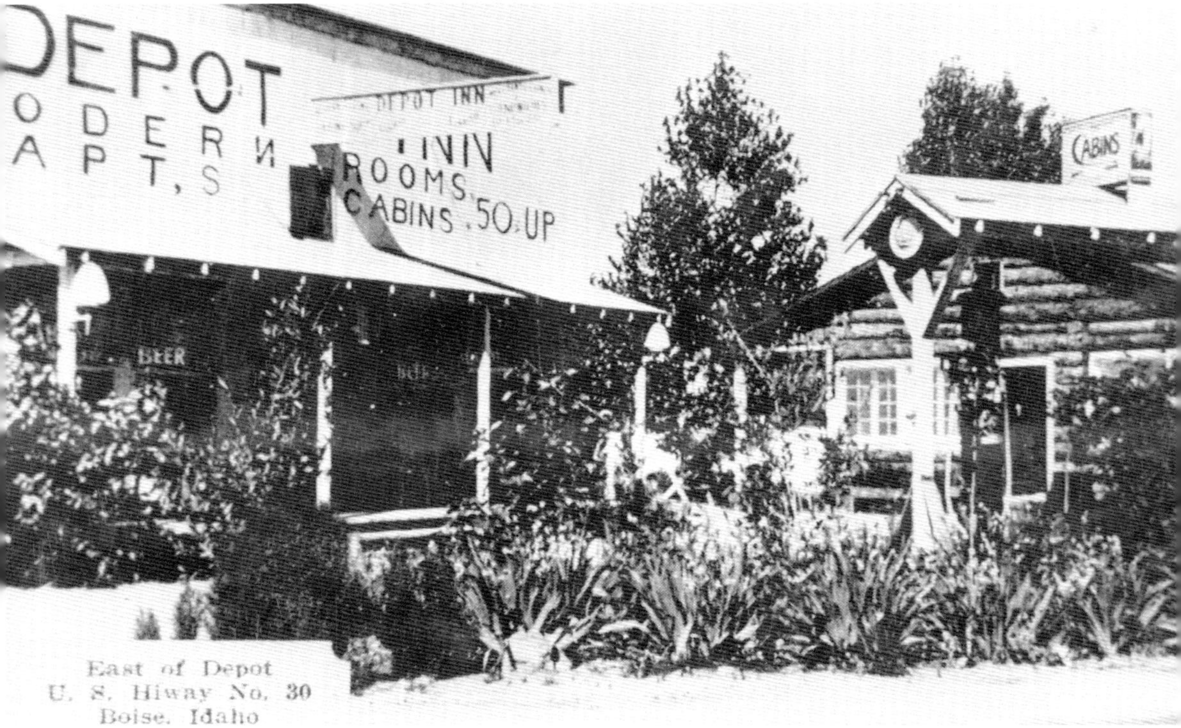

Depot Motor Court

Shown here is the tourist court managed by Diamond Tooth Lil. As a showgirl, she entertained at mining towns throughout the West, including Silver City in the Owyhee Mountains. Married nine times, among them to convicted murderer Diamondfield Jack Davis (he was later pardoned), she supposedly led a wild life and claimed to have drunk champagne with the Prince of Wales. In a 1943 interview, she stated, "We drank, but we didn't get drunk in those days. You can't have fun when you're drunk, and we were out for fun." Diamond Tooth Lil died in 1967 in California at age 89. (Courtesy of the Idaho State Historical Society.)

CHAPTER THREE

Movers and Shakers

Movers and shakers have the vision and courage to push a community forward. James Hawley, considered by many to be the best criminal lawyer of his generation in the West, came to Boise as a teenager in the early 1860s. From his modest start, he served in the territorial legislature and was eventually elected governor of Idaho. He was a successful defense lawyer—the firm he established in the 19th century remains in business today. The Columbian Club, originally established in 1892 to help provide Idaho's exhibits at the World's Columbian Exposition in Chicago in 1893, was a powerful advocate for civic improvement. The Columbian Club organized Boise's first lending library, established public playgrounds for children, and participated in many projects to beautify the city and enhance the lives of Boiseans.

In the 1960s, when downtown Boise was undergoing change and many old buildings were being demolished in the name of redevelopment, Billy Fong, a 40-year resident of downtown, challenged city leaders when he refused to leave his home. As destruction of downtown continued, Joan Carley bought and restored the 19th-century Pioneer Tent building, leading the charge for the preservation of historic buildings. Cecil Andrus, who has made Boise his home, is the only person elected to serve four terms as governor of the state. His influence broadened when he was named to serve as secretary of the interior in the Jimmy Carter administration.

Boise has become a vital, lively, and livable community through the efforts of those individuals who were not afraid to speak out to improve the economy, the environment, and the social conditions of the city.

James Hawley

James Henry Hawley, known as Idaho's "Grand Old Man," served one term as mayor of Boise (1903–1905) and was the ninth governor of Idaho (1910–1912). Hawley's parents, Thomas and Annie Carr Hawley, were originally from New York, but in 1847, the year James was born, they lived in Iowa. His mother died while James was a baby, and his father left his son with an uncle to follow the lure of gold to California in 1849. James remained in Iowa until 1861, then moved to California with his uncle. He was there only a short time before leaving to follow the gold rush to the Boise Basin. After a brief sojourn in Idaho, he returned to California and entered San Francisco City College, studying law with a local law firm.

Back in the Boise Basin by 1869, he became one of Idaho's leading attorneys, practicing law until the early years of the 20th century. Hawley specialized in murder cases. He represented the Sparks-Harrell cattle operation in 1896 during the sensational Diamondfield Jack Davis case. Davis was accused of the murder of two young sheep herders, John Wilson and Daniel Cummings. Hawley won him a full pardon. In 1907, Hawley and William E. Borah were the prosecutors in the trial of William D. "Big Bill" Haywood for conspiracy to assassinate former governor Frank Steunenberg. As J. Anthony Lukas wrote, no Idaho lawyer could match the length and breadth of Hawley's courtroom experience. His appearance, according to Lukas, was the model of an old-time Western lawyer, with none of the polish of Eastern attorneys. Casual in dress and appearance and not suave, Hawley had the ability to move a jury. He also made a name for himself in politics and as an author. He served in both houses of the territorial legislature, served as US district attorney for the Territory of Idaho, and authored the multiple volume *History of Idaho, the Gem of the Mountains* in 1920, which remains an indispensable aid for anyone interested in the state's history. He died in Boise at his home on Main Street in 1929, lauded by Sen. William Borah as a "remarkable trial attorney, who saved the necks of more men he defended and sent to prison more murderers he prosecuted, than any I know." (Courtesy of the Idaho State Historical Society.)

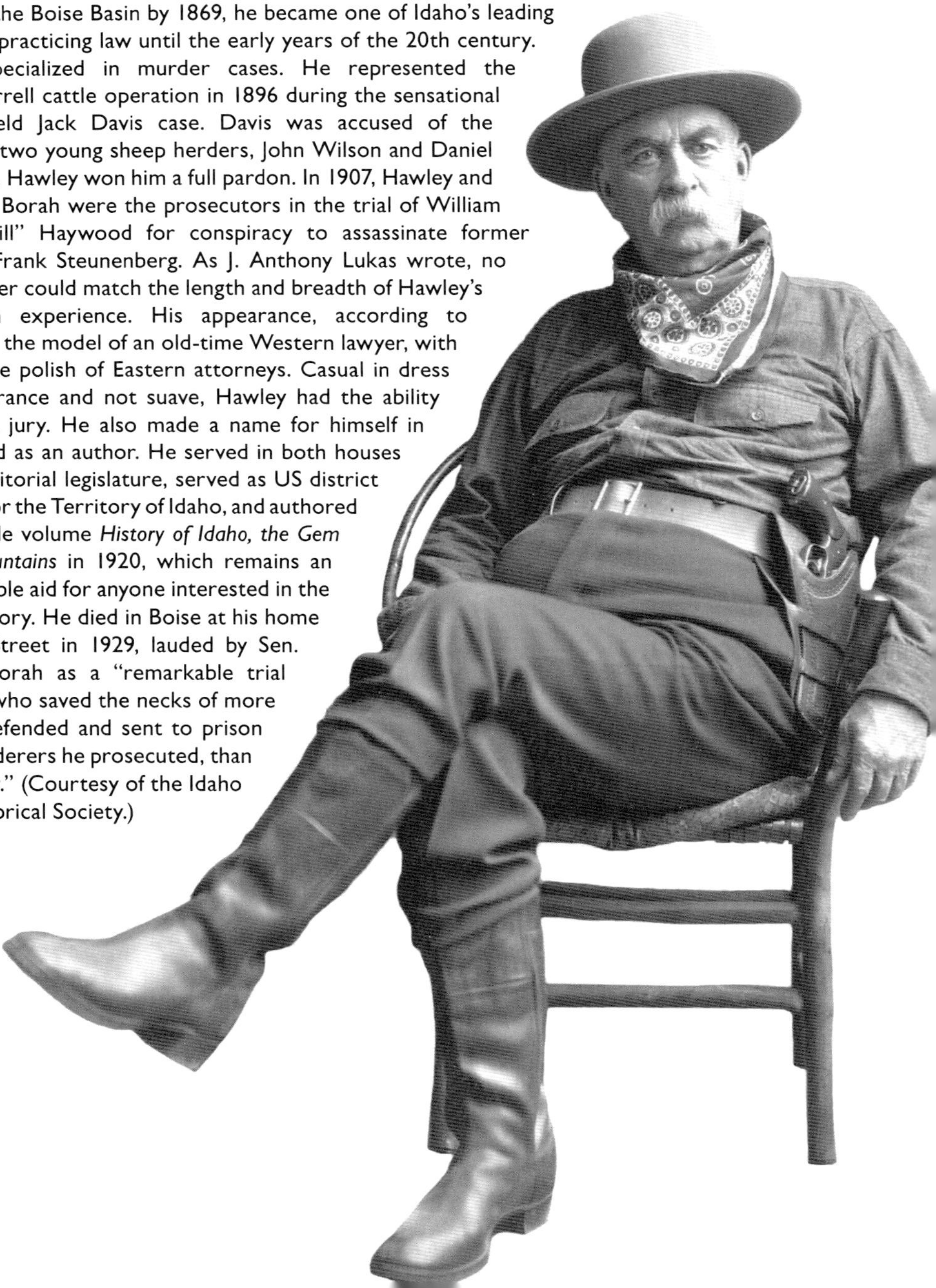

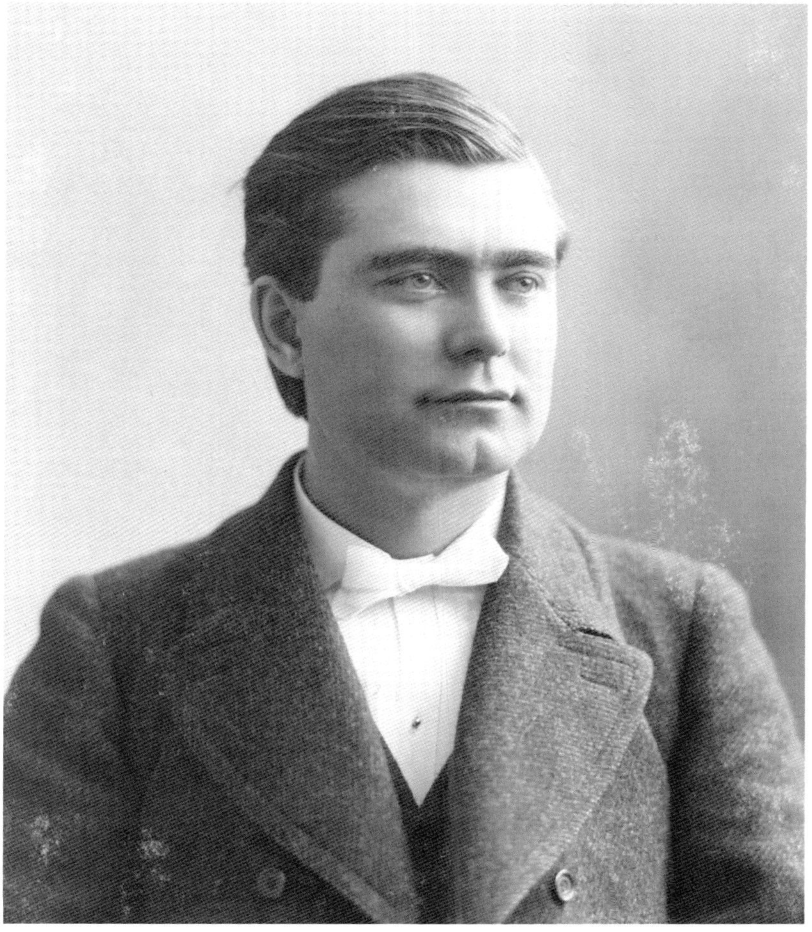

William Edgar Borah

A story about William E. Borah, which may be more myth than fact, says that late in 1890, he was heading to Seattle to start a law practice but ran out of funds when he reached Boise and decided to stay. The young attorney was born in Illinois in 1865. He left his home state for law school in Kansas, but dropped out after his freshman year due to illness. Continuing his studies under the direction of A.M. Lasley, his brother-in-law, Borah passed the bar examination in Kansas. He practiced law with Lasley for a few years before heading west. Arriving in Boise shortly after Idaho became a state, he opened a law office and soon earned a reputation as a notable attorney. In 1907, as a member of the prosecution team in the Haywood Trial (see page 44), Borah gained national attention. The same year, the Idaho legislature elected Borah to the US Senate, where he served with distinction for 37 years, longer than any other US senator in Idaho history. A well-known public speaker, Borah was nicknamed the "Lion of Idaho" and was considered the equivalent of Daniel Webster and William Jennings Bryan. A prominent progressive politician, he played a leading role in creating two constitutional amendments, the 16th, which established the graduated income tax, and the 17th, which allowed for direct election of senators. He was also a strong believer in avoiding "foreign entanglements," and may be most remembered for his role in keeping the United States out of the League of Nations after World War I. In 1895, he married Mary McConnell, who was the daughter of Gov. William J. McConnell. They had no children, but Borah engaged in a long-running affair with Alice Roosevelt Longworth (daughter of Theodore Roosevelt), with whom he fathered a daughter, Paulina, in 1925. (Courtesy of the Idaho State Historical Society.)

Mary McConnell Borah

In an interview long after William Borah's death, Mary "Mamie" McConnell Borah stated, "Politics was my life." Her father, William McConnell, was governor of Idaho, and she acted as her father's hostess and secretary. After her marriage to William Borah, she spent many years in Washington, DC. Known to her friends as "Little Borah," Mary lived to the age of 105. (Courtesy of the Idaho State Historical Society.)

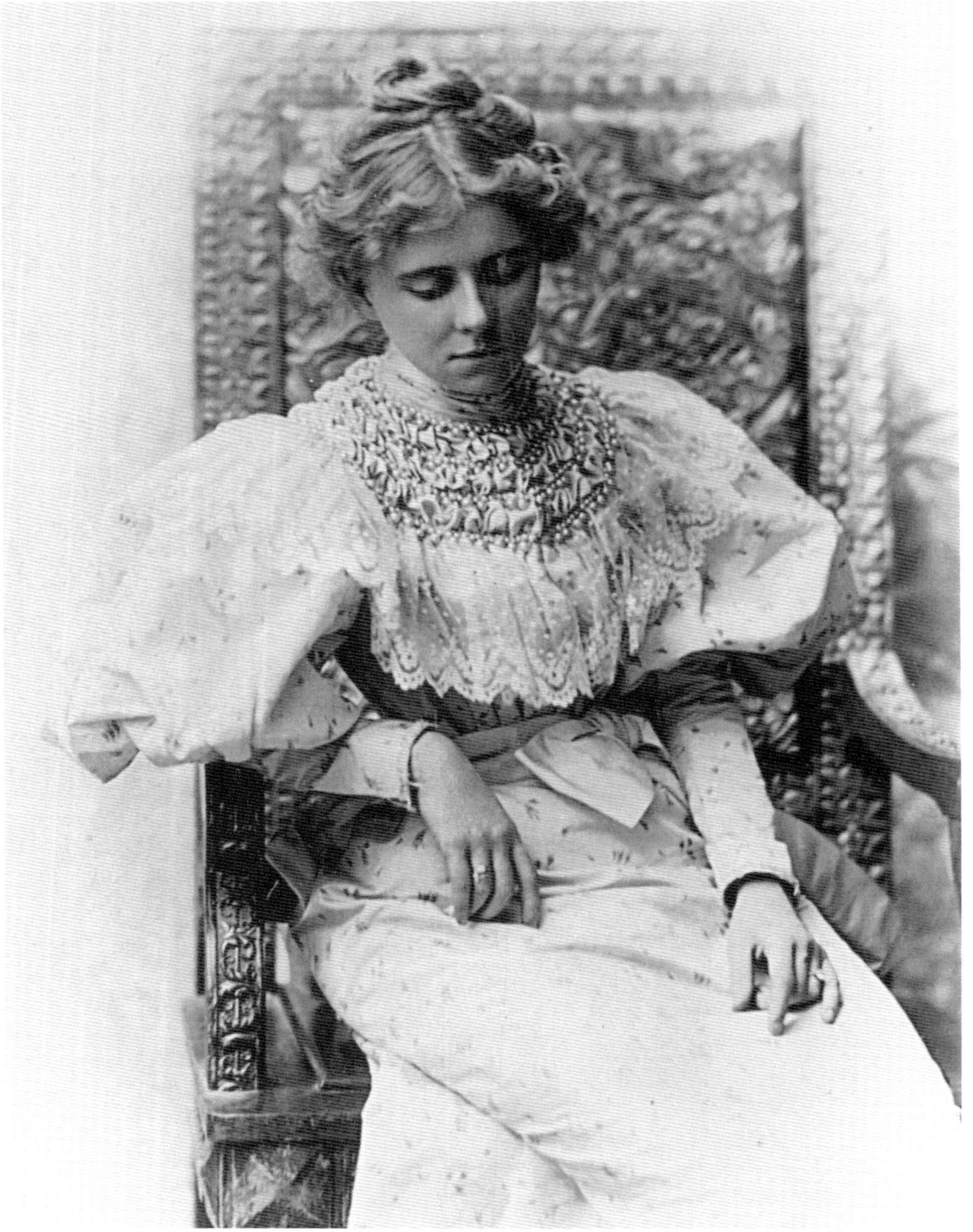

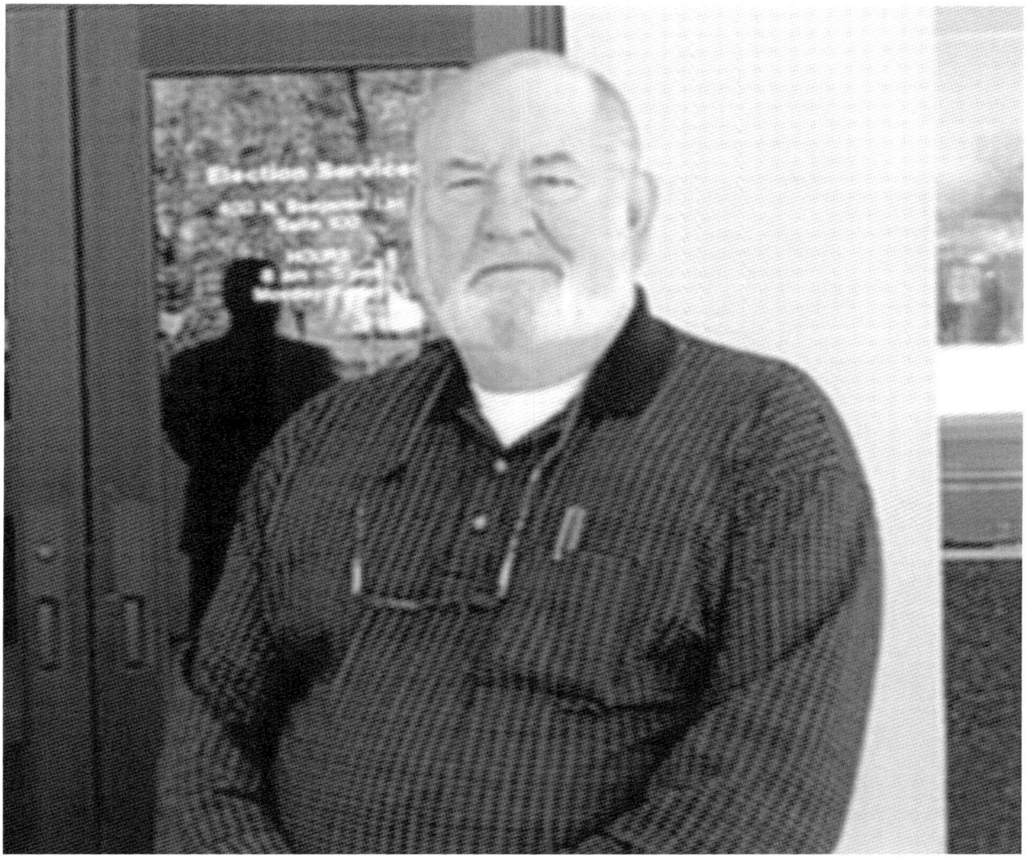

Vern Bisterfeldt

Soldier, police officer, county commissioner, and city council member, Vern Bisterfeldt began his career in Boise in 1959 when he was sworn in as a rookie policeman. He served almost 30 years in the Boise Police Department before retiring in January 1987. One day after he retired from the department, he was sworn in as an Ada County commissioner, serving for 12 years before poor health led him to resign in 1999. In 1994, tragedy struck when his daughter was murdered by her husband. Vern and his wife, Shirley, took on raising her two children and became active in the Grandparents as Parents organization. Bisterfeldt did not stay out of politics long; he was elected to Boise City Council on November 6, 2001. His public work spans almost a half-century, including service in the military. (Courtesy of the Idaho State Historical Society.)

Cecil D. Andrus

After serving as the state's chief executive from 1971 to 1977 and from 1987 to 1995—a total of four terms—Cecil Andrus holds the record as the longest-serving governor. Born in Hood River, Oregon, Andrus attended Oregon State University and served in the US Navy during the Korean War. When he was discharged from the service, he and his wife, Carol, moved to Orofino, in north Idaho, where he worked as a lumberjack and managed a sawmill. He considers himself "an accidental politician," becoming involved in politics when he sought to improve funding for education in the state. He also served as US secretary of the interior under Pres. Jimmy Carter from 1977 to 1981. Known for his activities to conserve wilderness, he considers one of his proudest accomplishments the funding of kindergarten in Idaho, which was passed in the legislature in 1975. (Both, courtesy of Cecil D. Andrus; below photograph by Dave Alexander.)

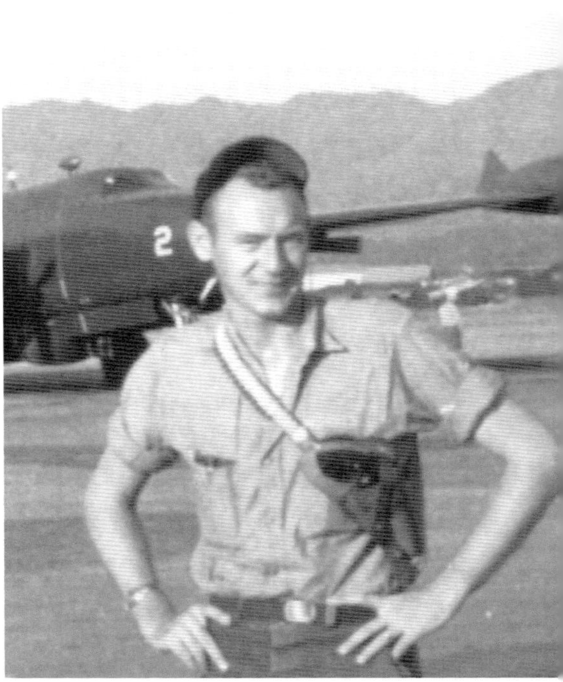

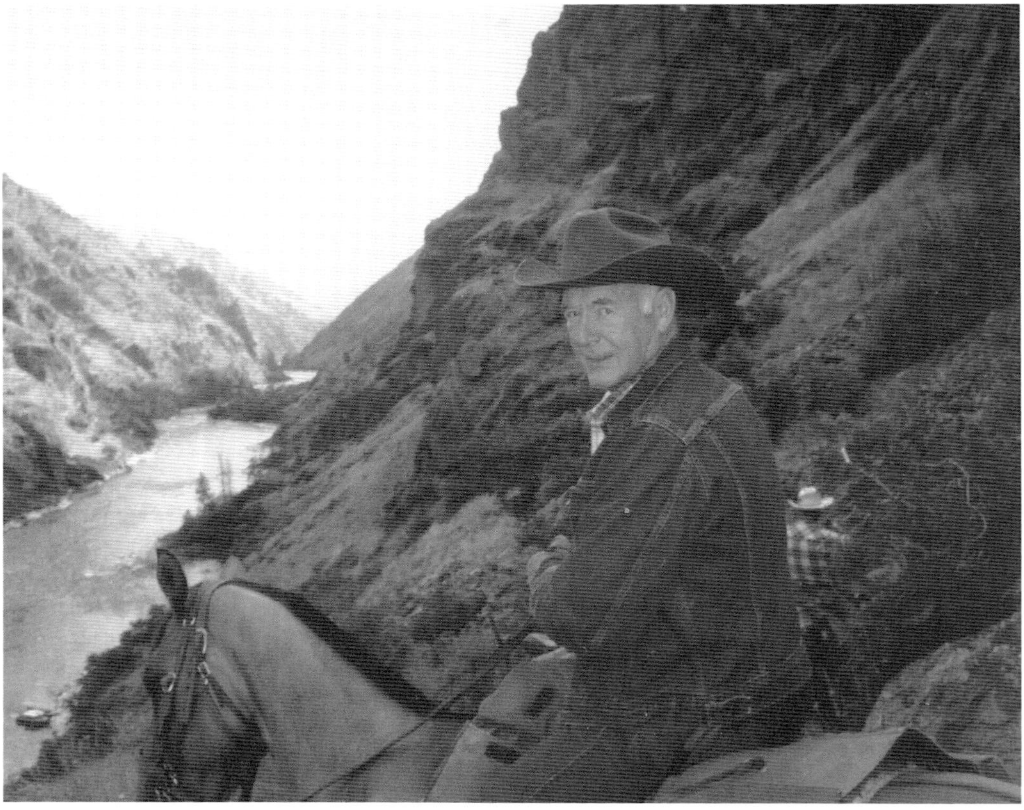

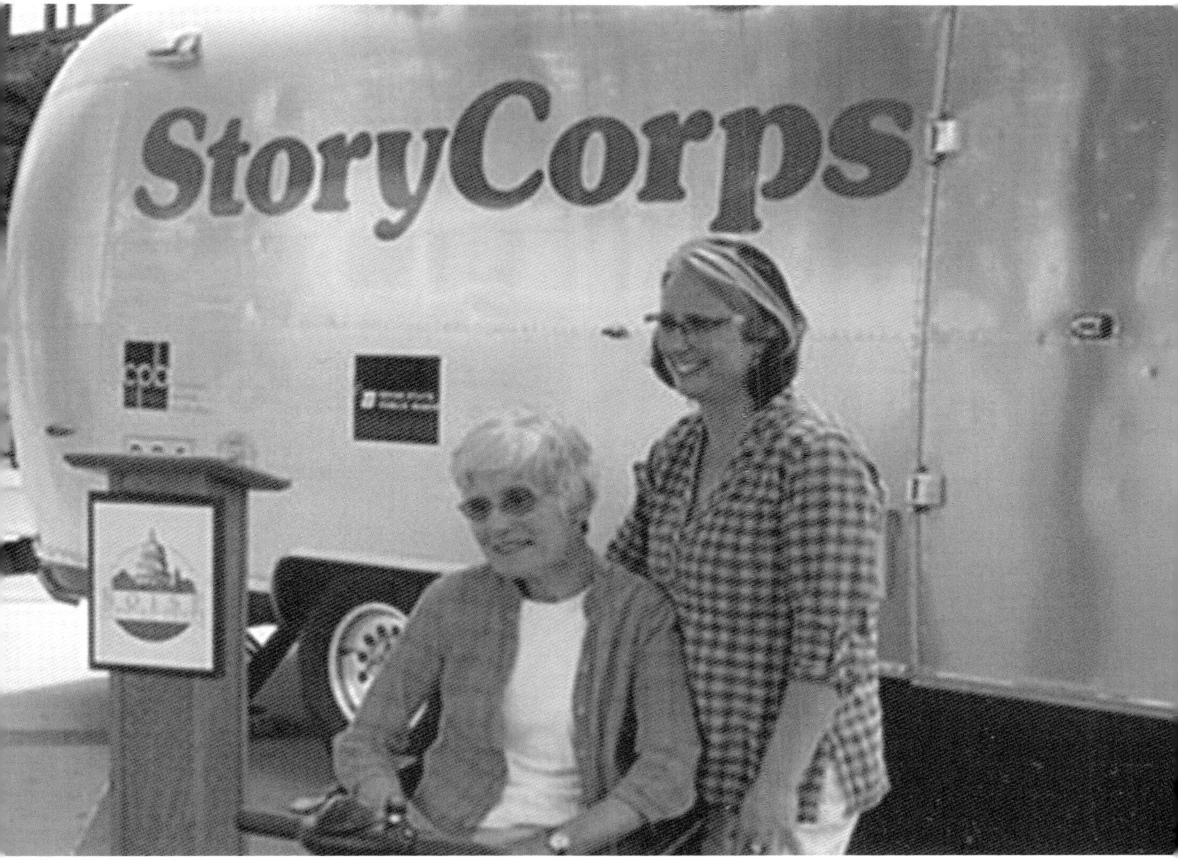

Marilyn Shuler

In 2013, as part of her keynote address for the 10th annual Change Your World Celebration at the Idaho Human Rights Education Center, Marilyn Shuler (left, with Marcia Franklin) quoted Eleanor Roosevelt: "Where, after all, do universal human rights begin? In small places, close to home—so close and so small that they cannot be seen on any map of the world."

Shuler has devoted her life to causes of human rights and the protection of those who cannot speak for themselves. Born in Portland, Oregon, just before World War II, she suffered from polio as a child and later experienced firsthand the discrimination that is often unthinkingly directed at those who are different. Polio victims were stigmatized, and in those days, no accommodations were made to the children who, if they could walk at all, had to use crutches and braces.

Shortly after arriving in Boise, she was elected to the Boise School Board, and served for several years, including a stint as chair in 1975–1976. She completed a master's degree in public administration at Boise State University in 1978, about the same time that she was appointed director of the Idaho Human Rights Commission by Gov. Phil Batt, a position she held for the next 20 years. Shuler was a leader in the movement to bring recognition of Martin Luther King Day/Human Rights Day to Idaho and was a cofounder of the Idaho Anne Frank Human Rights Memorial and the associated Human Rights Center for Idaho. She has advocated for foster children, establishing the John D. Shuler Memorial Fund after her husband's death to provide opportunities for them to engage in sports and other activities. Her advocacy and volunteer activities have continued into her retirement. (Courtesy of *Boise Weekly*, photograph by Skyler Barasanti.)

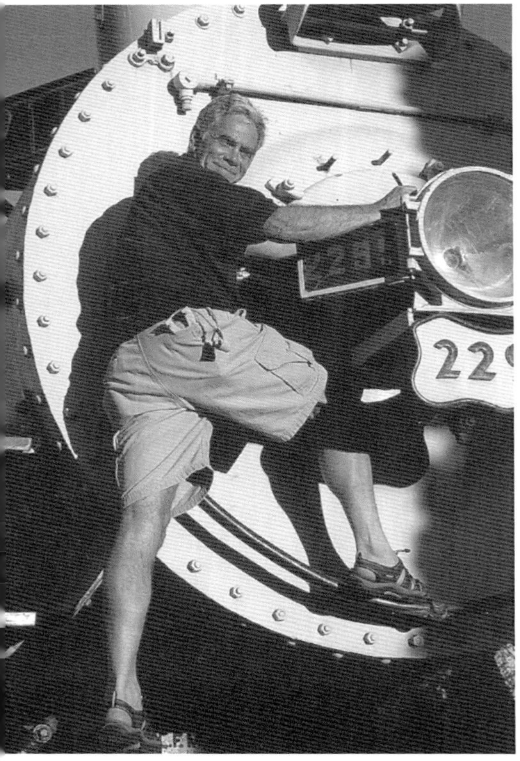

John Bertram

In 1969, when John Bertram arrived in town, Boise was on the front lines of a nationwide effort to modernize cities through a process known as urban renewal. The Boise Redevelopment Agency's efforts to update the city center with an indoor shopping mall called for clearing eight city blocks of historic buildings. Bertram, with experience in urban planning, had come to work in a program called VISTA, or Volunteers in Service to America. He also became involved in the burgeoning grassroots effort to save historic buildings in the downtown core. After his stint with VISTA, Bertram started his own business, Planmakers, which combined his training in urban planning and his passion for preservation and history to create comprehensive urban plans based on community heritage and resources. He encouraged developers and city leaders to consider historic structures as resources that could benefit business, bring tourism, and create a great quality of life, not only in Boise, but in communities throughout the state. Today, Bertram continues to work on many projects that preserve Boise's historic buildings. (Both, courtesy of John Bertram.)

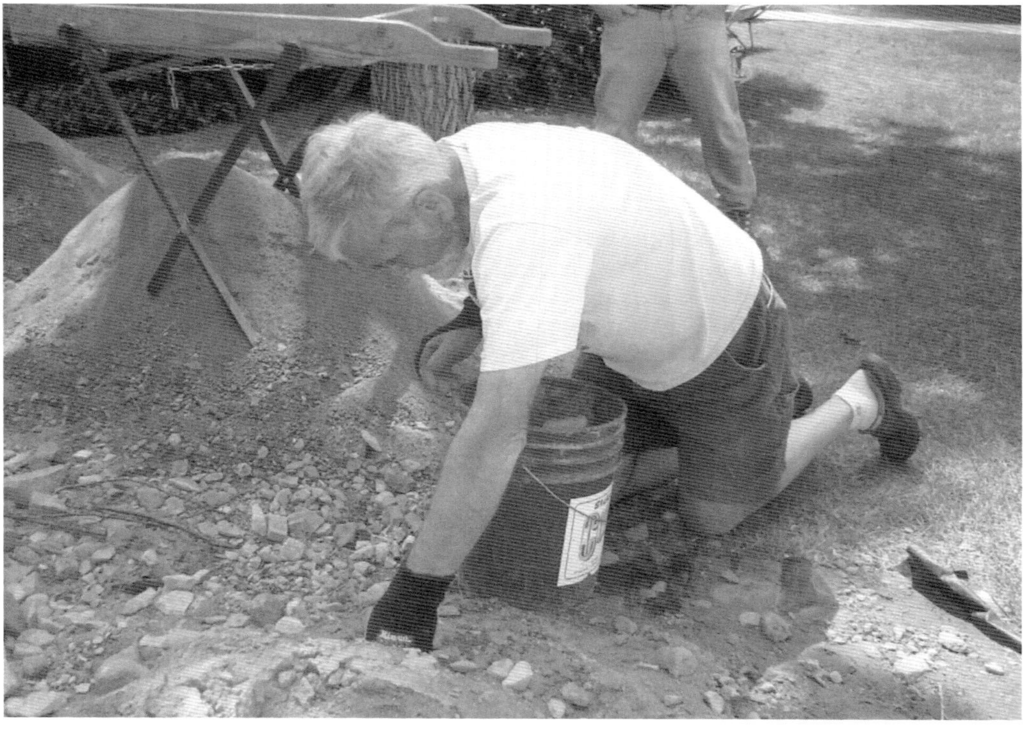

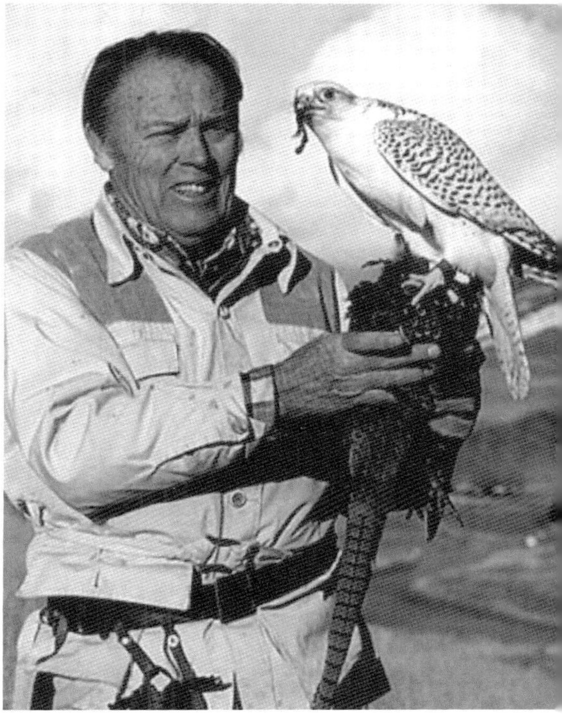

Morlan W. Nelson

A world-renowned expert on eagles and other birds of prey, conservationist and educator Morley Nelson, a native of North Dakota, made his home in Boise in 1948 as the Columbia Basin Snow Survey supervisor. As a child, Nelson developed a passion for raptors, which led him to a life committed to understanding and preserving raptors and their habitats. He was instrumental in establishing the Snake River Birds of Prey Natural Area and the World Center for Birds of Prey, the headquarters of The Peregrine Fund. Congress established the Snake River Birds of Prey National Conservation Area (below) in 1993. Renamed the Morley Nelson Snake River Birds of Prey National Conservation area in 2009 in Morley's honor, it protects one of the world's most dense concentrations of nesting birds of prey, including falcons, eagles, and hawks. (Right, courtesy of the Peregrine Fund; below, courtesy of the Bureau of Land Management, photograph by Bob Wick.)

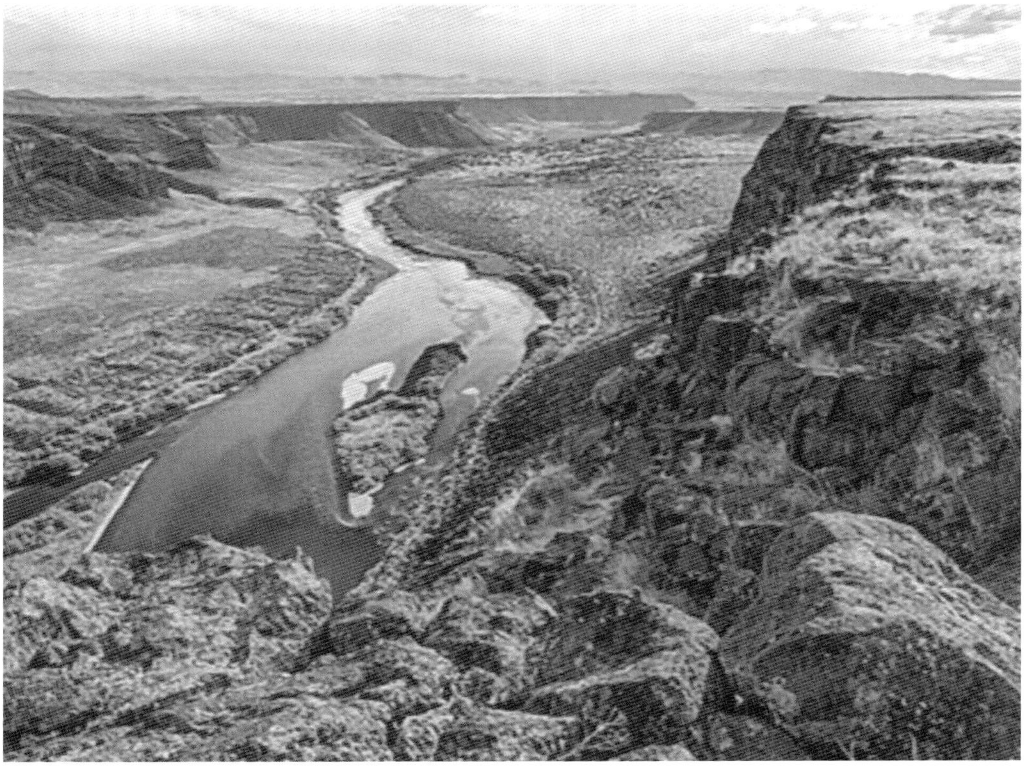

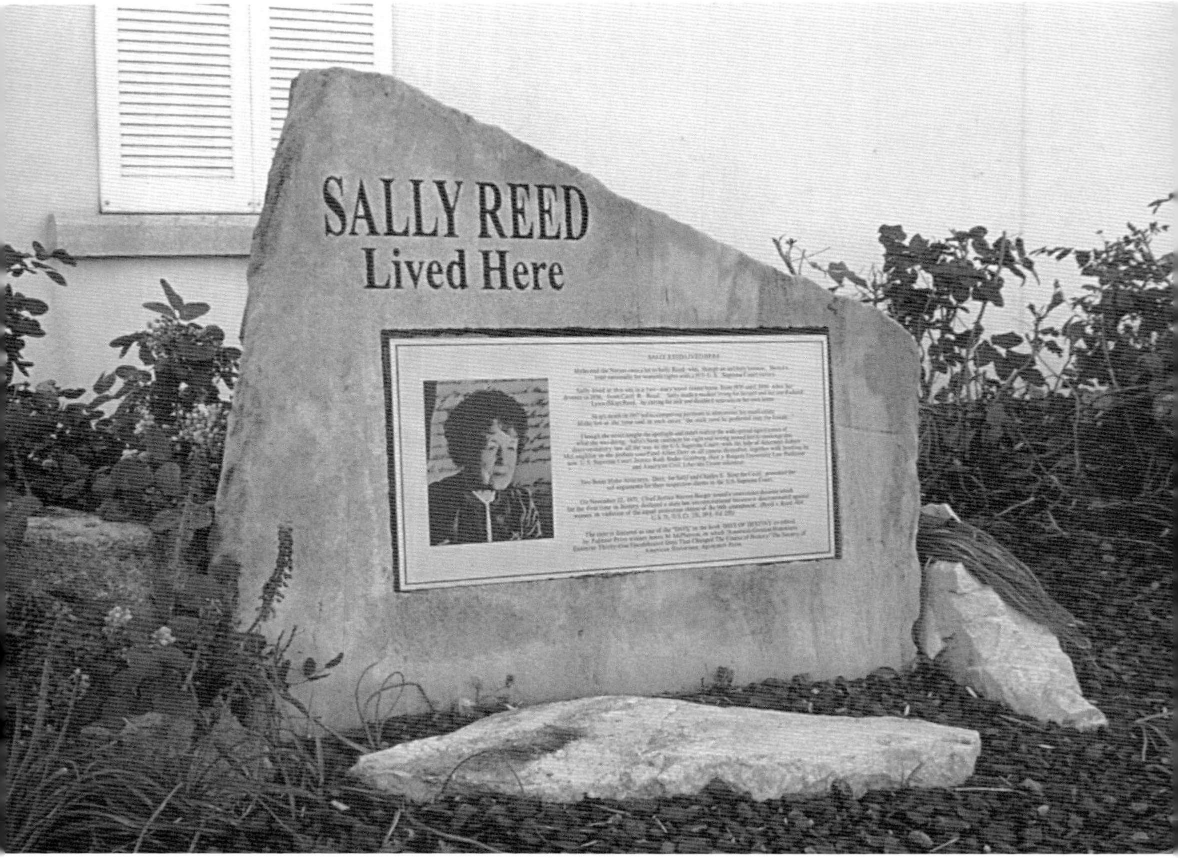

Mary Maxine "Sally" Reed

In 1969, Sally and Cecil Reed's 16-year-old son Skip committed suicide. The couple had divorced 11 years before and shared custody of the boy. Skip left a small estate, including his clarinet and a savings account. At the time, under Idaho law, men were given preference over women when both were equally qualified to administer an estate. Cecil Reed was named administrator by the probate court. Sally felt that her education and experience working as a secretary and bookkeeper made her more qualified for the task than her husband, who worked as a mechanic. She hired Boise attorney Alan Derr to appeal the decision. In Fourth District Court, Derr argued that the probate court's decision violated equal protection under the Idaho Constitution and under the 14th Amendment to the US Constitution. His argument won the case in the Fourth District, but when Cecil Reed filed an appeal with the Idaho Supreme Court, the original decision was upheld. The case was then brought to the US Supreme Court, where Derr, assisted by attorneys from the American Civil Liberties Union, successfully argued the case and won a victory for Sally Reed. *Reed vs. Reed* was the first time that the Supreme Court ruled against a state law that allowed gender discrimination. Sally Reed's case is now considered one of the most important decisions handed down by the US Supreme Court. (Authors' collection.)

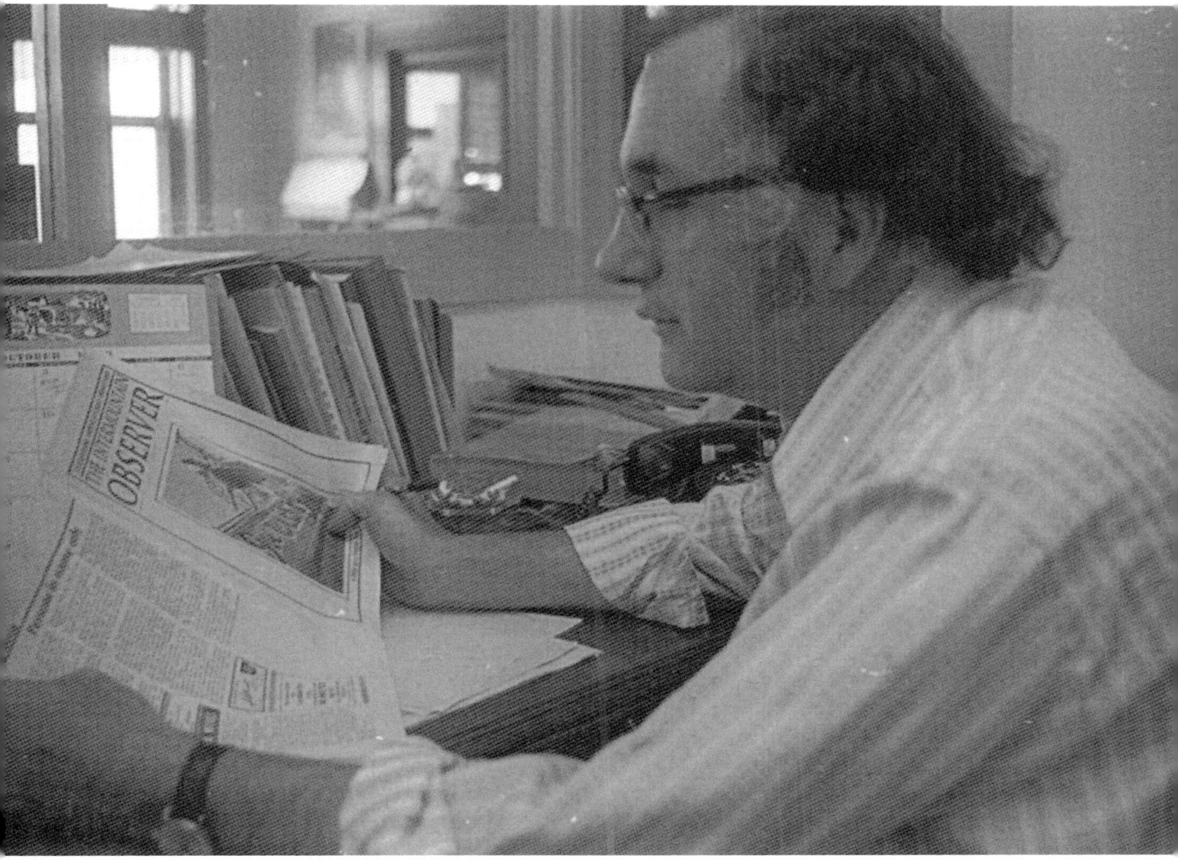

Samuel H. Day Jr.

Sam Day is remembered today as a leading light of liberal causes. In 1979, he gained national fame when, as editor of the *Progressive*, published in Madison, Wisconsin, he accepted an article that described the hydrogen bomb and then spent the better part of a year fighting a prior-restraint order from the federal government to publish it. Before his time at the *Progressive*, Day published a weekly newspaper in Boise called the *Intermountain Observer*, which featured the first photographs of mining activity on Castle Peak in the White Cloud mountains. The paper also published exposés on the misuse of public funds for the blind and the neglect of welfare programs for women and children, and advocated for the establishment of public kindergartens. In 1971, Day, in his own words, "crossed the line" by participating in a nonviolent but illegal protest in Boise, joining a group that linked hands to block traffic on the Capitol Boulevard Memorial Bridge at the same time that a nuclear test was taking place in the Aleutian Islands. (Courtesy of the Idaho Statesman Collection, Boise State University Library Special Collections Department.)

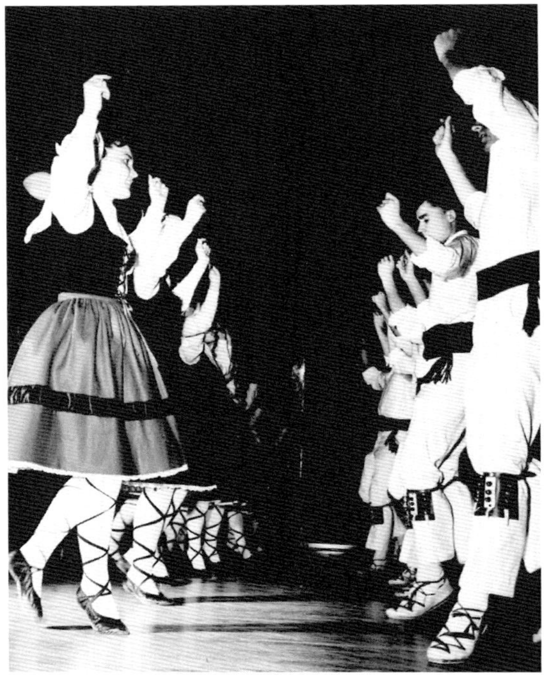

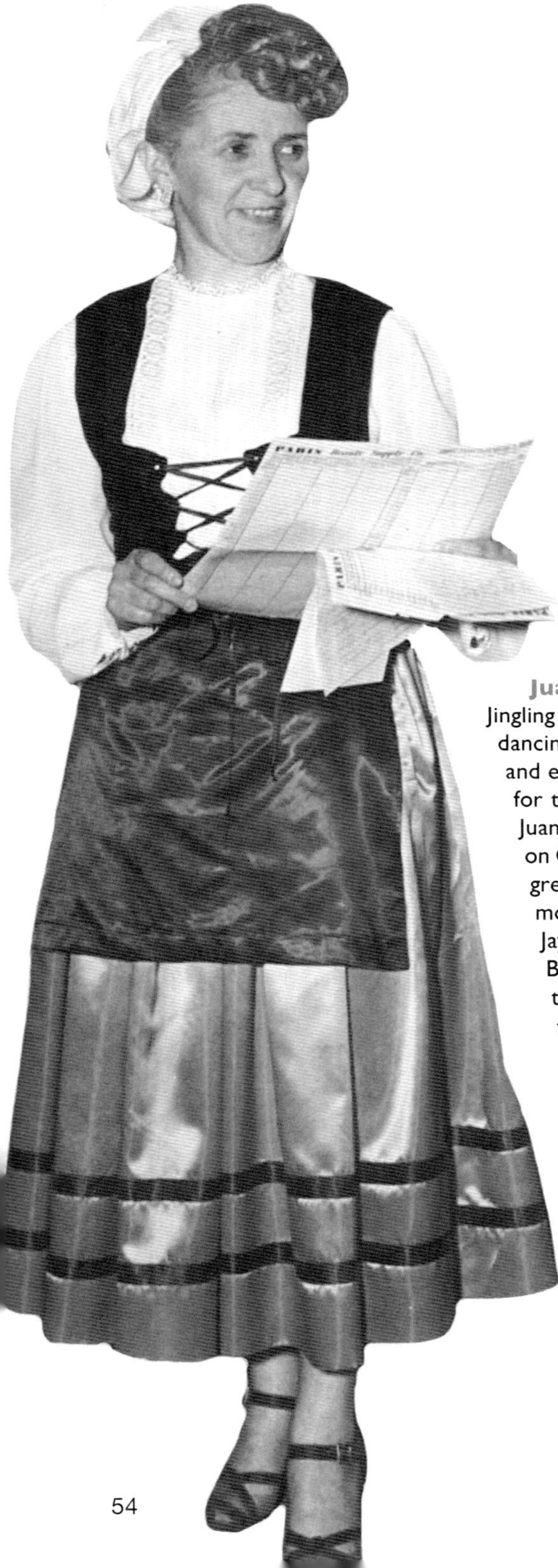

Juanita Hormachea

Jingling bells, swirling skirts, and high kicks are hallmarks of Basque dancing. Generations of Boiseans have enjoyed the vivacious and exuberant dances, all of which might have been lost if not for the efforts of Juanita "Jay" Hormachea. Juanita's parents, Juana Arriola and Juan Uberuaga, operated a boardinghouse on Grove Street near downtown Boise. Juanita, born in 1908, grew up in the close-knit Basque community and helped her mother run the boardinghouse. Outgoing and energetic, Jay loved the Sunday-afternoon dances hosted by various Basque boardinghouses. In 1947, she started to teach the traditional dances. In 1949 and 1950, she was invited to organize Basque dance performances for Boise's Music Week. The performances ignited an enthusiastic response. Jay's classes encouraged hundreds of young Boise Basques to celebrate their culture and heritage, and she is recognized for laying the foundation for Boise's famed Oinkari Basque Dancers. (Above, courtesy of the Basque Museum and Cultural Center; left, courtesy of the Idaho State Historical Society.)

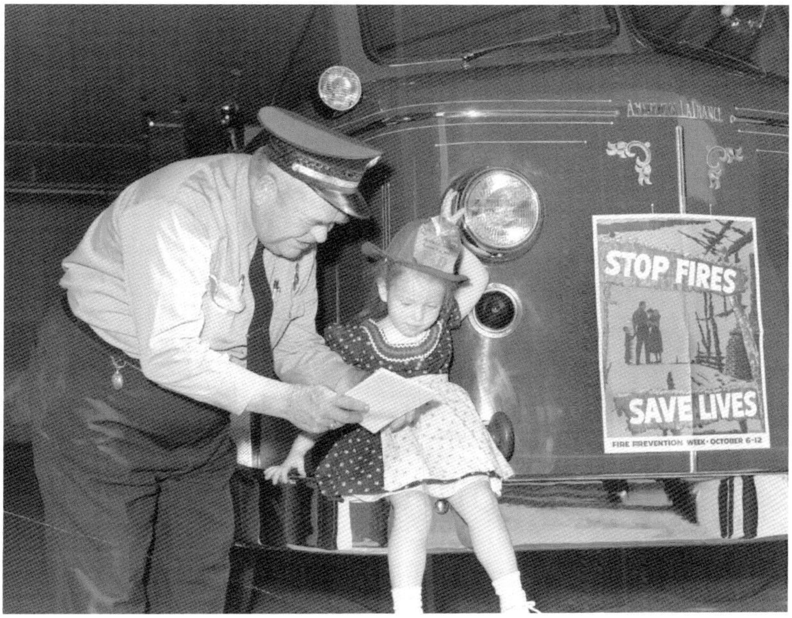

William F. Roach

William Frank "Doc" Roach (above) joined the Boise Fire Department in 1911 and had served for more than 50 years by the time he retired in 1965. He began his service when horse-drawn fire equipment was still in use (below) and ended as the department entered the age of modern communication and equipment. Doc Roach worked his way from the bottom up. He began as a firefighter and, after six years, became a fire dispatcher. In 1947, he was promoted to fire prevention captain and introduced an annual fire prevention week. In 1951, he became Boise's first fire marshal, a post he held until his retirement. Doc Roach educated hundreds of Boise citizens, bringing the fire-prevention program to schools and community clubs and establishing a program that is the foundation for today's public outreach. (Both, courtesy of the Doc Roach Collection, Boise State University Library Special Collections Department.)

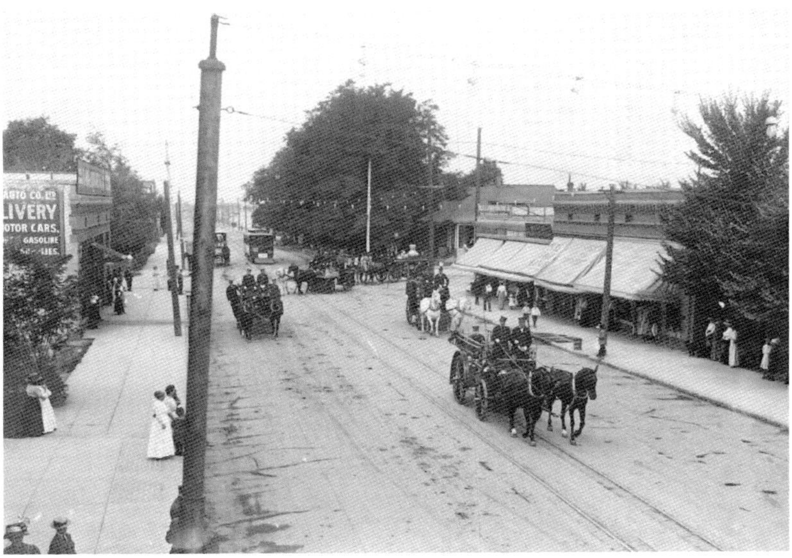

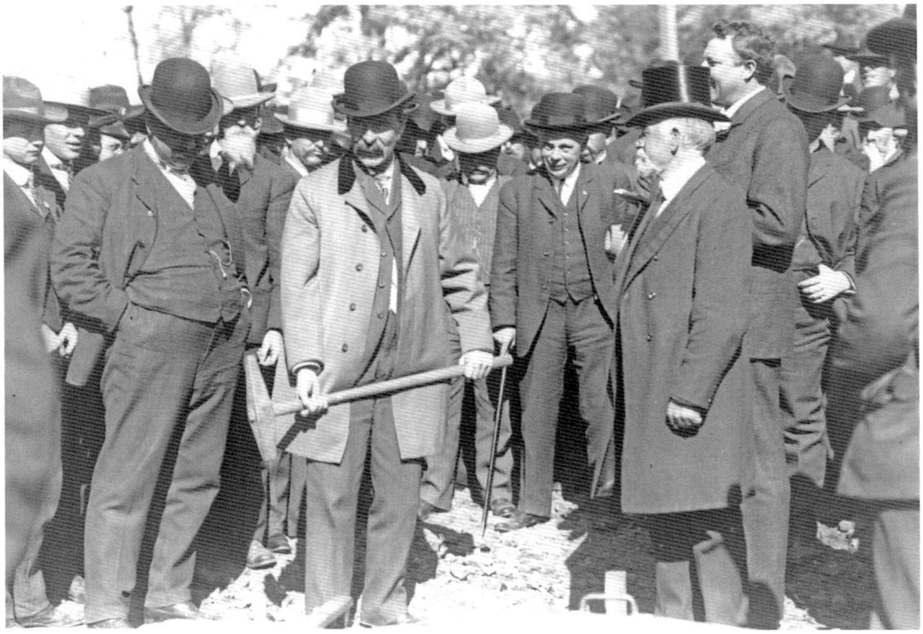

Harlan P. Ustick

Doctor, developer, and businessman, Harlan P. Ustick (shown above in top hat) is best known for platting the village of Ustick, west of Boise. Born in Ohio, he attended college at Miami University (Ohio) and medical school in Philadelphia. He practiced medicine in Ohio for a few years before moving to Chicago. Ustick headed west to Portland in 1890, finally landing in Boise in 1892. Once here, he opened his office, specializing in eye and ear conditions. Ustick had interests beyond medicine. He was one of the leading orchardists in the area and raised prunes, apples, and peaches. Involved in many civic projects, he and Watson Donaldson organized the Boise Valley Railway Company. The company promoted development of five- and ten-acre farms adjacent to the planned railway. (Both, courtesy of the Idaho State Historical Society.)

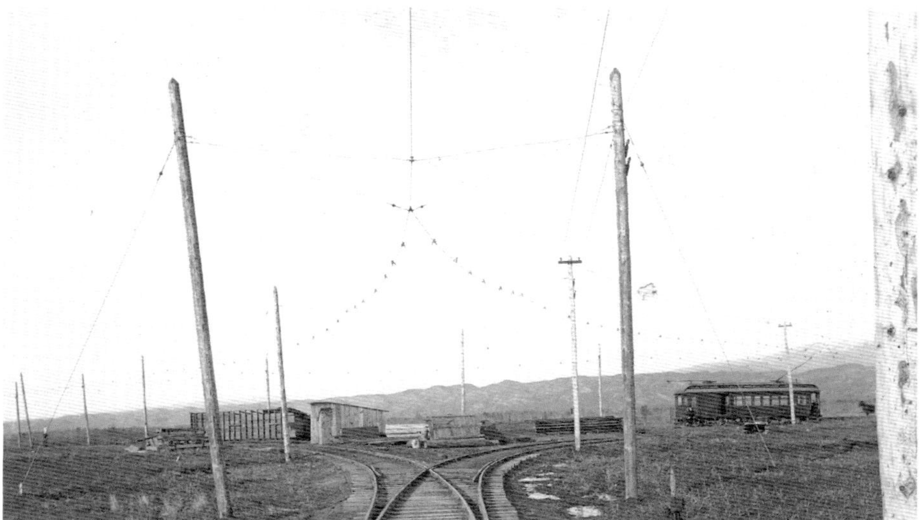

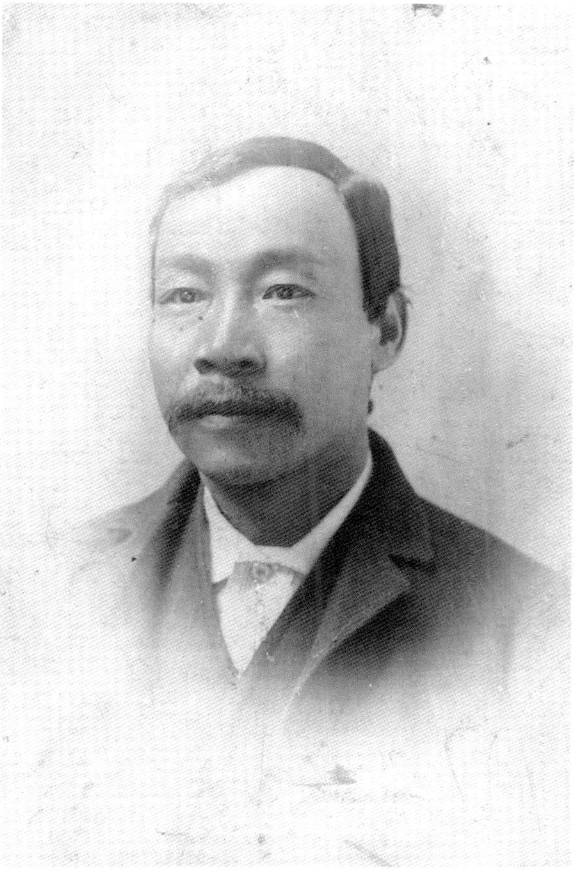

C.K. Ah Fong

"He is a Doctor," proclaimed the short headline in the local news column of the *Idaho Daily Statesman* on February 22, 1901. C.K. Ah Fong had been treating patients in southwest Idaho since his arrival in Alturas County more than 30 years earlier. Born and raised in the Guangdong province of China, Ah Fong Chuck received medical training through an apprenticeship with his father, Dr. Whey Fong Chuck. In the late 1860s, possibly due to violent political unrest in China, the two left for the United States. By 1869, the younger man was in Idaho, with his name transposed by immigration authorities to "C.K. Ah Fong." Dr. Ah Fong lived in and around the mining camps of Rocky Bar and Atlanta in present-day Elmore County before moving to Boise in the 1890s, where he opened the first of several offices downtown. He treated his patients for injuries (broken bones, lacerations, and gunshot wounds), venereal diseases, and chronic conditions like arthritis. Throughout his career, his patients included Chinese and Anglo residents, among them, according to most accounts, prominent businessmen, legislators, and at least one governor. In 1897, when the Idaho legislature enacted a law establishing a state board of medical examiners, Dr. Ah Fong, along with a number of other longtime physicians, was "grandfathered" in and approved to receive a medical license, but the law was declared unconstitutional. A new law was passed in 1899, and the new board refused to grant Dr. Ah Fong a license. He appealed the decision, carrying the case all the way to the Idaho Supreme Court, which overturned a previous court decision and granted the license, making Dr. Ah Fong the only licensed doctor of Chinese herbal medicine in the state and possibly the nation. He continued to treat patients until the early 1920s, when his son Herbert took over. Dr. Ah Fong died in 1927, but his family kept the office on Capitol Boulevard in operation until 1964. (Courtesy of the Idaho State Historical Society.)

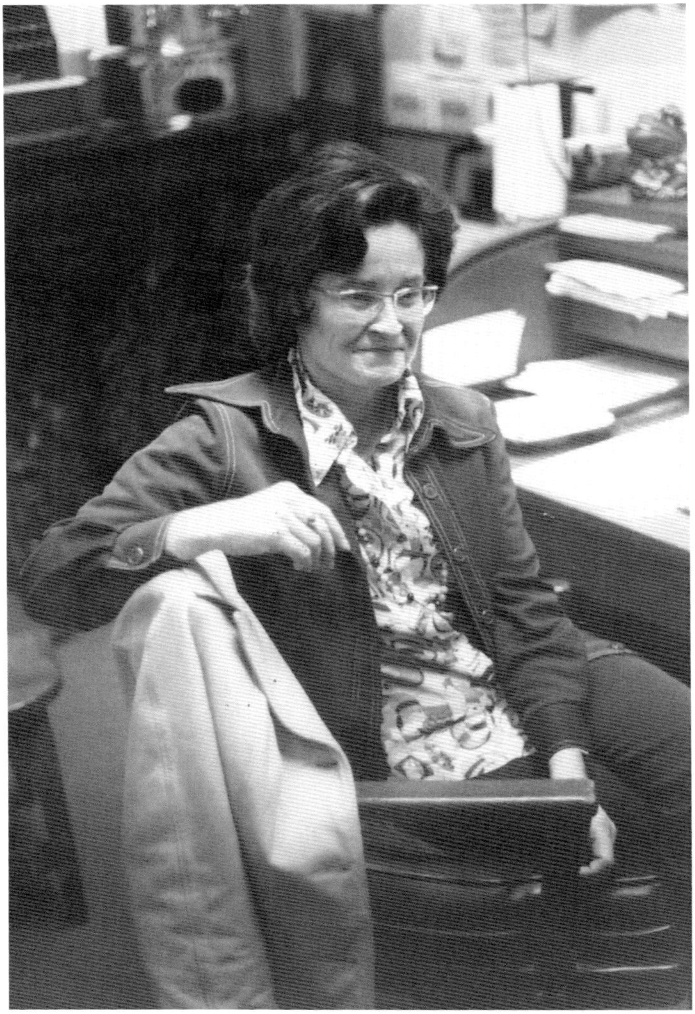

Joan Carley

Urban renewal projects of the 1960s and 1970s cleared 10 blocks of downtown Boise, taking with them a number of historic buildings. As in many communities at the time, urban renewal inspired a historic-preservation movement in Boise. Joan Carley was one of the leaders of the movement. A founding member of the Idaho Historic Preservation Council (now Preservation Idaho), she became a property developer in an effort to save Boise's historic buildings. She began with the purchase of the 1910 Pioneer Tent and Awning building in 1974. Within a few years, she had purchased several more blocks and developed a thriving commercial district with renovated historic buildings. Carley accomplished all of this with no previous experience in business or property development. She embarked on the project as a newly divorced woman with two children at home at a time when there were few female property developers. She had never purchased a building, never hired contractors, and had no experience with construction or renovation. But somehow she succeeded, and 40 years later, Old Boise at Sixth and Main Streets remains as a testament to her determination and hard work. Carley died in 2011, but her legacy remains. In 2013, the year of Boise's sesquicentennial, the city honored her by placing a plaque outside of the Pioneer Tent and Awning building, which still houses businesses and the offices of Old Boise. (Courtesy of Boise State University Special Collections Department.)

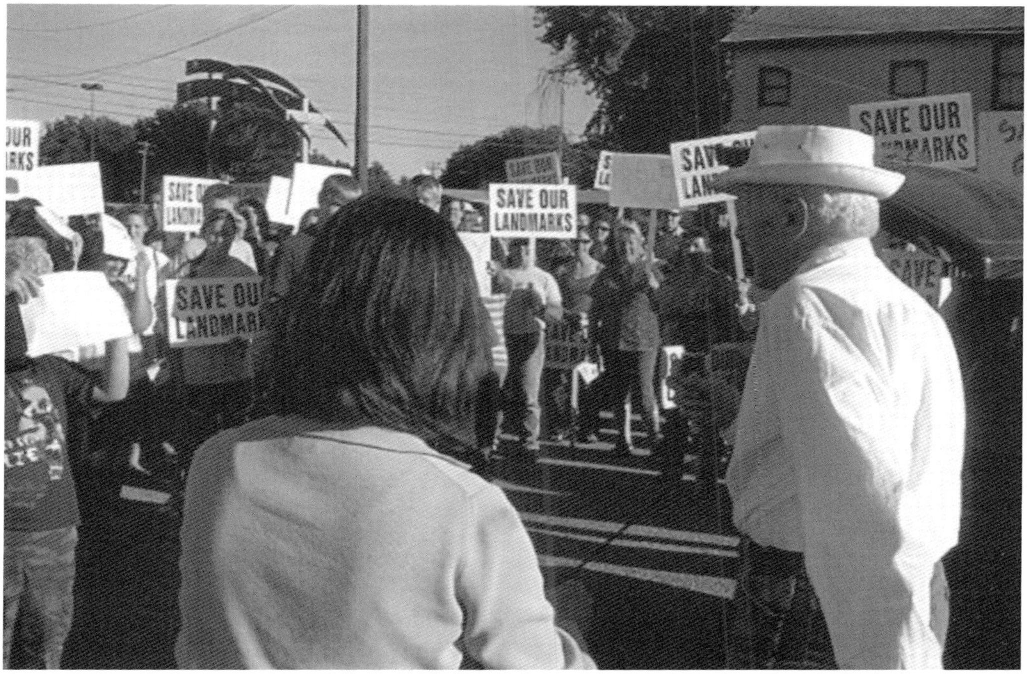

Preservation Idaho

This grassroots organization was formed in 1972 by Boise residents Joan Carley, Mary Lesser, Adelia Garro Simplot, and others. Preservation Idaho (originally called the Idaho Historic Preservation Council) is a statewide nonprofit group dedicated to the protection of Idaho's and Boise's heritage. (Both, courtesy of Preservation Idaho.)

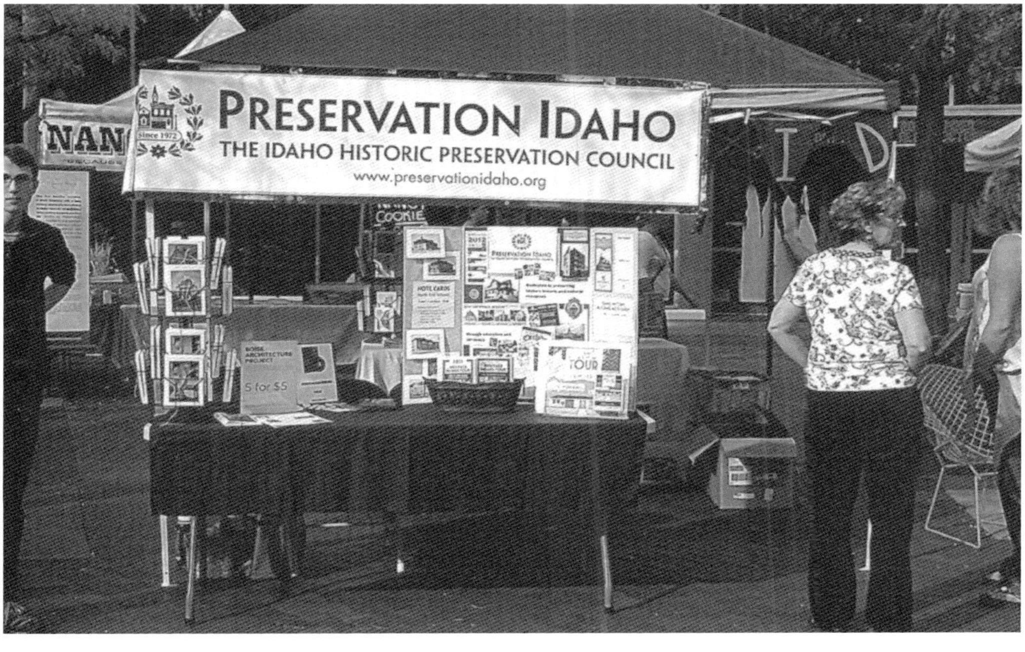

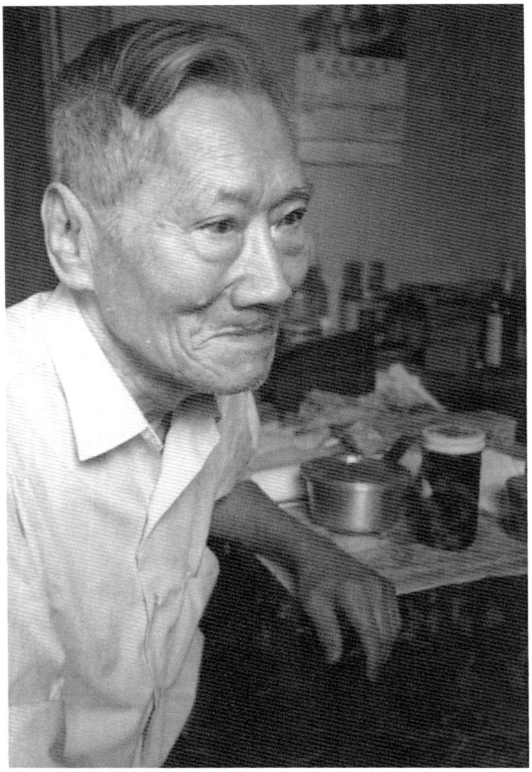

Billy Fong

Urban renewal became visible in Boise in the 1970s, when the central core was transformed as old buildings were demolished to make way for a proposed mall. The Hop Sing Tong Building, one of the few remaining buildings related to the Chinese population that once lived here, was a victim of the wrecking ball. The building's demolition made news when Billy Fong, 84, secretary of the Hop Sing Tong Society Club and former cook at the Golden Wok restaurant, refused to leave. Fong lived in the upstairs apartment for over 30 years. Even though his building was slated for demolition, he remained in his home, finally leaving when the wrecking ball approached his building. According to local legend, Fong threw out the white flag of surrender and left. (Courtesy of Idaho Statesman Collection, Boise State University Library Special Collections Department.)

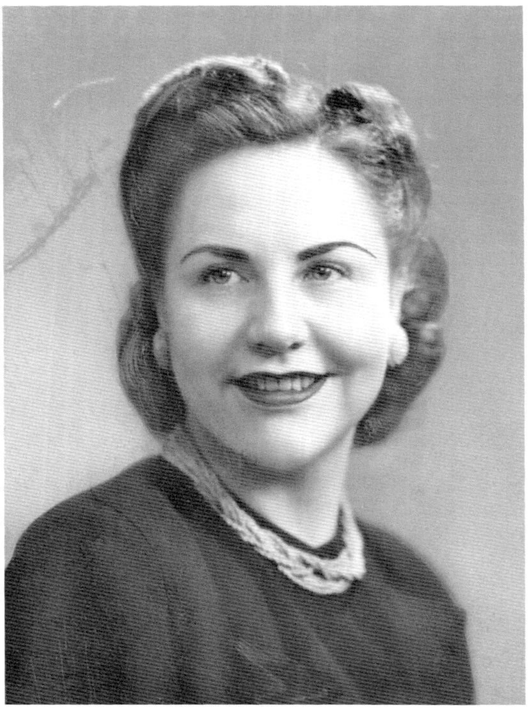

Edith Miller Klein

Edith Miller Klein paved the way for female attorneys and politicians. Born in the north Idaho town of Wallace, she was encouraged by her parents to attend college. Klein entered the University of Idaho in 1932 and graduated in three years with a degree in business administration. Over the next several years, she taught school and worked as a secretary. In 1943, she moved to Washington, DC. She attended law school, earned her law degree in 1946, passed the bar in the District of Columbia, and moved to Boise in 1946. Her Idaho law career began in 1947, and she served as an attorney and a judge. Interested in politics, Klein ran for office in 1948, kicking off a 20-year career in the Idaho legislature. She was responsible for authoring and sponsoring landmark legislation related to children and women's rights. (Courtesy of the Idaho State Historical Society.)

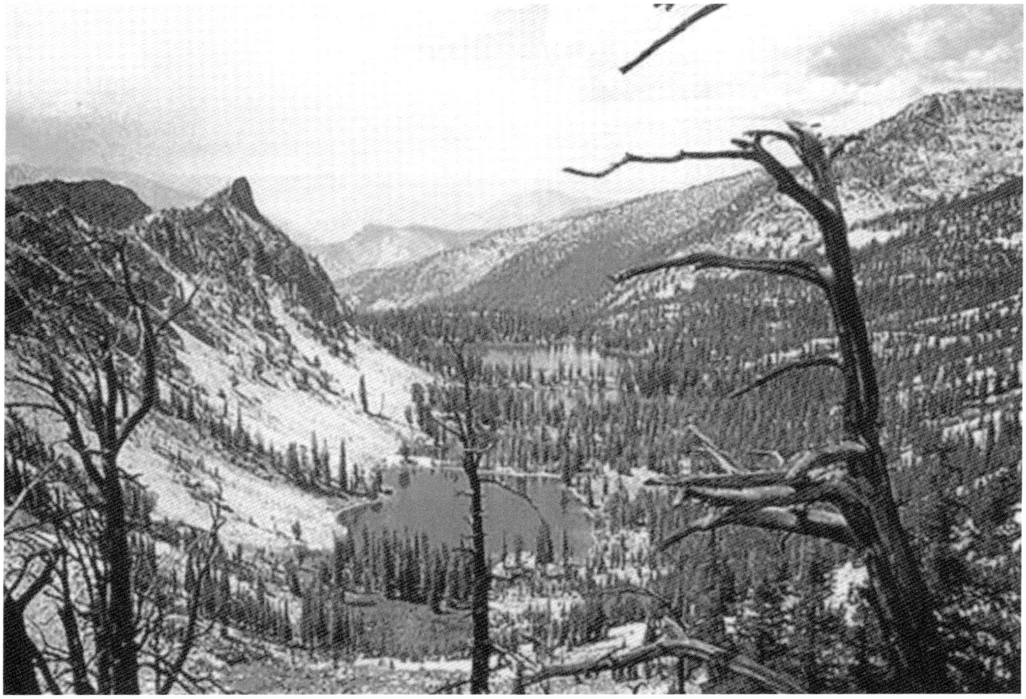

Frank Church

A third-generation Idahoan, Frank Church was born in Boise in 1924. His father owned a sporting-goods store and took Frank and his brother hiking, fishing, and hunting in the Idaho mountains. Frank cultivated a love for the outdoors that would lead him to work for the preservation of wilderness areas in Idaho. He attended Stanford University on an American Legion scholarship, and in 1950, graduated from Stanford Law School. He was admitted to the bar that year and practiced law in Boise. Interested in politics, he was elected to the US Senate in 1956 as a Democrat at age 32 and served until 1981. He was an advocate for protection of civil rights, the elderly, equal rights for women, and wilderness preservation. He died in 1984 at the age of 59.

The largest forested wilderness in the Lower 48 states was originally called the River of No Return Wilderness (above) when it was designated in 1980. The name was changed four years later to honor Senator Church. (Courtesy of Frank Church MSS56, Boise State University Library Special Collections Department.)

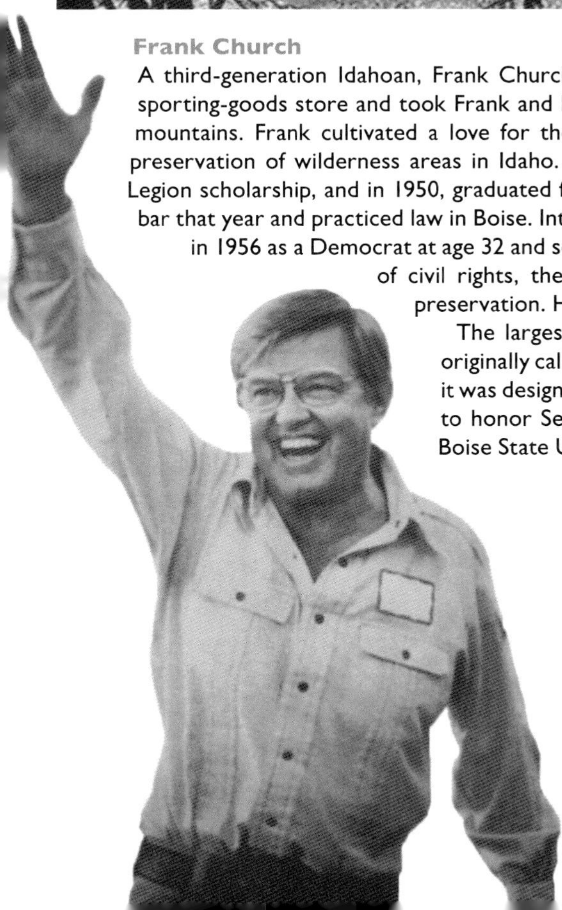

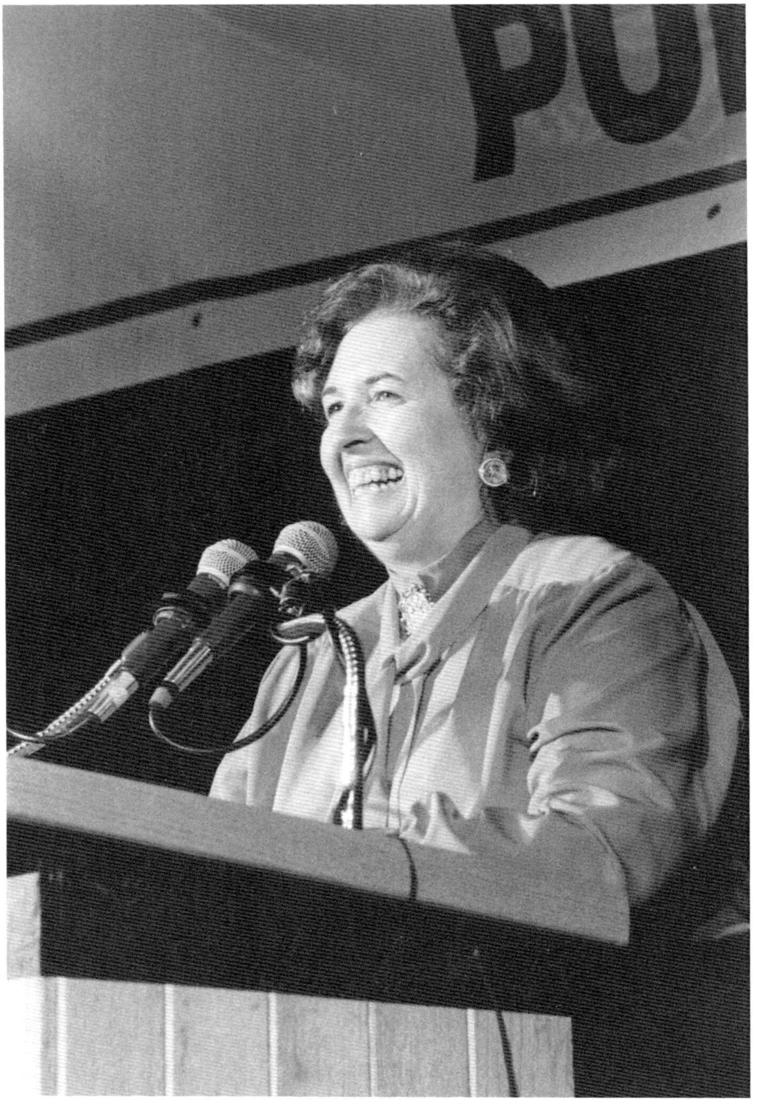

Bethine Church

Known as the matriarch of the Democratic Party, Bethine Clark Church was born into politics. Her father, Chase Clark, was an Idaho governor and federal district judge; she was the niece of Idaho governor Barzilla Clark and the cousin of D. Worth Clark. She was born in Mackay in 1923, but her family moved to Boise, where she attended Boise High School. Bethine and Frank Church were married in 1947 and raised two children, Frank Forrester Church IV and Chase Clark Church. Bethine, a partner to Frank throughout his political career, moved back to Boise in 1989 and was active in politics. A gracious woman, filled with energy and exuberance, she was, in the words of Cecil Andrus, "a force of nature." She worked on projects that were important to her, including education and promoting home health care and the preservation of Idaho's rivers and landscapes. She founded the nonprofit Sawtooth Society and the Frank Church Institute at Boise State University, which hosts yearly public-policy conferences. Bethine died in 2013 at age 90. (Courtesy of Frank Church MSS56, Boise State University Library Special Collections Department.)

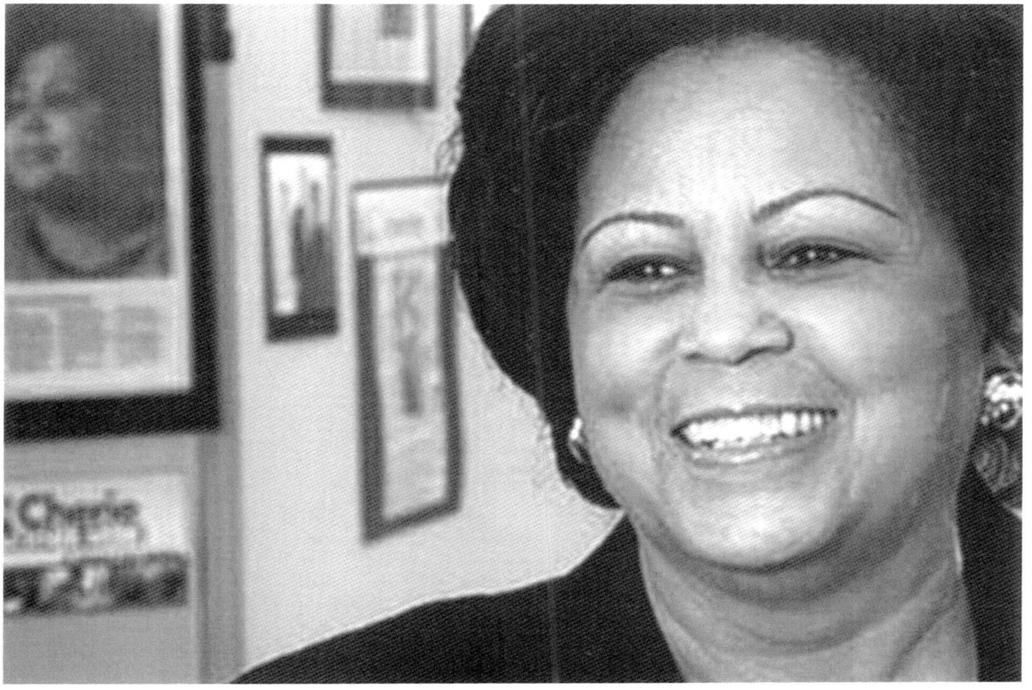

Cherie Buckner-Webb
Buckner-Webb, a fifth-generation Idahoan, has an impressive resume that speaks to her many accomplishments as a politician, business owner, and singer. Her great-grandfather Rev. William Riley Hardy moved to Boise around 1908 and founded St. Paul's Missionary Baptist Church. Her mother's family came to Boise during the Depression from Arkansas. Cherie was born in 1951 and grew up in Boise's North End. Her mother, Dorothy, was involved in the community and worked as a lecturer and civil-rights activist and was a role model for Cherie. After graduating from Boise High School in 1968, Cherie enrolled in George Fox University in Newberg, Oregon, and graduated four years later with a degree in management and organizational leadership. She returned to Boise and in 1974 received her master's degree in planning and social work administration from Northwest Nazarene University in Nampa. She worked for the next 36 years in her field, finding time to marry, have two children, and found a business. In 2010, she ran for office as a Democrat in the Idaho state legislature and won the seat with 68 percent of the vote. With this election, she became the first African American Idaho state legislator. Her political accomplishments continued when she won the Idaho Senate seat for District 19 in 2012. In addition to her political and business interests, she is an accomplished vocalist and recipient of the 2004 Idaho Excellence in the Arts award. (Courtesy of Idaho Public Television.)

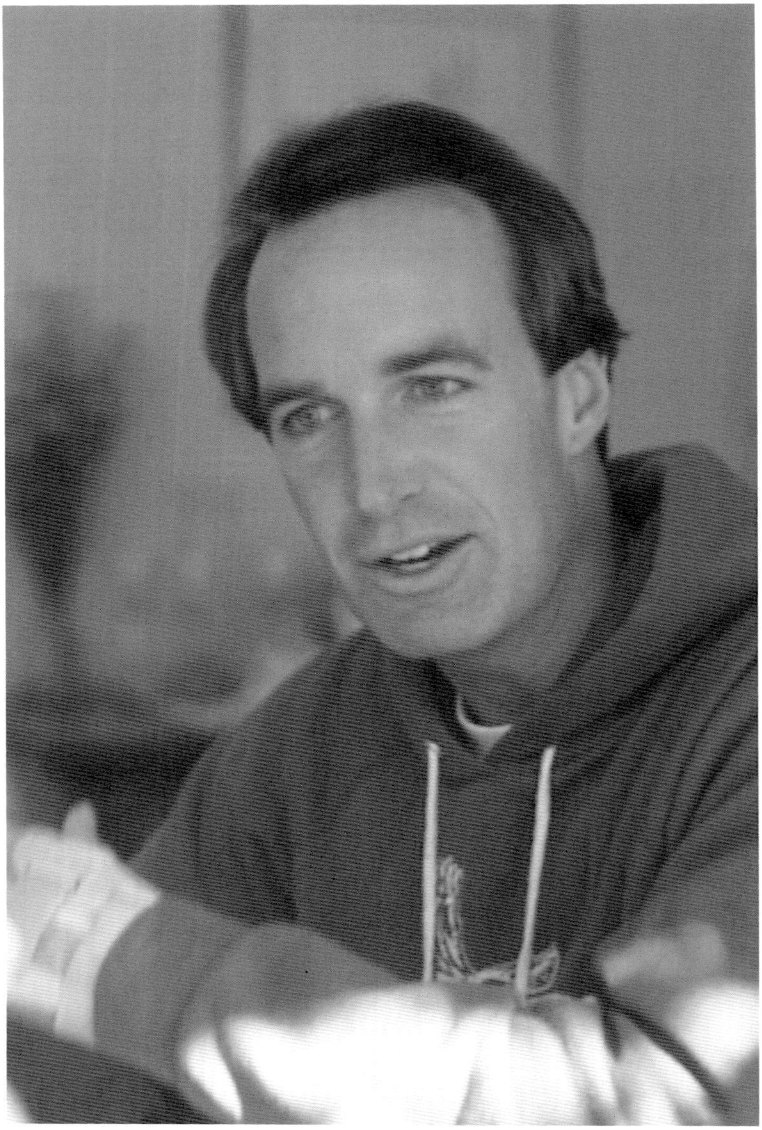

Dirk Kempthorne

Kempthorne was just 34 when he was elected mayor of Boise in 1986. He served for six years, then ran for and won a US Senate seat. Entering office on the tail of the economic decline of the 1980s, his goal as mayor was to strengthen the economy. His administration also dealt with the revitalization of downtown. Boise's core had experienced drastic changes in the 1970s, when many historic buildings were demolished for urban renewal. Kempthorne later said, "Some very beautiful, historic buildings were demolished in the name of urban renewal. It was like a grin was missing some of its front teeth as you drove through downtown Boise." Under Kempthorne, downtown began to rebuild, in part because the Boise Metro Plan was amended to allow the building of a mall in the suburbs, but still within the city limits. New businesses and companies were attracted to the city, and the economic situation improved. In his later career, he served as governor of Idaho and secretary of the interior. (Courtesy of Idaho Statesman Collection, Boise State University Library Special Collections Department.)

CHAPTER FOUR

Learning from the Best

In 1863, when Idaho was organized as a territory, advancement of education was called for in the Organic Act, which asserted that each township should help establish and maintain a sound system of free public schools. Laws passed in the first legislative assembly provided for a territorial superintendent of public instruction. The territorial laws did not provide for constructing school buildings, so until the school code was revised in 1879 to provide for construction, classes were held in private homes, stores, churches, and any other place with sufficient space. Boise had subscription schools, or select schools. One of the first was taught by Miss Frank A. Call and Mrs. M.J. Pufferies, who ran a select school for $4 a month in "a desirable location aside from the bustle of business." Good teachers were important, and an editorial in the local newspaper claimed that teachers were one of the most useful members of society. Boise has been lucky to have a long history of dedicated and passionate educators, such as Cynthia Mann, Helen Miller, and Merle Wells. They inspired, challenged, and taught thousands of Boise students.

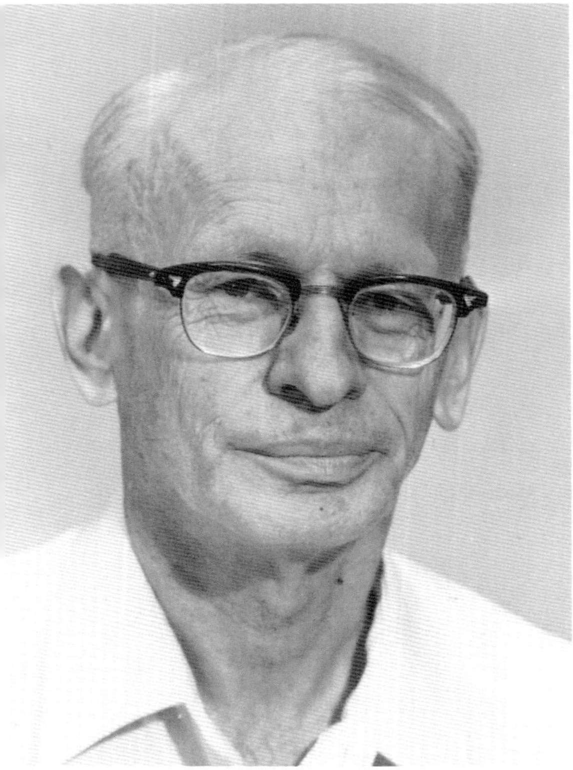

Merle W. Wells

Born in Lethbridge, Alberta, Canada, in 1918, Merle Wells moved to Boise in 1930, where he lived for most of the rest of his life. He graduated from Boise High School, then attended Boise Junior College (BJC) and the College of Idaho (C of I). Although he intended to pursue a law degree, his history classes in Boise with Dr. Eugene Chaffee inspired him to pursue a Ph.D. in history at the University of California, Berkeley. Merle left Boise briefly in the 1940s, but soon returned, teaching at C of I and BJC. In 1959, H.J. Swinney, the new State Historical Society director, hired Merle as historian and archivist. He stayed on for 40 years—even after his retirement in 1987. He drafted the law creating a state archives; set up the State Historic Preservation Office; and wrote the text for more than 200 historical highway signs. A legendary storyteller, Wells could start to answer a history-related question as he left Boise, only finishing up as the car pulled into Sandpoint, Seattle, or Sacramento. A research room at the Idaho State Archives is named in his honor. (Left, courtesy of University Archives Collection, Boise State University Library Special Collections Department; below, authors' collection.)

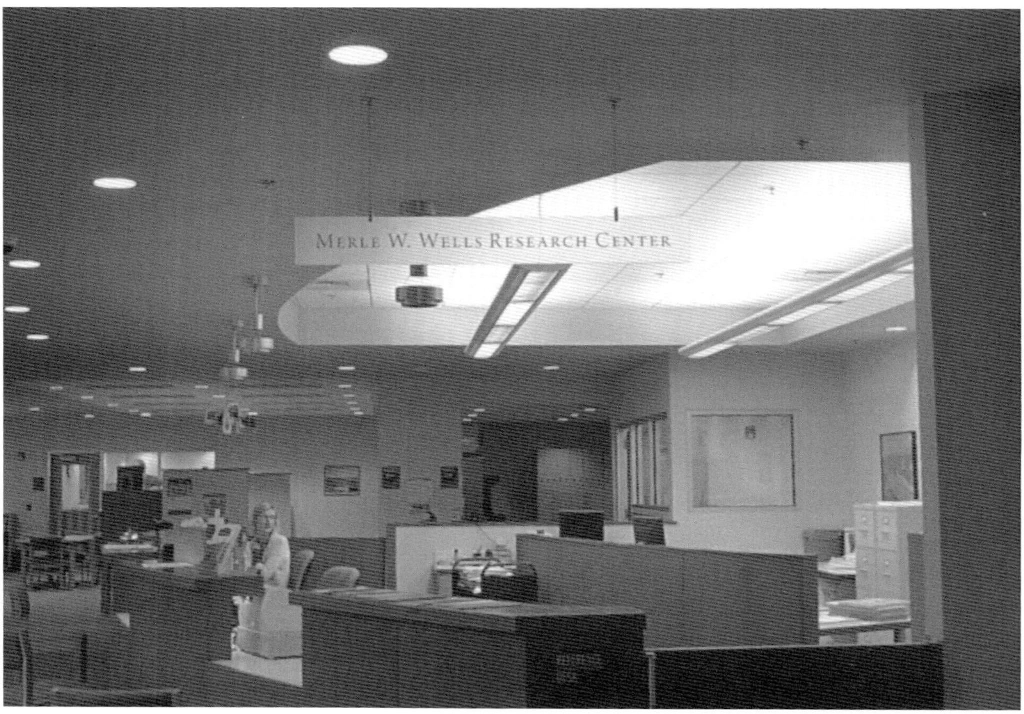

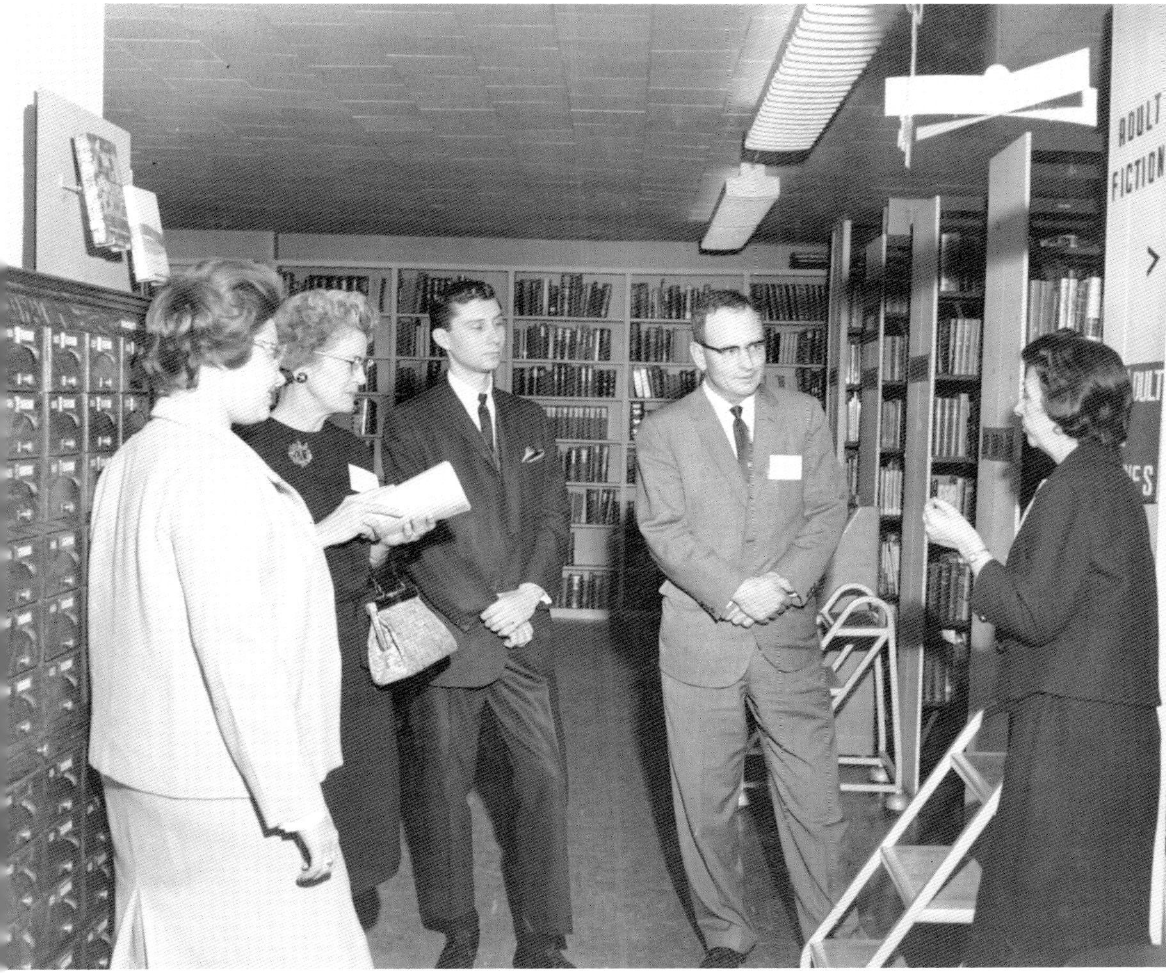

Helen Miller

Hired by the Idaho State Library Board in 1962, Helen Miller (far right) served as state librarian for 18 years, the longest tenure of anyone in the position to date. Under her direction, the state library increased support of library services to local communities, expanded from a small area in the basement of the State Historical Museum to its own building at Third and State Streets, supported scholarships for the training of professional librarians, and moved library systems into the era of information technology, from card catalogs to computers. In the winter of 1962, Miller drove to Idaho from the East in the Volkswagen Beetle that was her trademark car. The basic model had no radio or heater, so she hung a transistor radio from the rearview mirror, wore the warmest coat and snow boots that she could find, and made the trip. She was stopped once by a snowstorm in Wyoming, but arrived in time to start her new job on January 15, 1962. (Courtesy of the Idaho Commission on Libraries.)

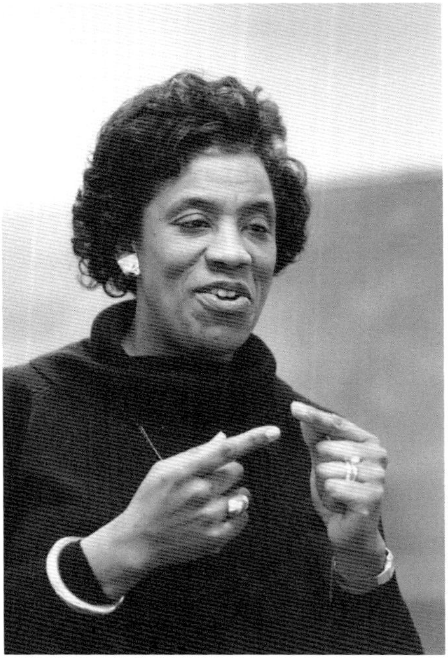

Mamie Oliver

Rev. Dr. Mamie Oliver (left) has been widely recognized for her contributions to public service and the study of African Americans in Idaho. She moved to Boise with her husband, Rev. H. Lincoln Oliver, when he was hired as pastor of St. Paul Baptist Church. Rev. Dr. Oliver became the first African American professor in Idaho when Boise State University hired her as assistant and associate professor in the Department of Social Work in 1972. During her tenure at BSU, she and her students completed foundational research on the history of African Americans in Idaho. Rev. Dr. Oliver is the author of several articles including "Idaho Ebony: The African American Presence in Idaho State History" and Idaho Ebony: Boise's Black Baptists: Heritage, Hope and Struggle." She is currently the pastor of Mountain View Community Fellowship. Below, the building where the Rev. H. Lincoln Oliver first served as pastor was moved to Julia Davis Park and is now the location of the Idaho Black History Museum. (Courtesy of University Archives, Boise State University Special Collections Department.)

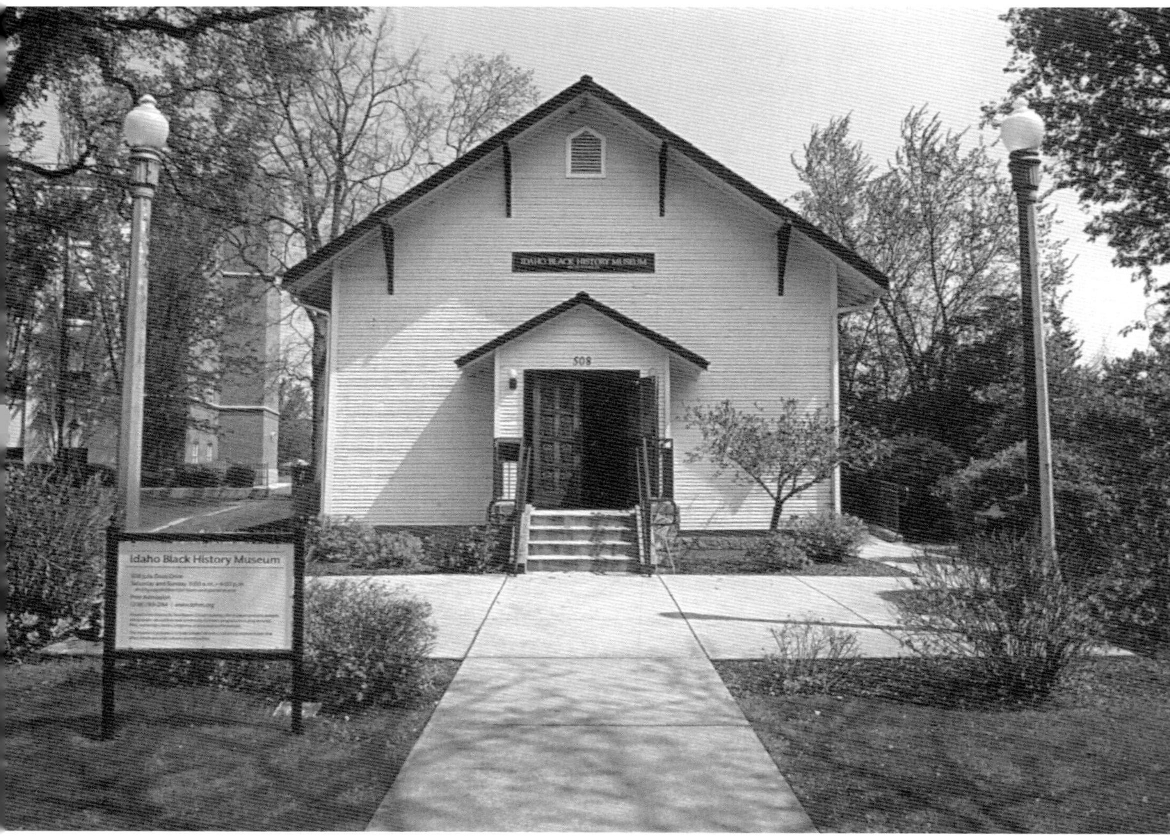

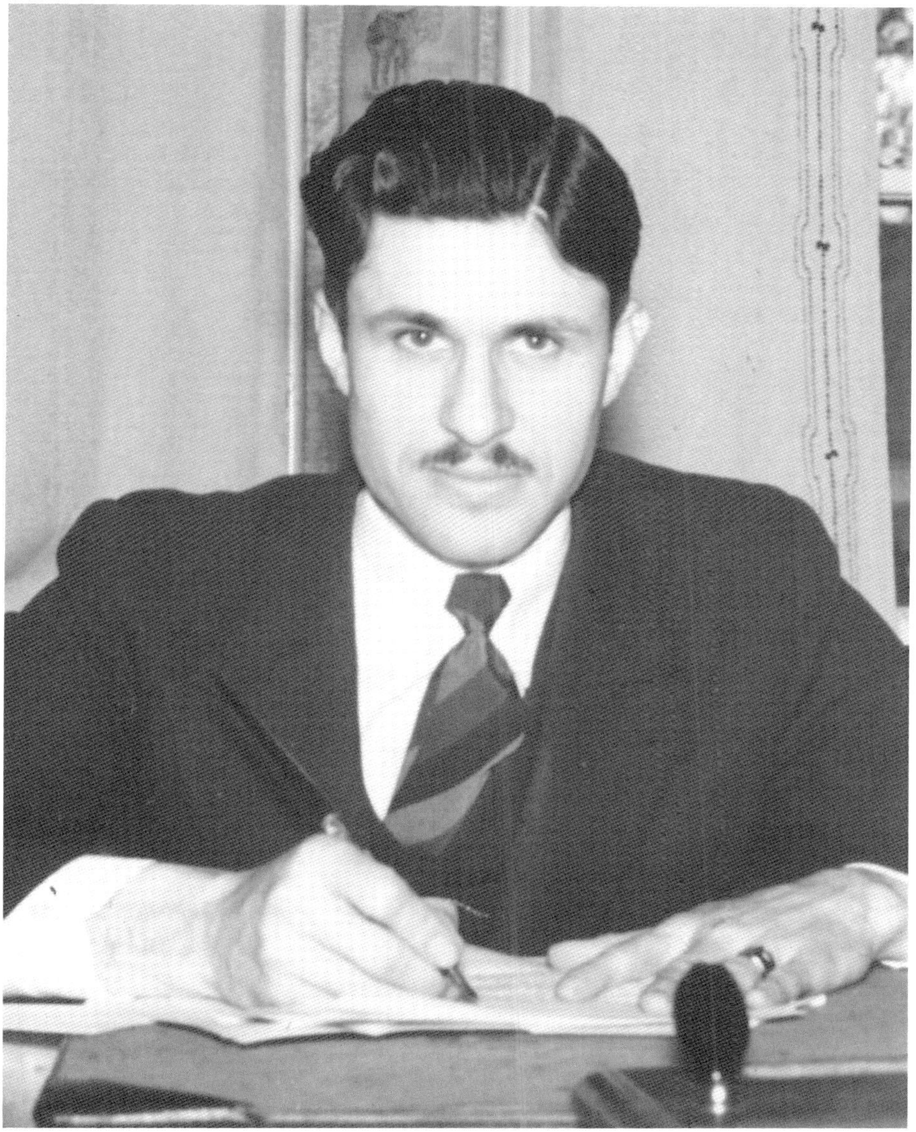

Eugene Chaffee

On September 6, 1932, the predecessor to Boise State University, Boise Junior College, opened its doors to its first students, 41 men and 37 women. Boise resident Eugene B. Chaffee was hired to teach history. Born in 1905 in Aurora, Nebraska, Chaffee moved with his family to a 40-acre farm west of Boise in 1916. He graduated from Boise High School in 1923 and attended the College of Idaho and Occidental College before receiving a master's degree in history from the University of California, Berkeley. Returning to Idaho, he was supervisor of music for Meridian schools and principal of the Ustick school prior to his appointment at Boise Junior College. A popular teacher, he was selected by the students as their faculty advisor and in 1936 was named president of the college. He would lead it for the next 32 years. According to historian Merle Wells, Chaffee's dedication and talent for inspiring community support made the college a four-year institution and laid the foundation for the university. (Courtesy of Boise State University, Special Collections Department.)

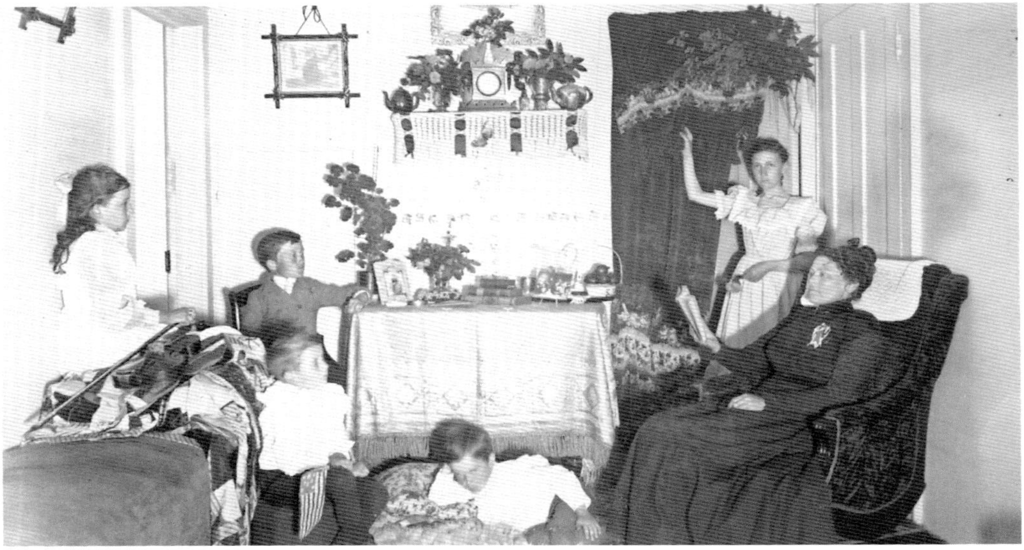

Cynthia Mann

The gravestone of beloved teacher and philanthropist Cynthia Mann is inscribed, "It Was Happiness to Serve." Born Cynthia Pease in 1853 in Kentucky, she moved first to Illinois and then Kansas. Mann arrived in Boise around 1880 and taught at public schools in Boise and surrounding towns. She was a member of the Columbian Club and the Business Woman's Club and a founding member of the Pioneer Chapter of the Daughters of the American Revolution. Her legacy to the city was the donation of a block of land on Warm Springs Avenue for The Children's Home Society of Idaho in 1908. At the time of her death in 1920, she was remembered as the "children's friend" and one of the most beloved women in the city. (Courtesy of the Idaho State Historical Society.)

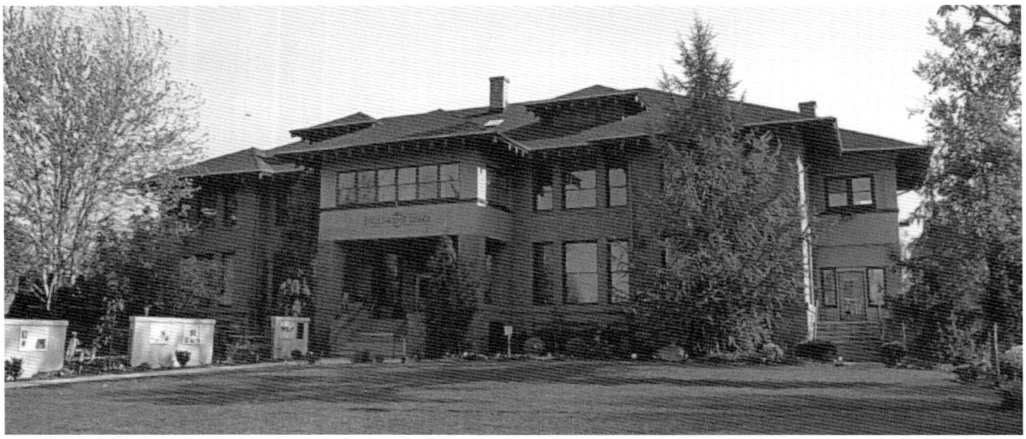

Children's Home Society of Idaho

After Cynthia Mann's generous donation of land to the Children's Home Society of Idaho, a variety of activities were held to raise funds for the building, including balls, tag sales, and donations. Designed by the Boise architectural firm of Tourtellotte & Company, construction of the building began in 1910. The cornerstone was laid on May 14 and the building was completed and opened in December 1910. It was used as an orphanage until the late 1960s. It is still owned by the Children's Home Society, whose mission is to improve the lives of children in the community. (Authors' collection.)

CHAPTER FIVE

The Arts from A to Z

In 1907, Clarence Darrow, the 20th century's most famous attorney, arrived in Boise as defense counsel for mine union organizer William "Big Bill" Haywood and his colleagues George Pettibone and Charles Moyer, all standing trial for conspiring to murder former governor Frank Steunenberg. Finding more cultural refinements than he had expected, Darrow later proclaimed Boise to be the "Athens of the sagebrush." Situated 350 miles from Salt Lake City and 349 miles from Portland, Boise has always had to create its own art and culture. James A. Pinney brought famous actors and actresses to Boise. When he opened his new Columbia Theater in 1892, one of the highlights was the appearance of Julia Marlow, a leading Shakespearean actress of the time. She appeared with her company's production of *As You Like It*.

Mary Hallock Foote, an author and illustrator, lived in the region for 12 years. During that time, the desert landscape inspired her drawings of Western life. Contemporary author and Pulitzer Prize winner Anthony Doerr makes Boise his home.

Music Week is a favorite Boise event. It was established in May 1919 by Eugene A. Farner, director of musical activities at St. Michael's Episcopal Cathedral and St. Margaret's School. He also served as director of the Boise Civic Festival Chorus. During the weeklong event, community members produced their own programs, which were offered free to the public. This tradition has continued to the current day and is the basis for rich entertainment throughout the city. Boise's rich musical scene has also been fed by the talents of jazz pianist Gene Harris and singer, songwriter, and saxophonist Curtis Stigers.

Local theatrical groups have played an important role in Boise. In the heyday of the Pinney Theatre, local productions featuring local players were often on the schedule, and the tradition continued into the 20th century. The Idaho Shakespeare Festival, founded in 1976, has established a national reputation. Today, it offers internships, workshops, and traveling productions, bringing theater to small towns all over the state.

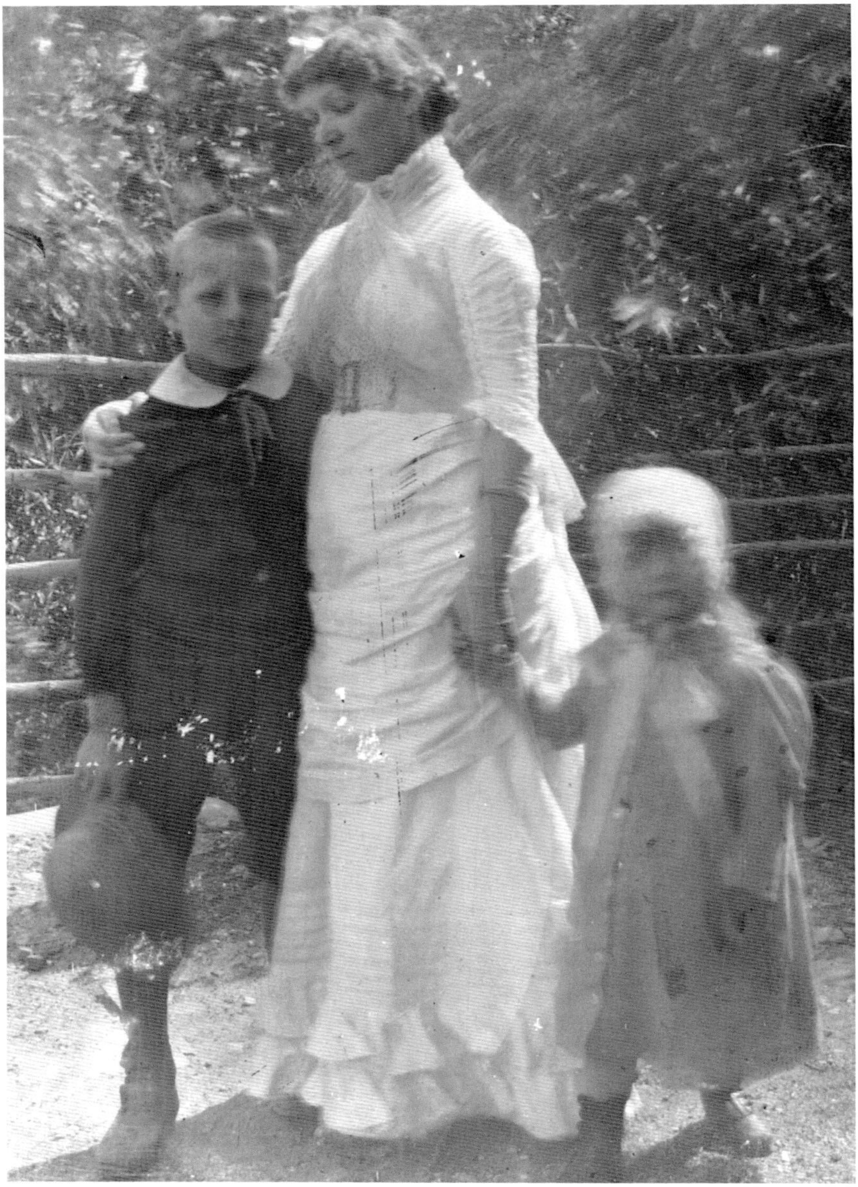

Mary Hallock Foote

Mary Hallock Foote, one of the most famous women artists of her time, arrived in Idaho in 1884. Her husband, Arthur Foote, a mining engineer, came to Idaho to build dams and canals on the Boise River for agricultural irrigation. The Footes lived in the Boise area for 12 years as Arthur tried, with little success, to raise money for the construction of a major canal. The project, called the New York Canal, finally took shape under the US Reclamation Service in the early part of the 20th century. During the years the Footes were in Idaho, Mary, an accomplished author-illustrator, worked as a correspondent for *Century* magazine, writing and illustrating stories and essays about the life she experienced in the West. Her life became the controversial inspiration for Wallace Stegner's Pulitzer Prize–winning novel *Angle of Repose*. (Courtesy of the Idaho State Historical Society.)

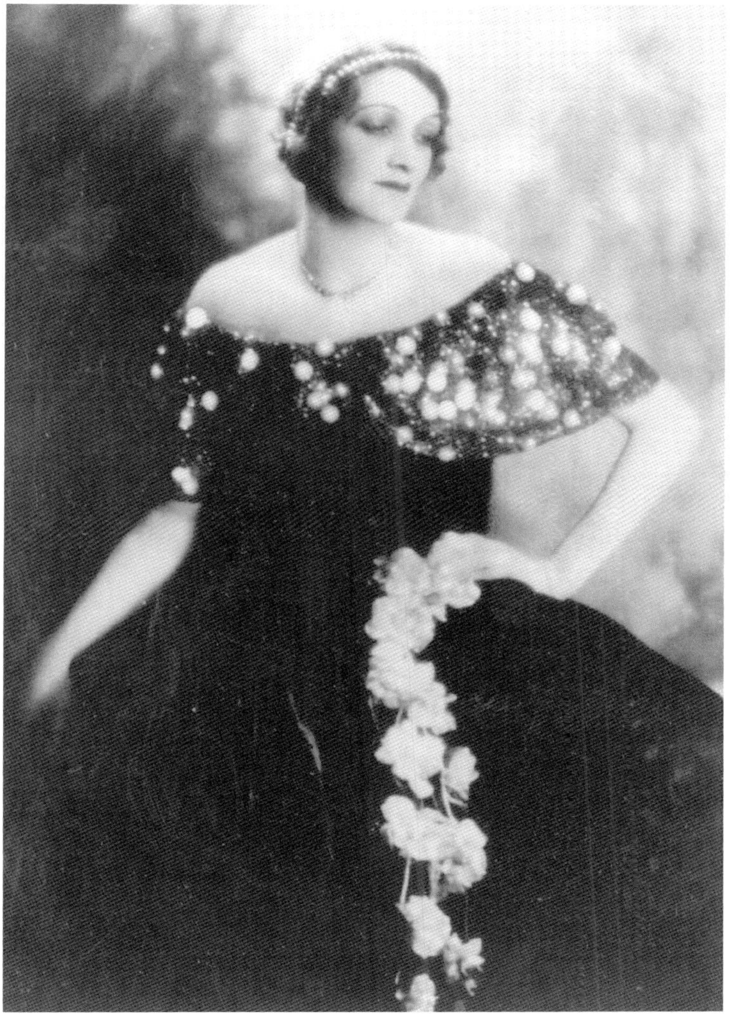

Lucille Lippincott

"Especially noted was the applause of the lyric art of Signorina Lippincott who, in the part of Violetta, clearly demonstrated vocal gifts of the highest order perfectly harmonized with an excellent mastery of dramatic art." This praise for Boise's "Prima Donna" was published in an Italian newspaper in January 1929 and quoted in the *Idaho Daily Statesman* on May 12, 1929. The daughter of Albert and Emma Lippincott, Lucille was born in Silver City, Idaho, in 1896. She attended grade school at St. Margaret's Hall, a school for girls in Boise. Her father, a doctor, moved the family to New York sometime later, where Lucille received private voice lessons before attending the Institute of Musical Art (now The Julliard School), graduating in 1919. She continued her studies in Europe for several years before her debut in Italy in 1929 as Violetta in *La Traviata*. Lippincott performed as a concert singer in Europe and the United States throughout the 1930s. She opened a studio in the Pinney Building in the 1950s and added a second studio in Twin Falls. Although she never achieved the national and international acclaim that her early career seemed to promise, she trained many young singers who later remembered her with affection. Lippincott was a staunch supporter of the arts in Boise and Idaho through her continued activities on committees for the Tuesday Musicale and Boise's Music Week. She died in Twin Falls on July 31, 1967. (Courtesy of the Idaho State Historical Society.)

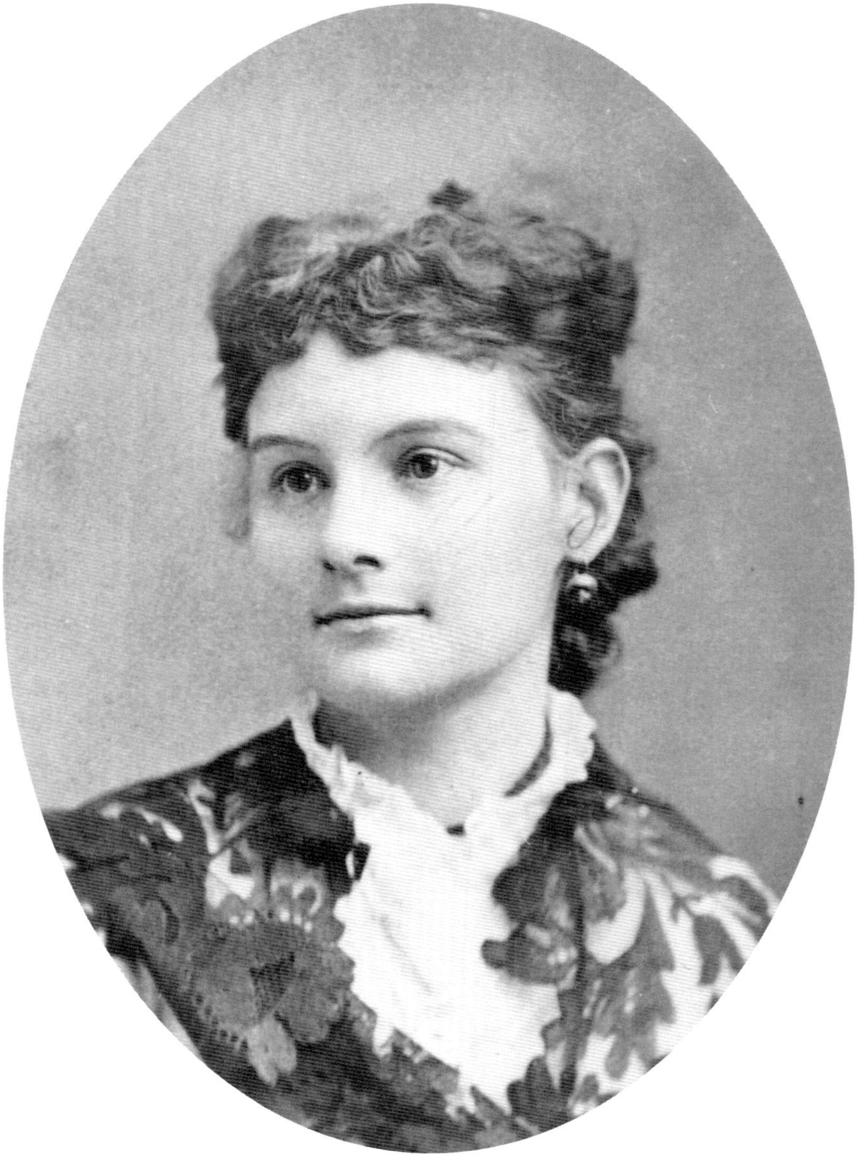

Emma Edwards Green

Artist Emma Edwards Green is best known for her design of the original Great Seal of the State of Idaho. The seal was created in 1891 by an act of the state legislature and is the only state seal originally designed by a woman. (In 1957, the seal was revised and modernized by Paul B. Evans.) Emma, the daughter of John C. Edwards, a former governor of Missouri and a founder of Stockton, California, came to Boise in 1888. She made Boise her home and taught in schools in many southwest Idaho communities, including Bruneau, Atlanta, Pine, and Rocky Bar. She opened an art studio in Boise, where she taught painting and drawing and exhibited her work. She married James G. Green, a miner, and traveled with him to mining towns throughout Idaho. Emma specialized in landscape paintings and was known in particular for the scenes she painted during the Thunder Mountain mining boom of the early 20th century. (Courtesy of the Idaho State Historical Society.)

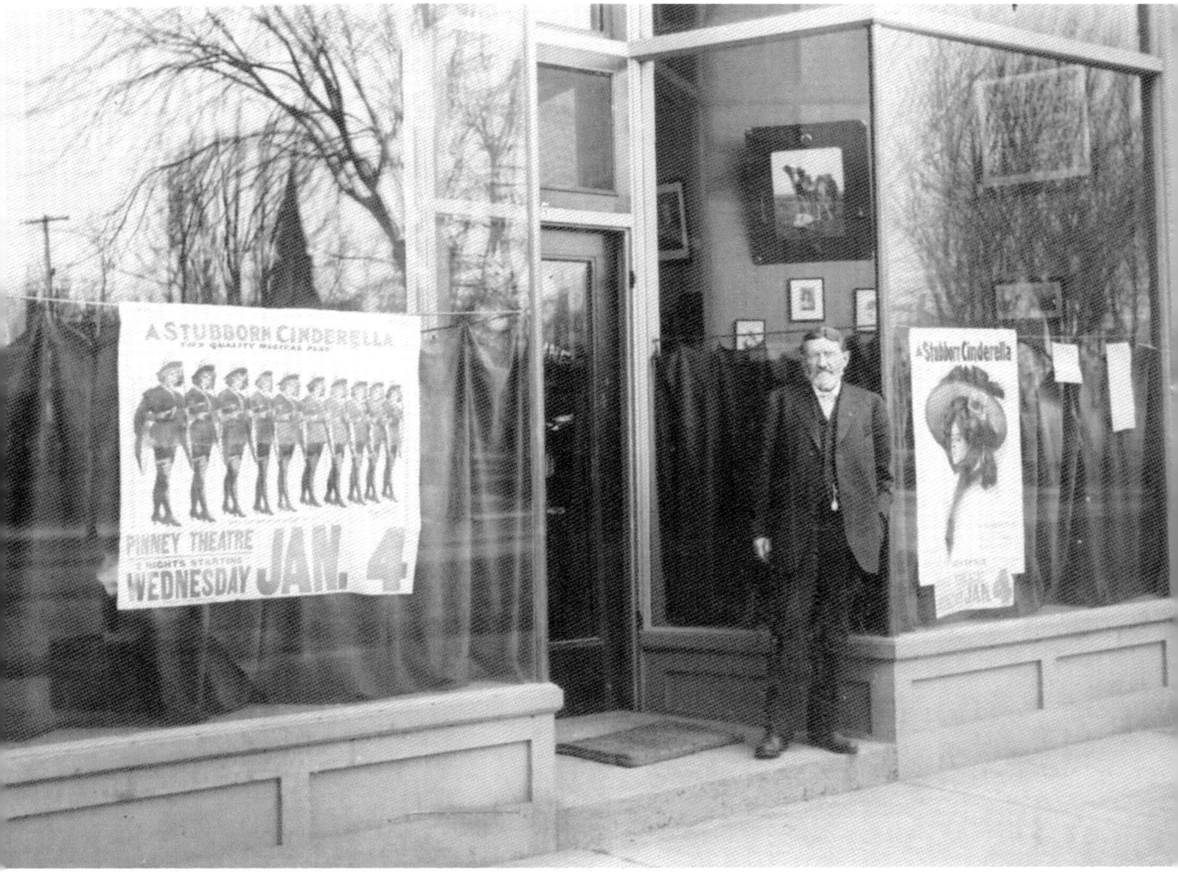

James Pinney

Pinney was lured to Idaho by the mining boom. Born in Ohio, he began his career as a clerk, but left to follow the gold trail west to California, then to the new Idaho Territory. Settling in Idaho City, he was appointed postmaster by Pres. Abraham Lincoln and opened a mercantile store. In 1873, he relocated to Boise and became involved in civic affairs, serving five nonconsecutive terms as mayor. Under his leadership, Boise built a new city hall, a fire station, and a sewer system; acquired the land for Morris Hill Cemetery; and extended the city limits for the first time. Pinney's true passion was for the theater. In 1888, he undertook management of Peter Sonna's opera house, located in the second floor of a hardware-store building. Then, four years later, he built the ornate Columbia Theater on Jefferson Street. The Columbia's success led Pinney to build an even more elaborate venue. In 1908, he commissioned Seattle architect E.W. Houghton to design a grand theater building, located across Jefferson Street from the Columbia Theater. Building-supply issues and design changes caused delays, but the new theater opened on September 18, 1908, with the play *The French Chef.* Over the next 60 years, Boiseans attended concerts, plays, community events, and movies at the Pinney. The theater closed its doors for good following the run of Elvis Presley's 1967 musical *Double Trouble*. James Pinney was at work in his theater office when he collapsed and died on February 4, 1914. (Courtesy of Erstad-McLeod Families.)

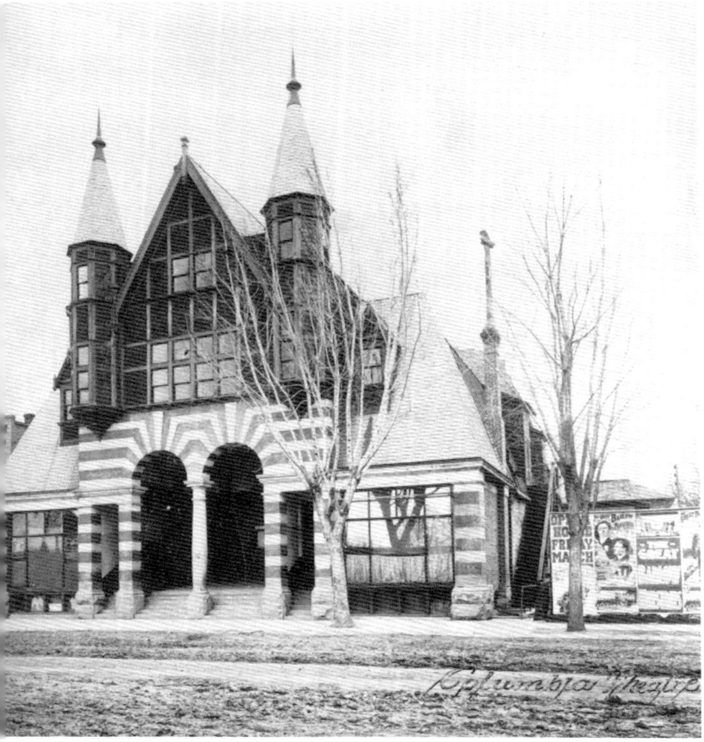

Columbia Theater

James Pinney built the ornate Columbia Theatre on Jefferson Street, between Eighth and Ninth Streets, in 1892. Hundreds of actors and musicians performed on its stage until it was torn down in 1908. (Courtesy of the Erstad-McLeod families.)

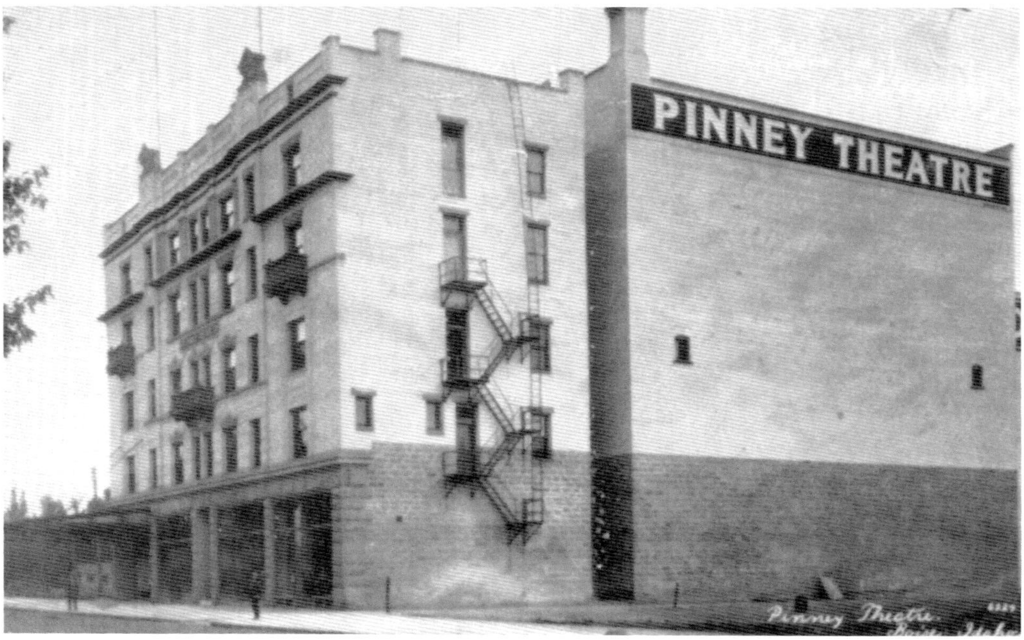

Pinney Theater

The popular Pinney Theater provided years of entertainment for Boiseans. (Courtesy of the Erstad-McLeod families.)

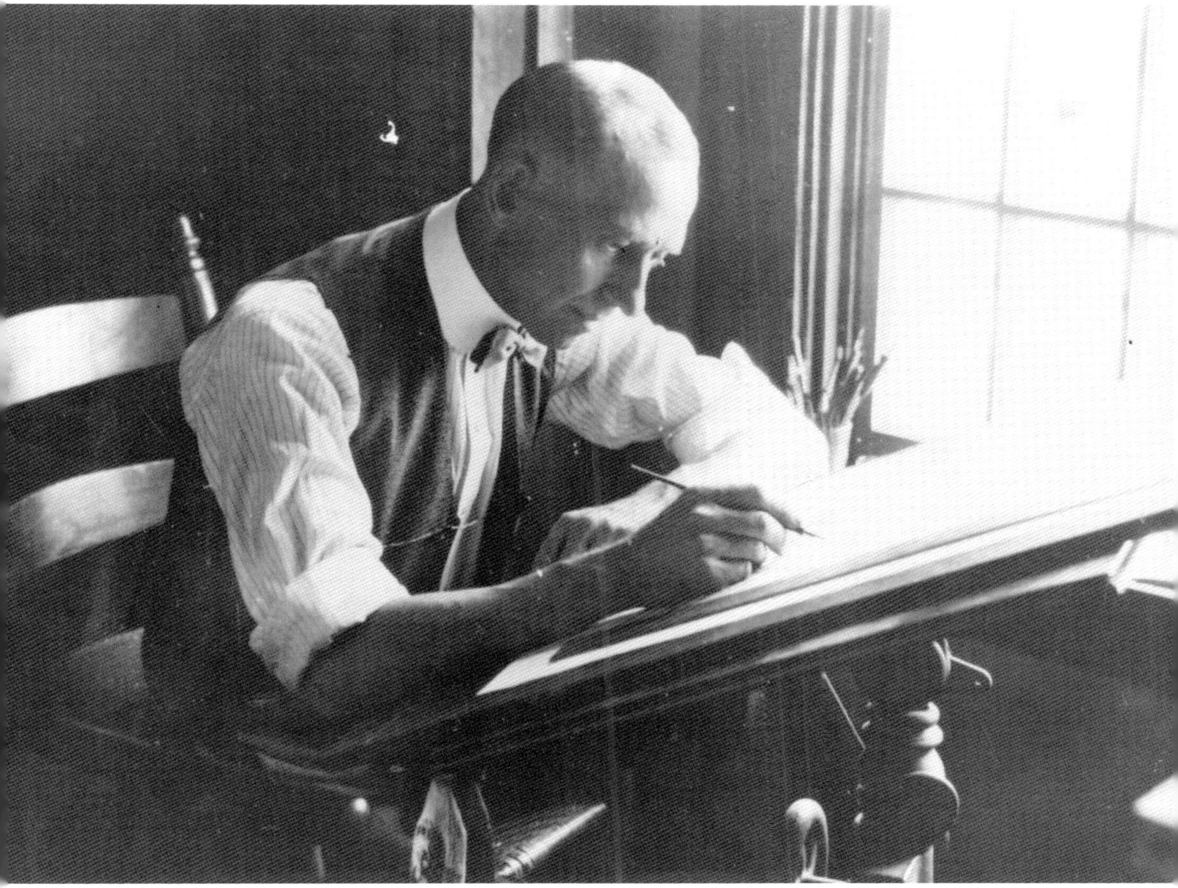

Nick Villeneuve

Political cartoons on the pages of the *Idaho Daily Statesman* drawn by Nick Villeneuve caught readers' eyes during the 1910s. Hired as the first local cartoonist for the paper, his cartoons graced the front pages in the World War I years. The talented artist was born in Star, Idaho, in 1884. When he was three, his family moved to Boise, which remained his home throughout his life. A popular artist, actor, and musician, Villeneuve left Boise in 1902 with the intention of attending the Chicago Art Institute. He could only attend for three months before his finances were exhausted. Back in Boise, Nick began work for a local promotional magazine until he was hired by the *Statesman*. After the war, he worked as a freelancer and as a draftsman and illustrator for the Idaho Power Company from 1926 until his death in 1947. (Courtesy of the Idaho State Historical Society.)

Jean B. Wilson

In 1902, James Pinney sold his Pioneer Book Store to Edward J. Phelps. On July 4, 1904, when a fire destroyed the building and much of the stock, Phelps sold out. Over the following decades, the business was bought and sold many times. In 1925, it was purchased by Ernest and Estella Ayres, who named it Ayres Book Shop. A few permutations later, it became The Book Shop.

In the 1950s, store owners Harry M. Schuppel and Thomas Fisher hired Nancy Stringfellow as manager. Nancy wrested control of the store from them, converting a mishmash of books of indifferent selection to a well-organized collection of interest to readers of all ages. People flocked to the store to find not just the latest bestsellers, but the best of what to read. In the early 1960s, Stringfellow hired newly widowed Jean B. Wilson as a part-time employee in the children's department. Wilson stayed on as a full-time employee, becoming manager when Nancy retired in 1971. In 1979, she bought the store. Both Stringfellow and Wilson were voracious readers who found their true calling at The Book Shop, creating a store that was beloved by Boiseans and admired by bookworms across the nation. Stringfellow died in 1994; that year, Wilson sold the store to her son Dan and his wife. Like many independent bookstores, The Book Shop fell victim to the competition of big chain stores and online shopping. It closed for good in 2000. Jean Wilson died in 2001. People who knew them remember Nancy Stringfellow for her sharp wit and unfiltered cigarettes, and Jean Wilson for her warm smile and chocolate-chip cookies. Both are remembered for matching the right book to the right reader—even when the reader did not have a clue herself. (Courtesy of Sally Mitchell, *Idaho Statesman* photograph.)

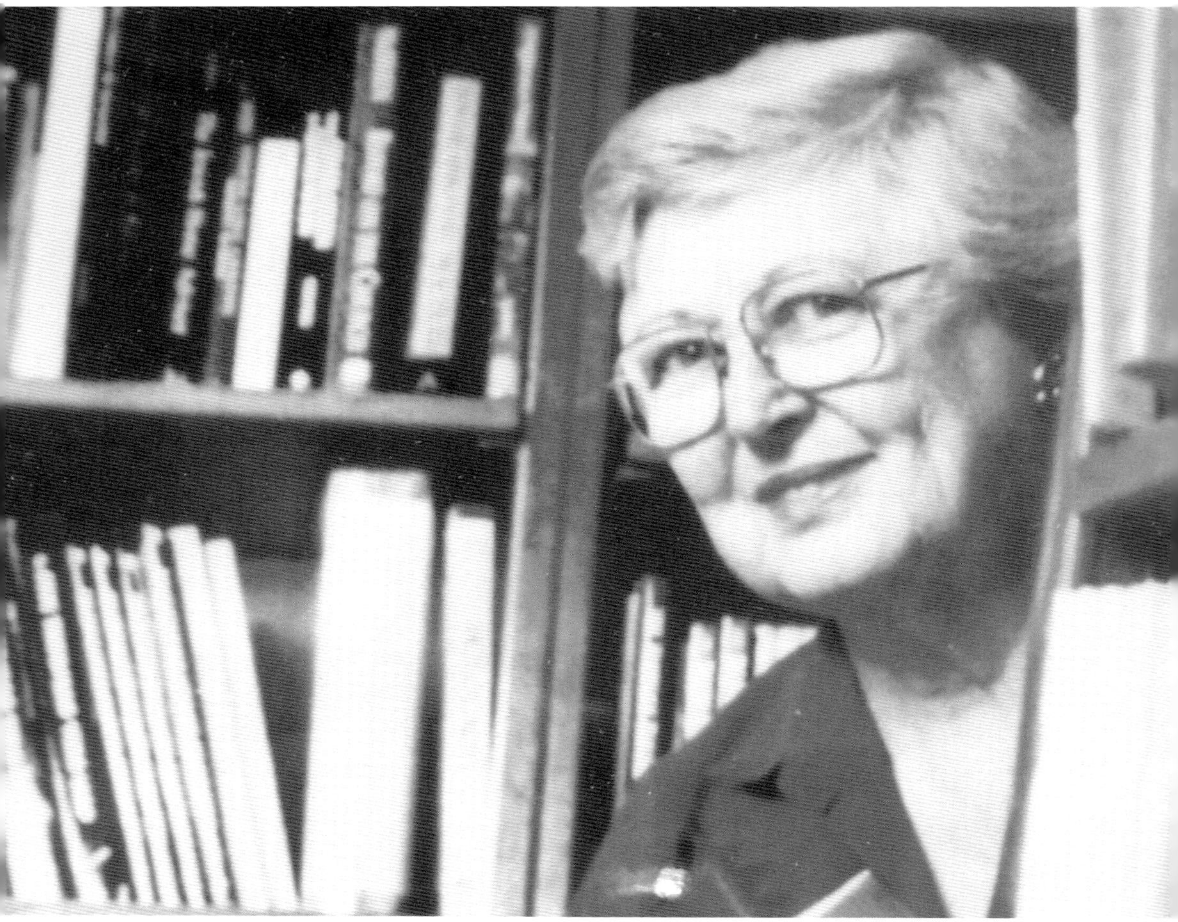

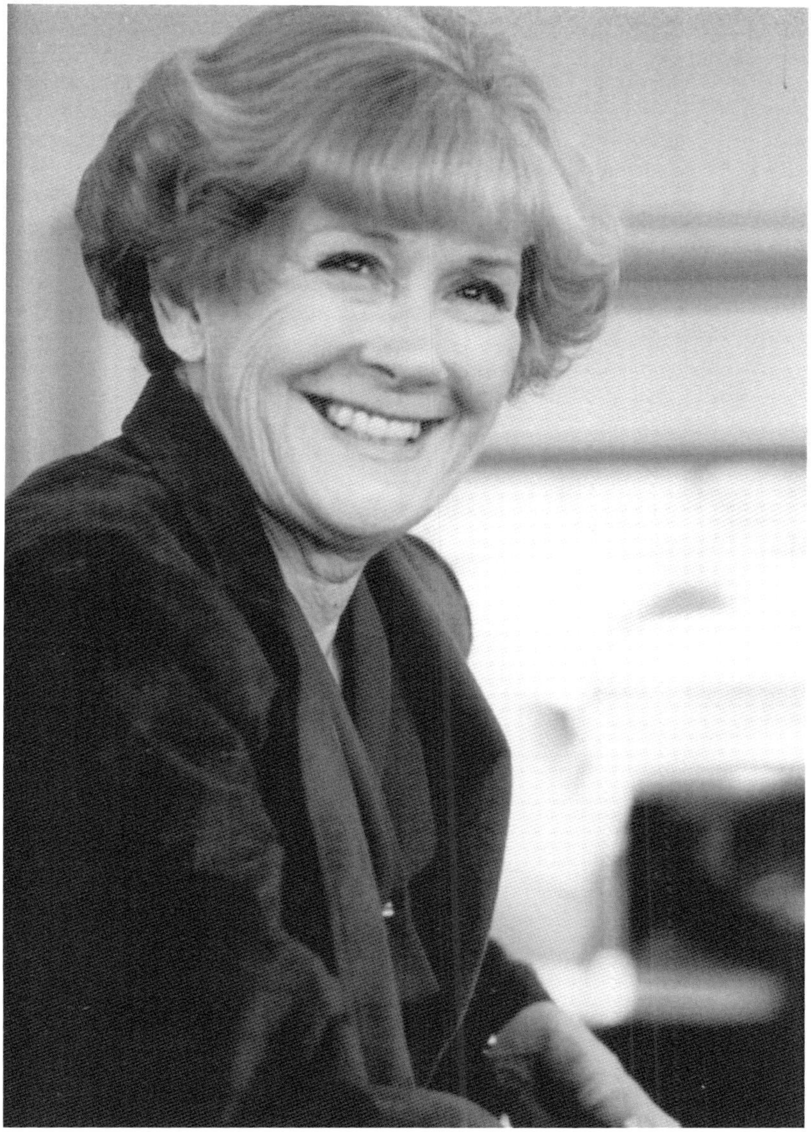

Velma Morrison

Velma Mitchell grew up on her grandmother's farm in rural California, near Tipton. By the late 1950s, Mitchell was the owner of The Broiler, a successful restaurant in Bakersfield, when Harry Morrison became a regular customer. The two were married on July 1, 1959. Harry's plan for the recently completed Ann Morrison Park included a site for a civic auditorium, a venue for the performing arts, but that idea never came to fruition. Instead, after Harry's death in 1971, Velma took steps to make his dream a reality. Over the next 13 years, working with her close friend Fred Norman, she developed community support for the project through sponsoring special performances of plays and musicals, encouraging donations from major sponsors, and setting up community fundraisers. The work culminated in 1984 with the opening of the Morrison Center for the Performing Arts. In 2009, as part of the center's 25th anniversary celebration, it was renamed the Velma V. Morrison Center for the Performing Arts. (Courtesy of Boise State Archives, Boise State University Special Collections Department.)

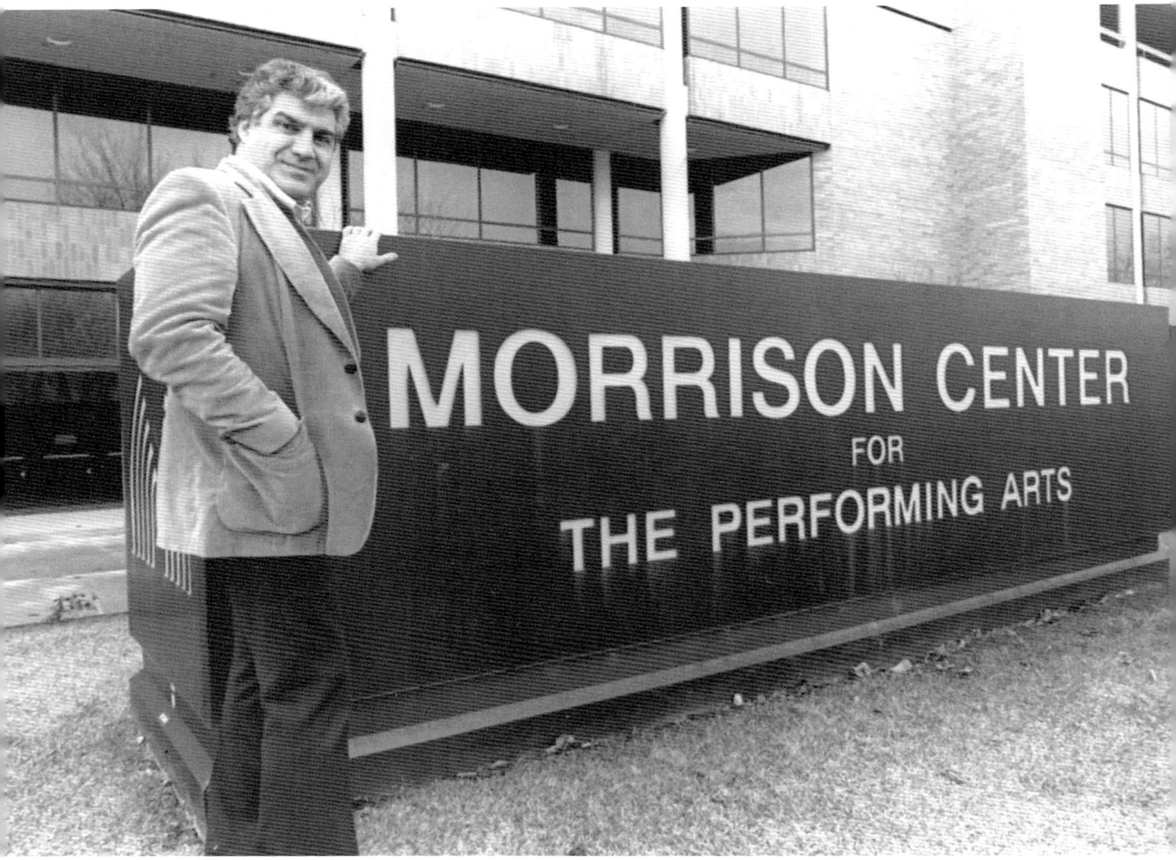

Fred Norman
Norman attended Boise Junior College on a football scholarship in the 1950s, but left Boise shortly after graduation. He returned in 1969 and began a career at Boise State, working at various times as director of the student union, as the Broncos' quarterback coach, and as a professor in the theater department. Everyone who knew him agreed that he was passionately enthusiastic about everything he took on and was endowed with the energy to achieve the most challenging of goals. When he and Velma Morrison met, the perfect match of determination, enthusiasm, and energy allowed them to achieve the goal of bringing the Morrison Center for the Performing Arts to life. After it was built, Norman served as its executive director for 15 years, and continued to direct local productions before retiring in 1999. (Courtesy of Boise State Archives, Boise State University Special Collections Department.)

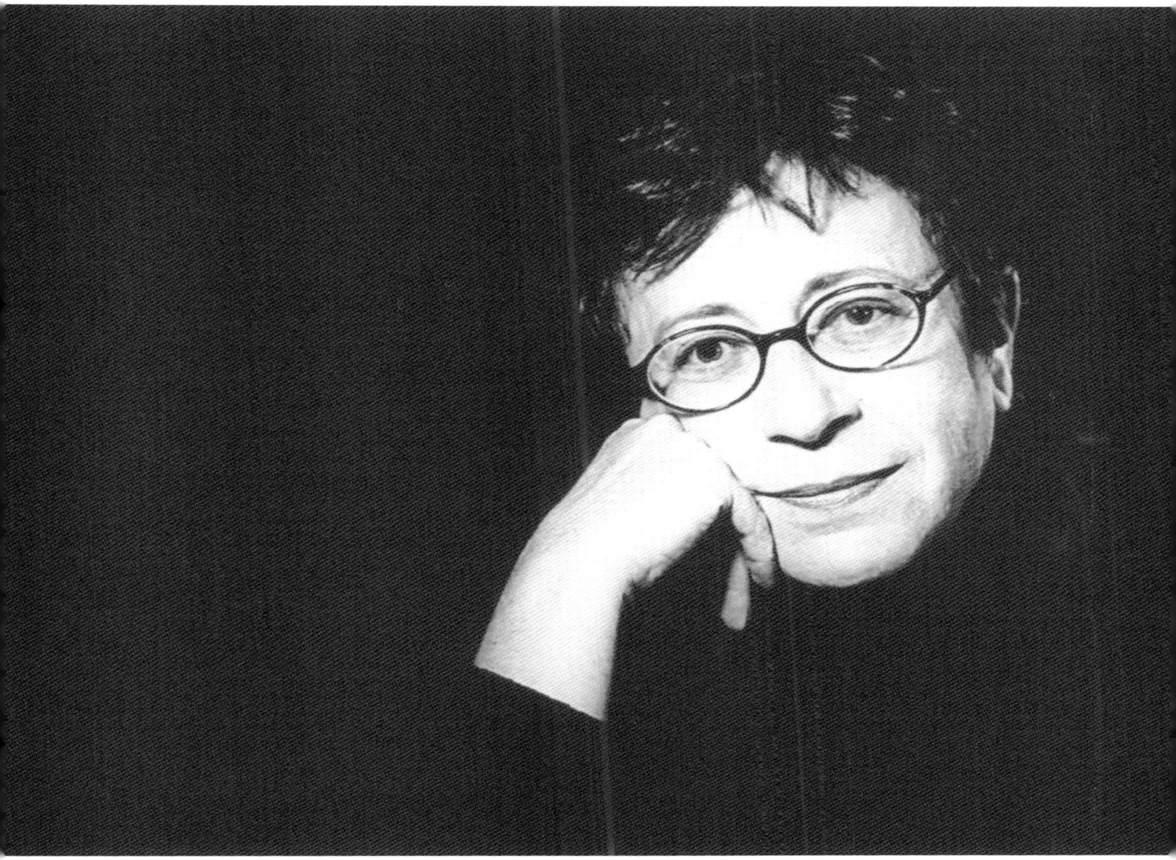

Surel Mitchell
Artist Surel Mitchell arrived in Boise in 1977. Over the next 34 years, she became a driving force behind the visual arts community. She served on both the Boise City and Garden City Arts Commissions, was involved in organizing and judging many arts exhibits, and influenced artists through her own work and her desire to promote opportunities for art. Her work was exhibited in galleries across the United States. The Boise Visual Chronicle, a collection of work by local artists sponsored by the City of Boise, includes one of her contributions. She received many honors during her life, including the Idaho Governor's Award for Excellence in the Arts (2000) and the Mayor's Award for Excellence in the Arts (2011). Mitchell, who died in 2011, was an advocate of the live/work concept, and resided for a number of years in the home that also housed her Garden City studio. After her death, her home became Surel's Place, a live/work studio for local artists working on special projects and for artists with a regional or national reputation who come to work with a local institution. (Courtesy of Rebecca Mitchell Kelada, photograph by Deborah Hardee.)

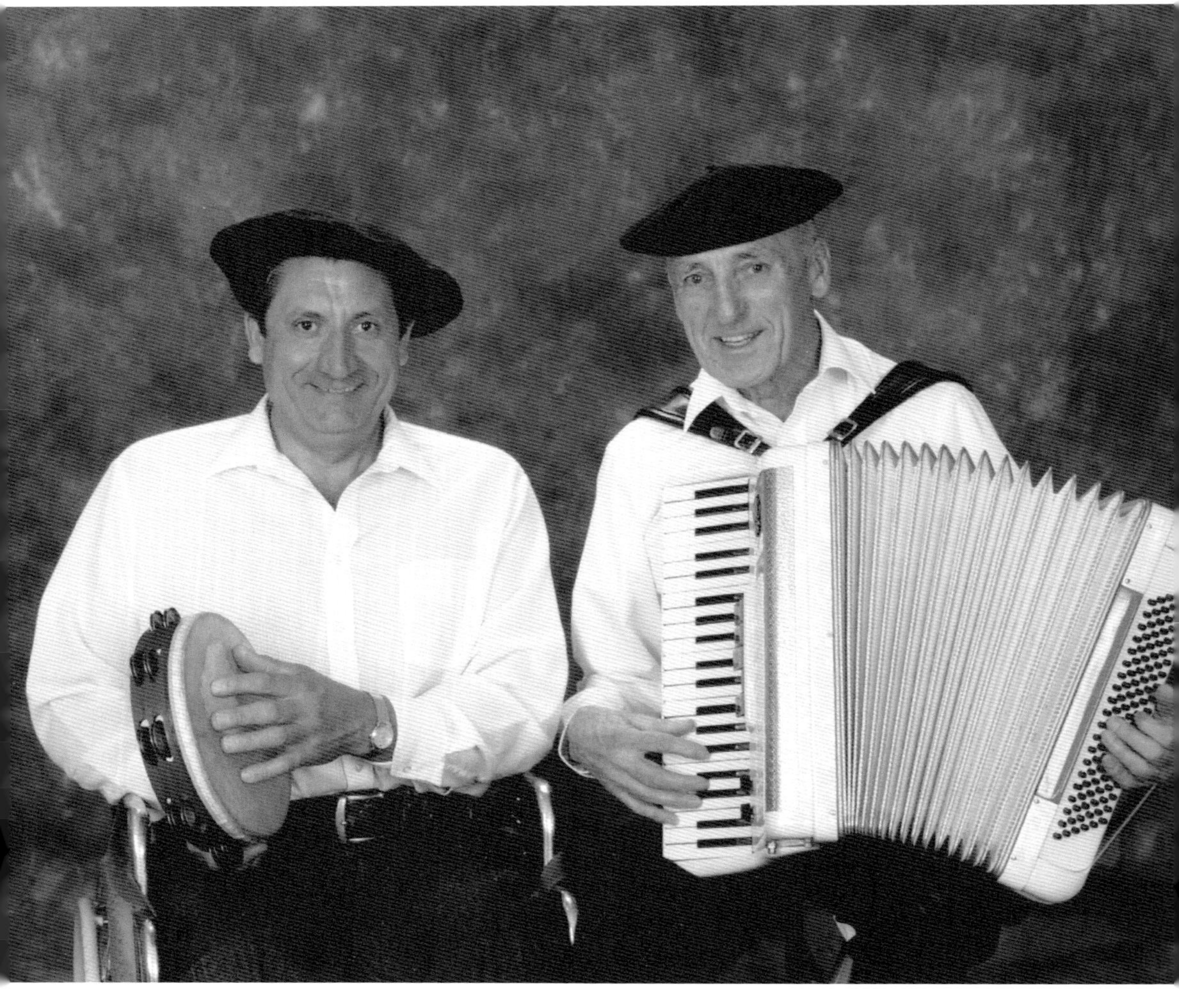

Jimmy Jausoro

Jausoro (right), shown here with Juan Zulaika, was a beloved member of Idaho's Basque community and a world-renowned musician. His parents, Tomas and Tomasa Jausoro, raised Jimmy in the boardinghouse they owned in the neighboring town of Nampa. He started playing the accordion at the age of 10, and after six months of lessons, learned to read music. He quickly became a proficient player and was invited to perform Basque music at private parties and at other boardinghouses. By the time he was 15, he was entering music contests and performed on radio station KWG in Portland, Oregon, after winning an amateur contest. Jausoro's professional job was working for the Union Pacific Railroad, but music was his passion. He formed the Jim Jausoro Orchestra in 1957, and the group performed until 2000. Jausoro passed away in 2004. As Patty Miller, director of the Basque Museum and Cultural Center, noted, Jausoro provided "a lifetime of dedicated practices, performances and service to the Basque communities in the West." (Courtesy of the Basque Museum and Cultural Center.)

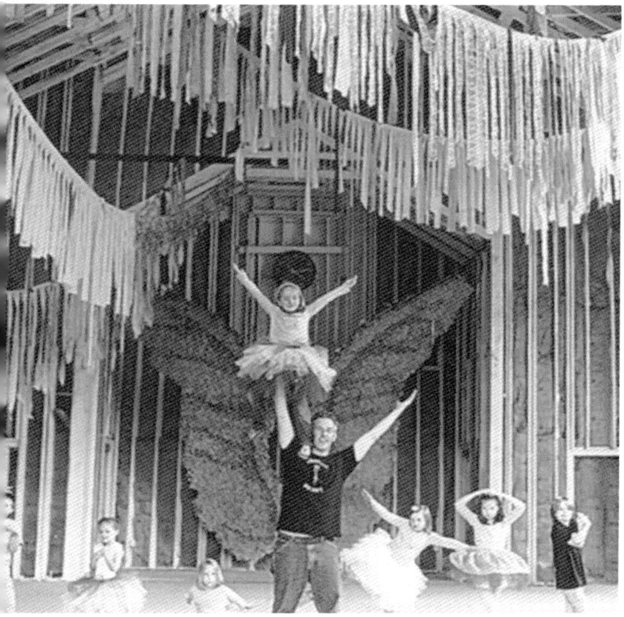

Jon Swarthout

Swarthout has been inspiring children through dance for almost 20 years. A Boise native Swarthout left at age 16, attending the North Carolina School of the Arts and the Houston Ballet Academy. He danced professionally with the Joffrey Ballet and the Oregon Ballet Theater before moving to the Feld Ballet in New York City, a tuition-free public school where students receive rigorous academic and dance training. He returned to Boise, where he danced with Ballet Idaho. By 1998, ready for a change, Swarthout created Dance Rascals, a program incorporating some of the ideas of the Feld Ballet, teaching children how to use dance to broaden their experience and understanding. (Courtesy of Jon Swarthout, photograph by Melanie Folwell.)

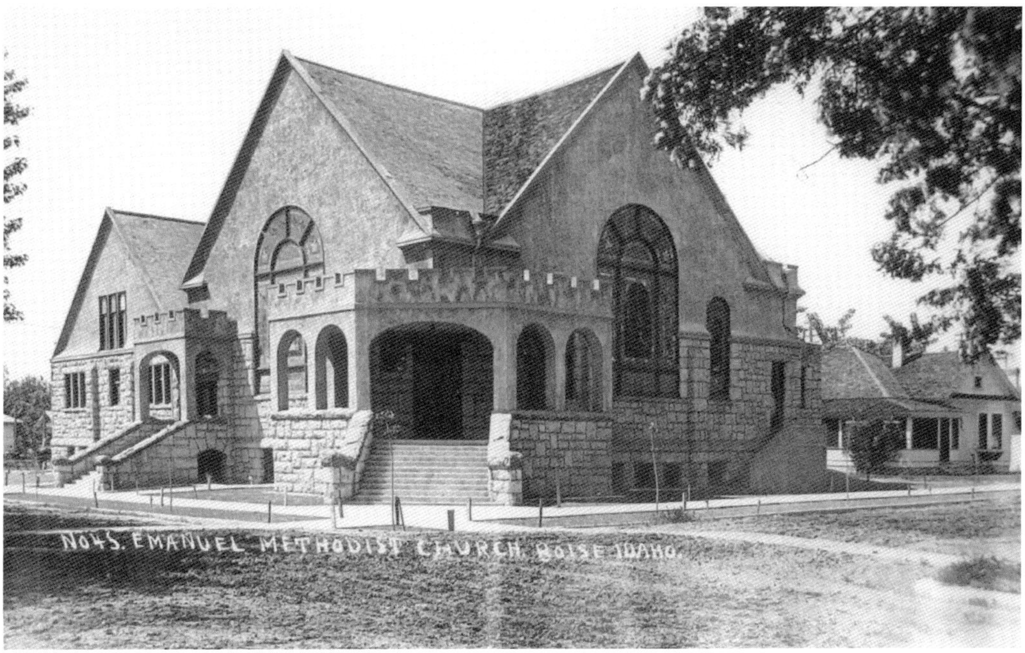

TrICA

Dance Rascals evolved into TrICA (Treasure Valley Institute for Children's Arts). A home for the organization was found at the abandoned Immanuel Methodist Episcopal Church in Boise's North End in 2007. Erected in 1907, the building was sold in the 1970s to a developer who planned to renovate it into apartments. When that project failed, the building stood vacant for years, suffering the not-unexpected fate of use as a meth lab. Grants, donations, and sweat equity have nearly completed its transformation into an arts center with offices for TrICA. (Authors' collection.)

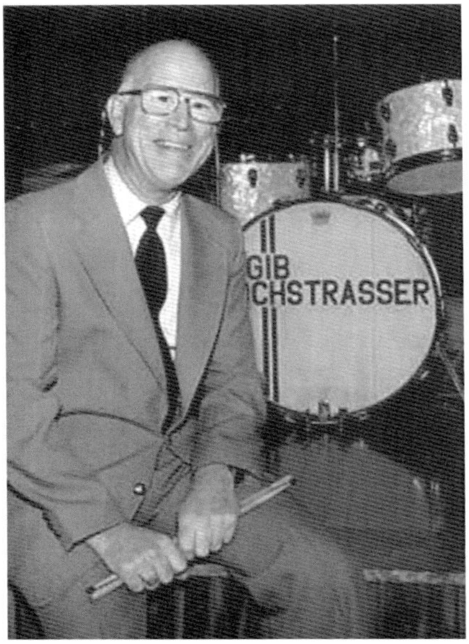

Gilbert Hochstrasser

Many Boiseans remember tapping their toes and moving their feet to the beat of "Gib" Hochstrasser and his King of Swings Jazz Band. He played with numerous bands through the years and later formed his Boise-based big band. The *Idaho Statesman* described Hochstrasser as "a looming presence in Boise music circles, a beloved drummer and band leader who celebrated big-band music through the buffeting winds of popular music tastes." He died in Boise in November 1999 at age 72. (Courtesy of the Idaho Jazz Society.)

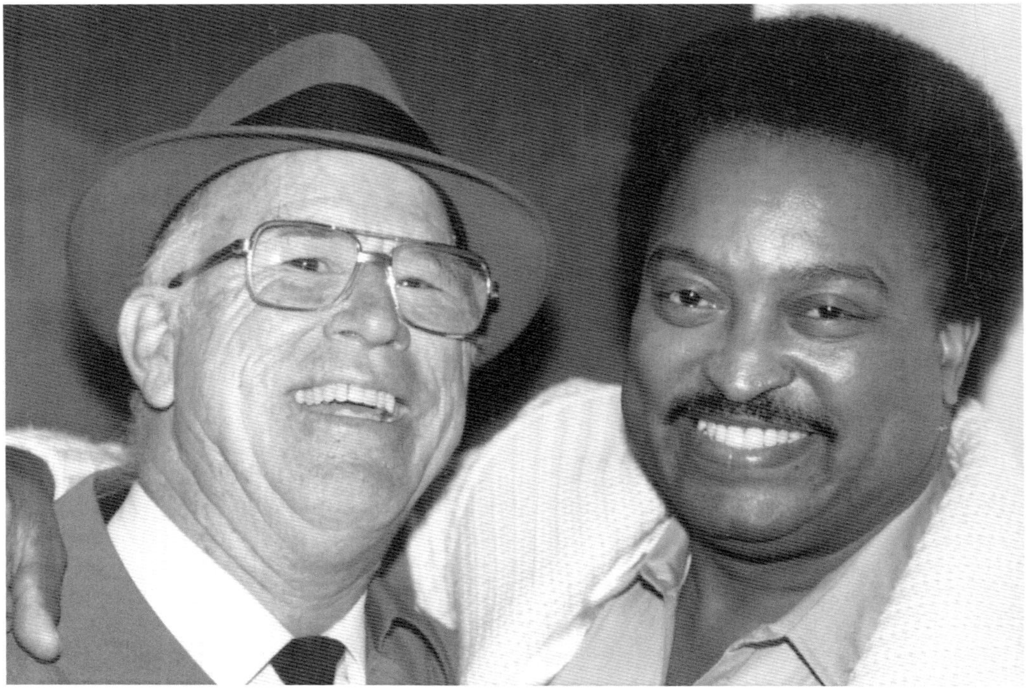

Gene Harris

Acclaimed jazz pianist Gene Harris (right, pictured with Gib Hochstrasser) retired to Boise in 1977. A Michigan native, he was a Grammy-nominated musician who played on more than 80 recordings over a 40-year musical career. In 1996, he led a group of business leaders, educators, and musicians to found an endowment to provide scholarships for jazz musicians. The Gene Harris Jazz Festival at Boise State University was organized later to support the endowment. Although Harris died in 2000 from kidney failure, his legacy of music continues with the annual event. (Courtesy of the Gene Harris Jazz Festival.)

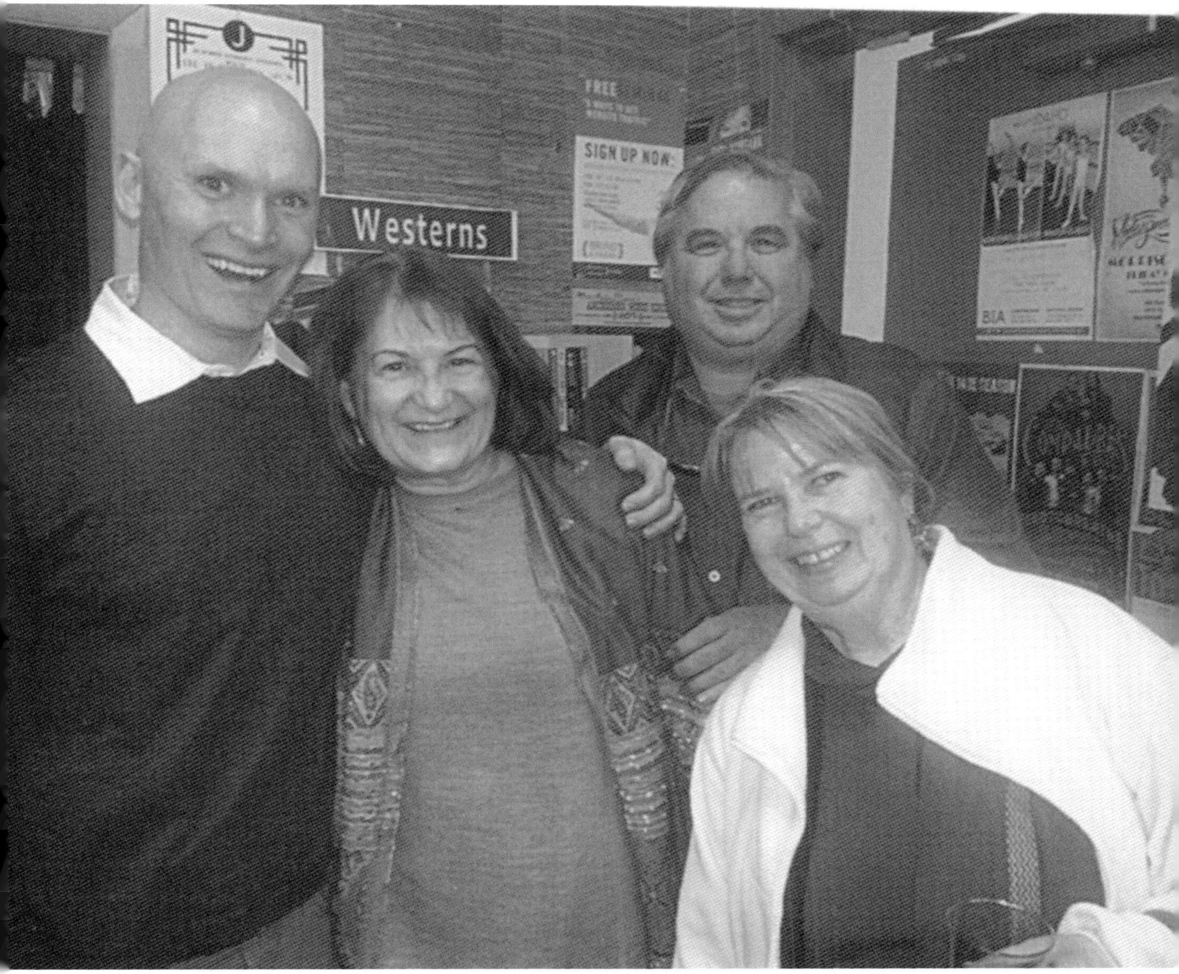

Anthony Doerr

Award-winning author Anthony Doerr calls Boise home. He was introduced to the city by his wife, Shauna Eastman. From this location, he writes fiction set in faraway locations such as China, Rome, and France. His life has been centered on words. He started writing when he was eight in his childhood home in Cleveland, Ohio. He studied history at Bowdoin College, where he met Shauna, and received his master of fine arts from Bowling Green State University in Ohio. He supported his writing by taking a variety of jobs. Doerr has been a cook in Colorado and worked on a sheep farm in New Zealand. He keeps a daily journal and uses his entries, combined with research and imagination, to create stories that resonate with readers around the world. His 2014 book *All the Light We Cannot See* was awarded the 2015 Pulitzer Prize for fiction. Here, Doerr (far left) poses with fans. (Courtesy of Alison Perry.)

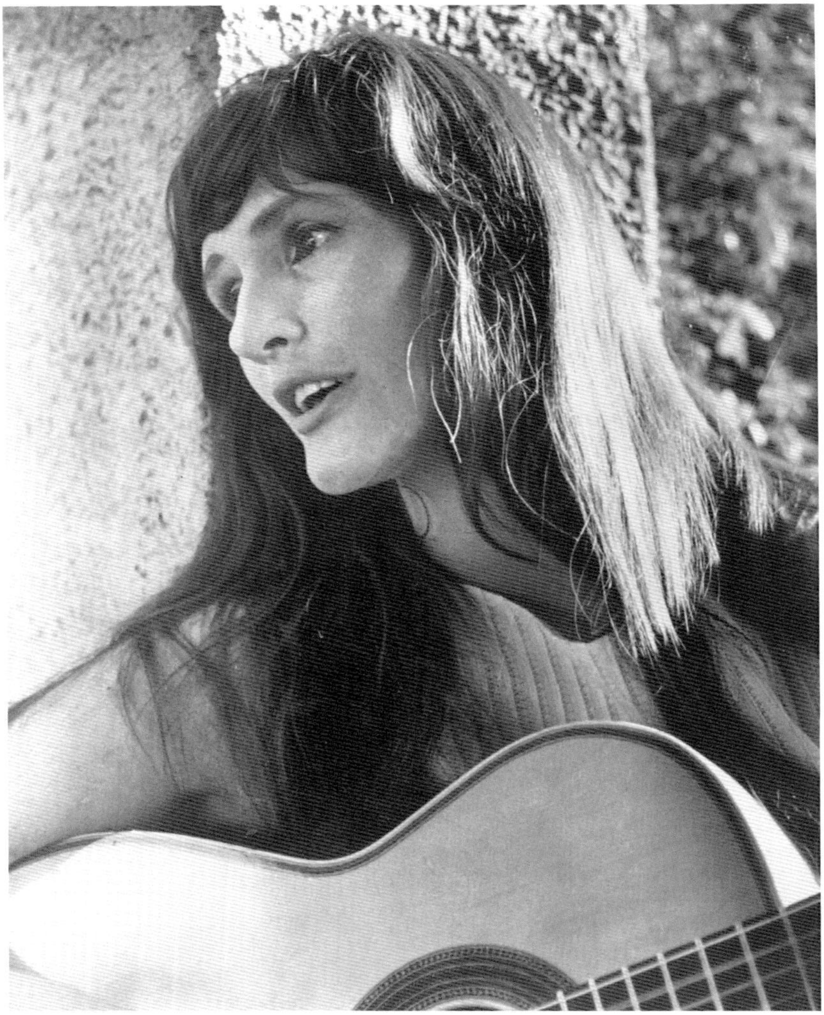

Rosalie Sorrels

Although often described as a folksinger, Rosalie Sorrels has referred to herself as a troubadour who uses songs of many styles and narratives in her storytelling. Born in Boise in 1933 to Walter and Nancy Stringfellow, Rosalie grew up in a home where music, literature, and drama were valued. Her early ambition was to become an opera singer. She married James Sorrels in 1952. A few years later, the couple moved to Salt Lake City, where he was employed as an engineer for the telephone company. The two shared an interest in folk music and were able to teach classes through the University of Utah. Rosalie, having received training in "song catching" through the university's folklore program, taught folk singing and song collecting, while Jim gave guitar lessons. They also began to perform, with Rosalie singing and Jim accompanying on the guitar and other instruments. From the late 1950s until 1965, Rosalie was engaged in performing, recording, and collecting songs and was an active member of the folk-music scene in Salt Lake City. Her marriage ended in 1965. Taking her five children with her, she became, as she describes, "A Travelin' Lady," performing at festivals and concert venues across the country, collecting and creating a body of work that has made her a national icon. She returned to Idaho in the 1990s and moved into the home her father built by hand on Grimes Creek. (Courtesy of the Idaho Statesman Collection, Boise State University Collection.)

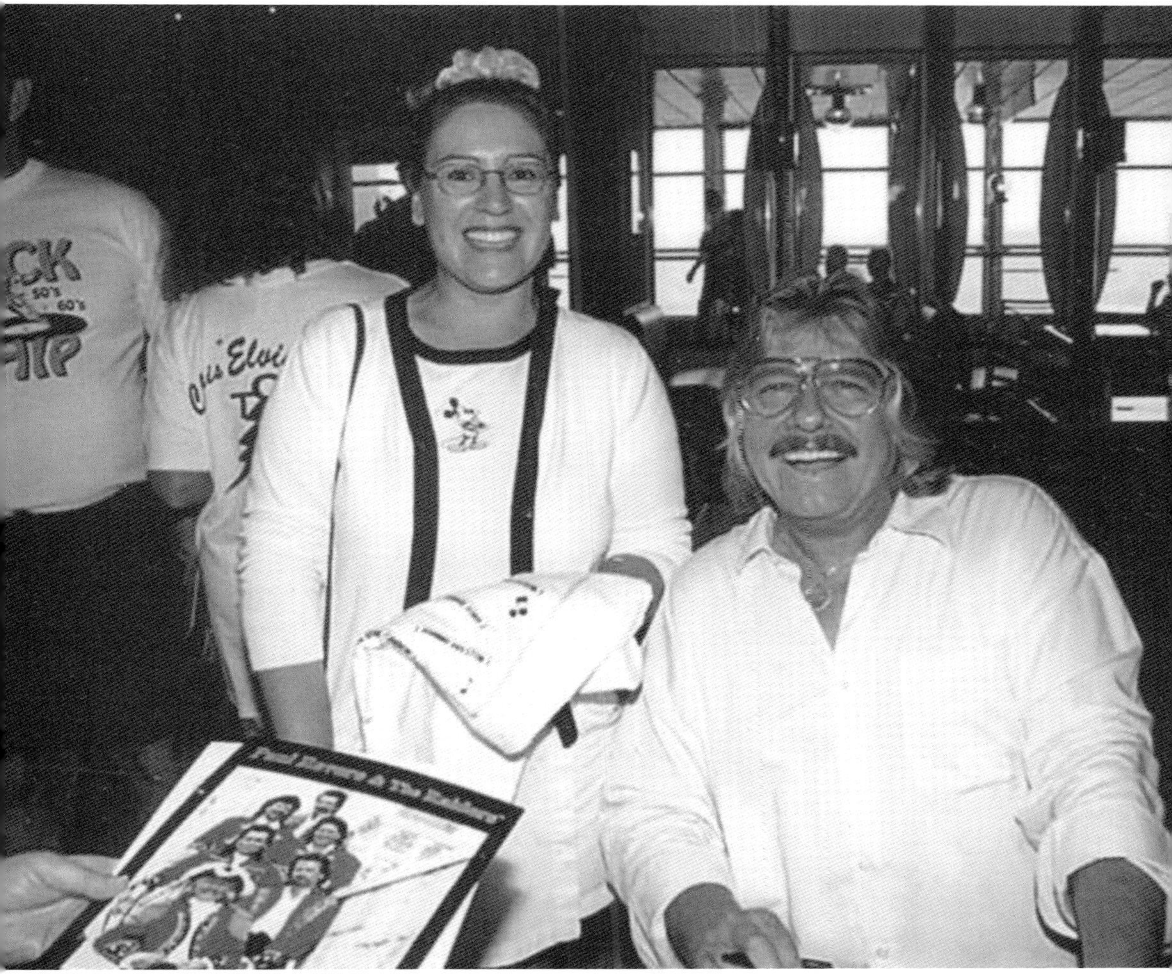

Paul Revere

By the time he was 19 years old, Paul Revere (born Paul Revere Dick) was an entrepreneur who owned three barbershops and a hamburger stand in Caldwell, a few miles west of Boise. But he also was a talented pianist, and his dream was to be a musician. In the late 1950s, with Mark Lindsay, he organized a band called The Downbeats. The group eventually moved to Portland and changed its name to Paul Revere and the Raiders, recording several songs and achieving a top-40 recording with "Like, Long Hair" in 1961. By the mid-1960s, the group had adopted Revolutionary War–style costumes and an energetic performance style. When television producer/host Dick Clark developed a new program based in California, *Where the Action Is*, he signed the group as the show's regular band. Between 1965 and 1971, Paul Revere and the Raiders produced a string of hits, including five in the top 10. When the band disbanded in the 1970s, Paul returned to Idaho and engaged in real estate and other business adventures. He also established the Ride to the Wall Foundation, which supports outreach programs for veterans. For many years, Revere and his wife lived in a home on Boise Avenue that featured a guitar-shaped swimming pool. Beginning in the 1980s, Paul Revere and the Raiders was reorganized with new members and began touring again. After many successful years on the road, Paul Revere passed away at his home in Garden Valley, Idaho, on October 9, 2014. (Courtesy of Alison Perry.)

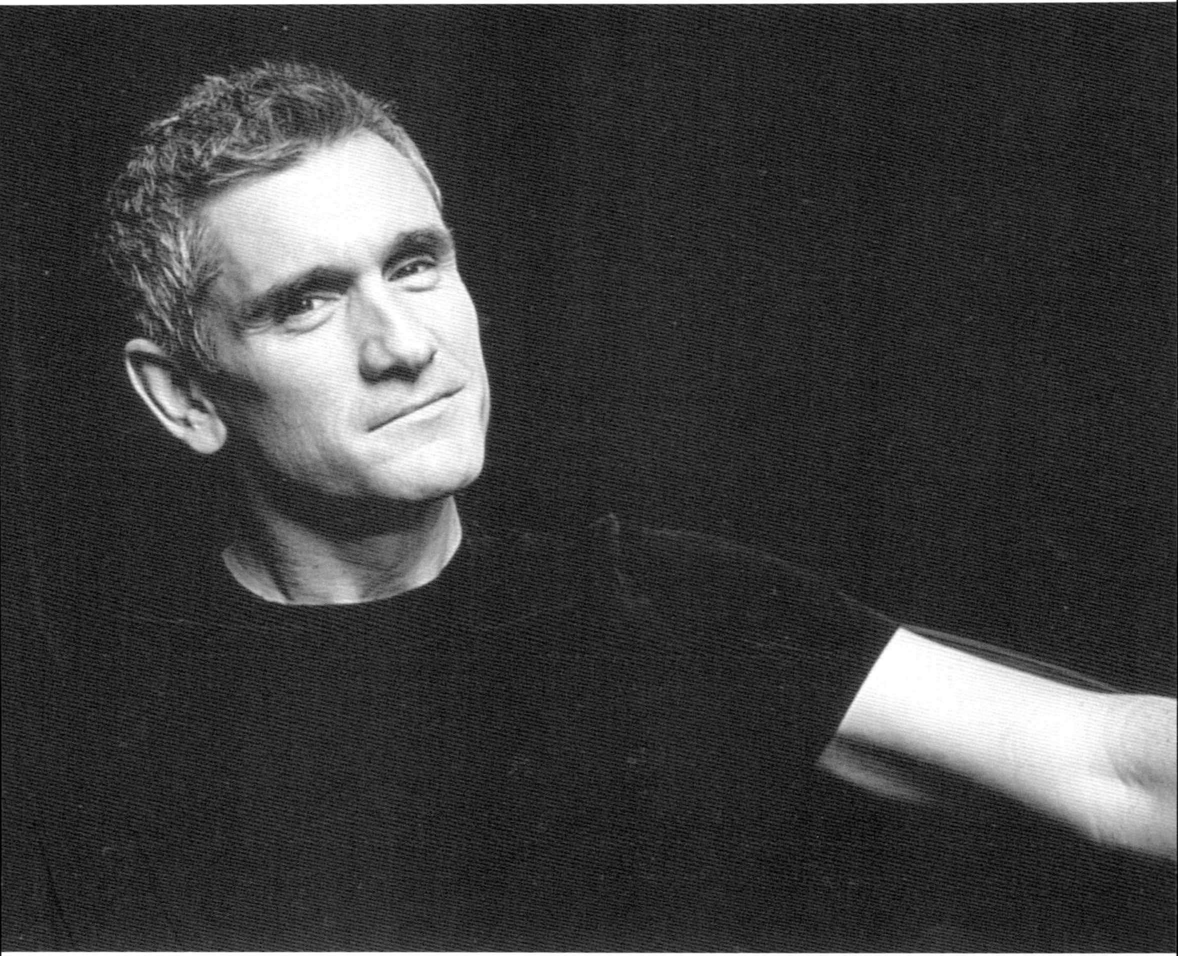

Curtis Stigers

Jazz singer Curtis Stigers grew up in Boise, attended Boise schools, and played in the school bands. He credits his junior high and high school band instructors for the part they played in helping him develop his talent. By the time he was in his teens, he was sneaking into the regular jam sessions hosted by pianist Gene Harris at the Idanha Hotel. In the late 1980s he moved to New York, and by 1991, had realized his dream, recording an album with a song that hit the top 40, "I Wonder Why," followed in 1992 with a song on the soundtrack for the Whitney Houston movie *The Bodyguard*. The evolution of his own interests brought him back to Boise, where he has developed an international following and has a full concert schedule every year. (Courtesy of Curtis Stigers, photograph by Mali Lazell.)

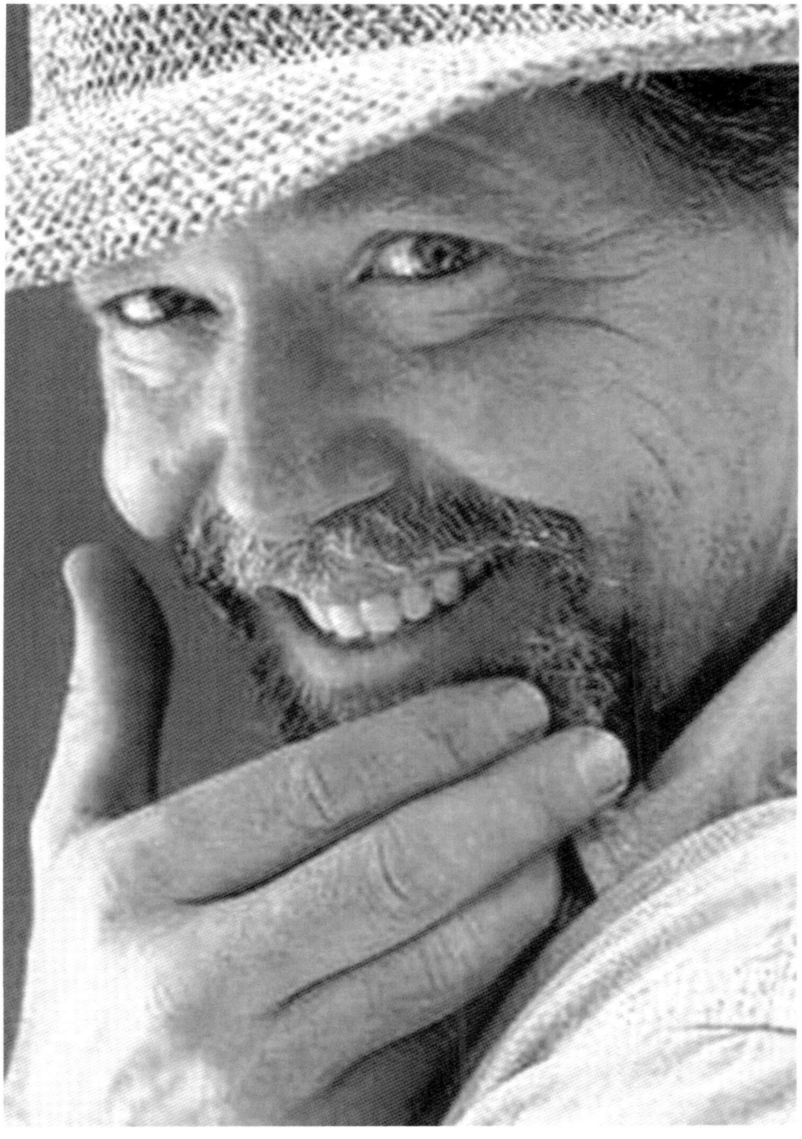

Dan Peterson

Idaho native Dan Peterson was well known to theater devotees in Boise. He took center stage at the Idaho Shakespeare Festival, Idaho Theater for the Youth, and the Boise Contemporary Theater. Born in Lewiston in 1953 to Gerald and Dixie Peterson, he and his family moved to Boise in 1968, where Dan attended Capital High School and became involved in the drama department. He attended Boise State University and graduated with a theater arts degree in 1978. A talented actor, Peterson delighted audiences not only in Boise, but around the state. He was a founding member of the Idaho Shakespeare Festival, which began in 1977. He was committed to theater and acting and was among the founders of the Idaho Theater for Youth in 1981. The group produced theater for young audiences around the state. With boundless energy and enthusiasm, Peterson entertained audiences not just on stage, but also through radio and television commercials. He shared his love of theater with thousands until his untimely death in 2008. (Courtesy of the Idaho Shakespeare Festival.)

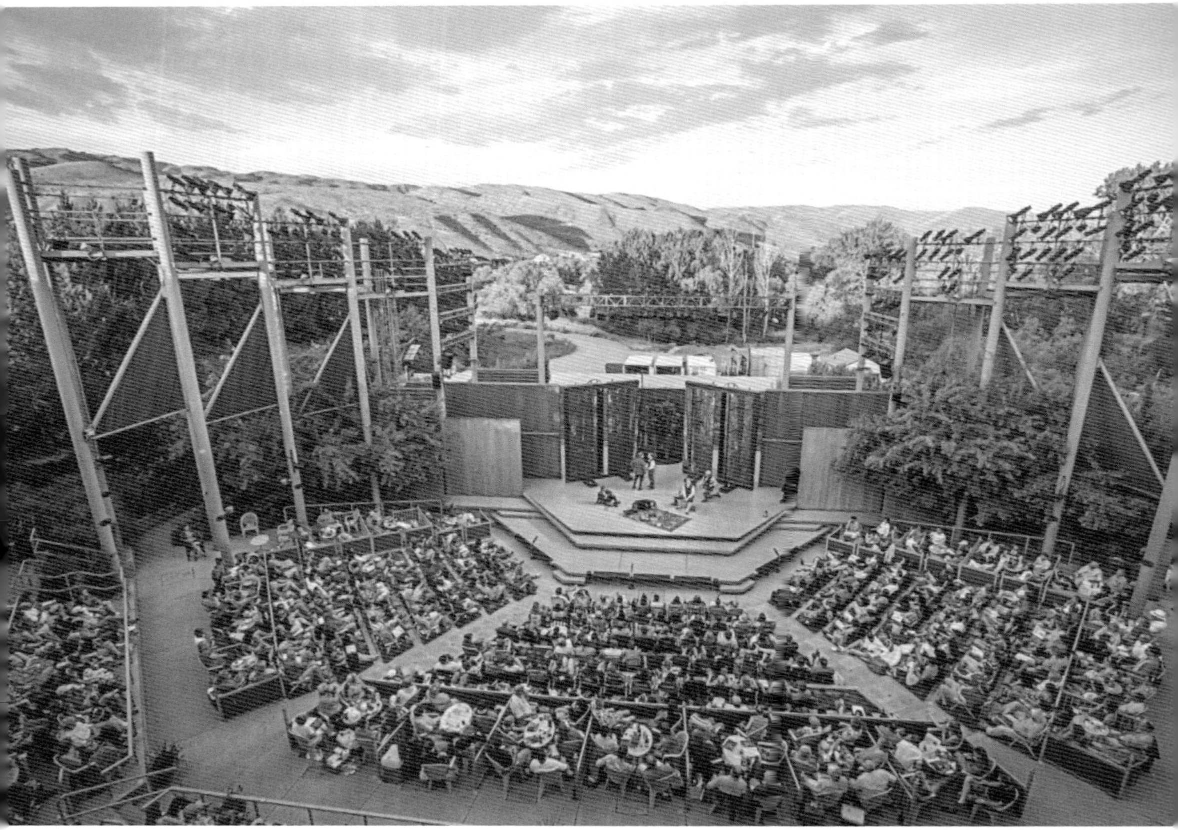

Idaho Shakespeare Festival

Dan Peterson was a founding member and part of a troupe of actors that has entertained thousands over the years. Since its beginnings in 1977, the Idaho Shakespeare Festival had its stage at various locations in Boise. In 1998, a permanent outdoor amphitheater was built adjacent to the Boise River. (Courtesy of the Idaho Shakespeare Festival.)

CHAPTER SIX

Keeping Boise Beautiful

Visitors to Boise often comment on the city's setting: a valley surrounded by mountains to the north and the desert to the south. The city was named for the cottonwood trees that lined the banks of the river, creating an inviting habitat for its early Native American inhabitants. Today, a network of trees softens the desert surrounding, and the Boise River cuts a swath through the center of the city. A 25-mile greenbelt system on both sides of the river is essentially the heart of the city. The greenbelt links people to neighborhoods, wildlife habitat, and downtown and is recognized as one of Boise's urban treasures. The oldest neighborhoods north and east of downtown contain a variety of historic buildings intermingled with modern and contemporary architecture. Mayor Dave Bieter's goal of creating the most livable city in the country does not appear to be an impossible dream, but it is not easily achieved. Boise struggled over a 20-year period as city leaders attempted to revive downtown after eight square blocks were leveled for an anticipated mall. At one point, after a large portion of the area had been cleared of buildings, downtown Boise was compared to Beirut. As progress on downtown revitalization stalled, a grassroots group was formed to save the remaining buildings. Leaders in the preservation movement included Joan Carley, Adelia Garro Simplot, Arthur Hart, and John Bertram. Other visionaries, such as Bill Onweiler, saw potential in cleaning up the Boise River and creating parks centered on the beautiful natural resource. Today, Boise reflects these efforts of beautification.

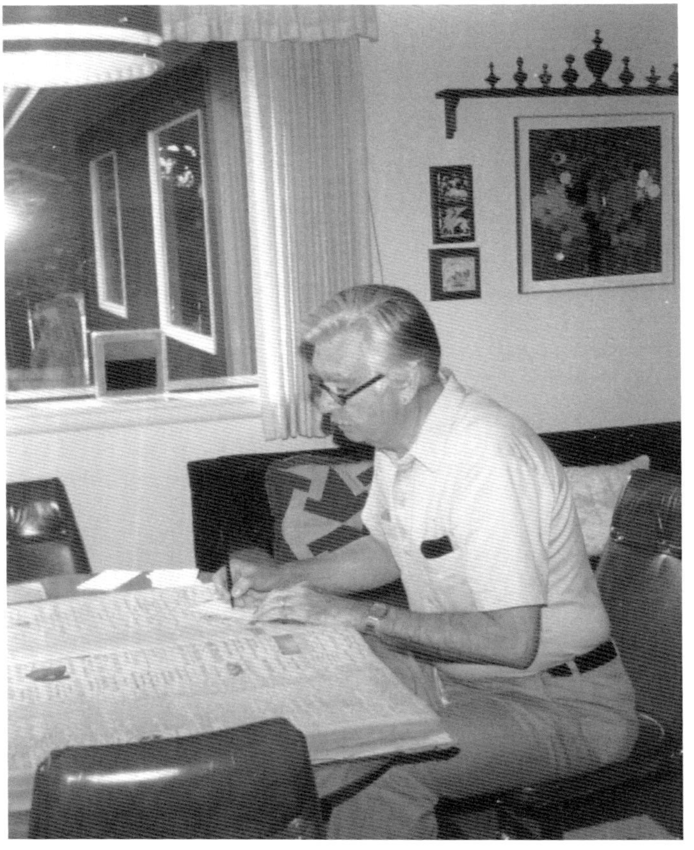

Arthur Hart

In 1968, Arthur Hart's friend Louie Attebery invited him to give a lecture at the College of Idaho in Caldwell. Hart, who had been on the College of Idaho faculty as director of the art department in the early 1950s, moved east in 1953, teaching first at Bay Path College for Women (now Bay Path University) in Longmeadow, Massachusetts, and then at Colby Junior College (now Colby-Sawyer College) in New London, New Hampshire. The exact topic of the lecture is not known now, but Hart remembers that there was no fee for the appearance. Instead, the college paid for a first-class airline ticket, and he was promised a pancake breakfast at the home of his good friend Lyle Stanford. The lecture was well attended. What Hart did not know was that someone in the audience had an epiphany. The Idaho State Historical Society needed a director, and, with Hart's rapport with the audience and strong presentation style, he seemed perfect for the job. "Someone," he remembers, "called Merle Wells, who was reluctantly serving as acting director of the Society, to come down and listen to me. Then they invited him to the pancake breakfast." The next thing he knew, Hart was repeating the lecture in Boise and meeting with the three-member board of trustees. After a brief consultation, the board voted to offer the job of director of the Idaho State Historical Museum to Hart. "There was no official form," he remembers. "One of the board members was the controller at Morrison Knudsen, so he got one of their applications for me to fill in, just to have the paperwork." For the next five years, Hart served as director of the museum, while Merle Wells was head of the society. In 1974, Wells stepped down, and Hart became director of the society, a position he held until he retired in 1987. Since then, he says, he has pursued his love of Idaho history, publishing more than 20 books, guiding tours to historic Silver City and other locations, and writing a weekly column on Idaho history for the local newspaper. Dee, his wife of 70 years, says that he has enough material to write columns for at least another 20 years. (Courtesy of Arthur Hart.)

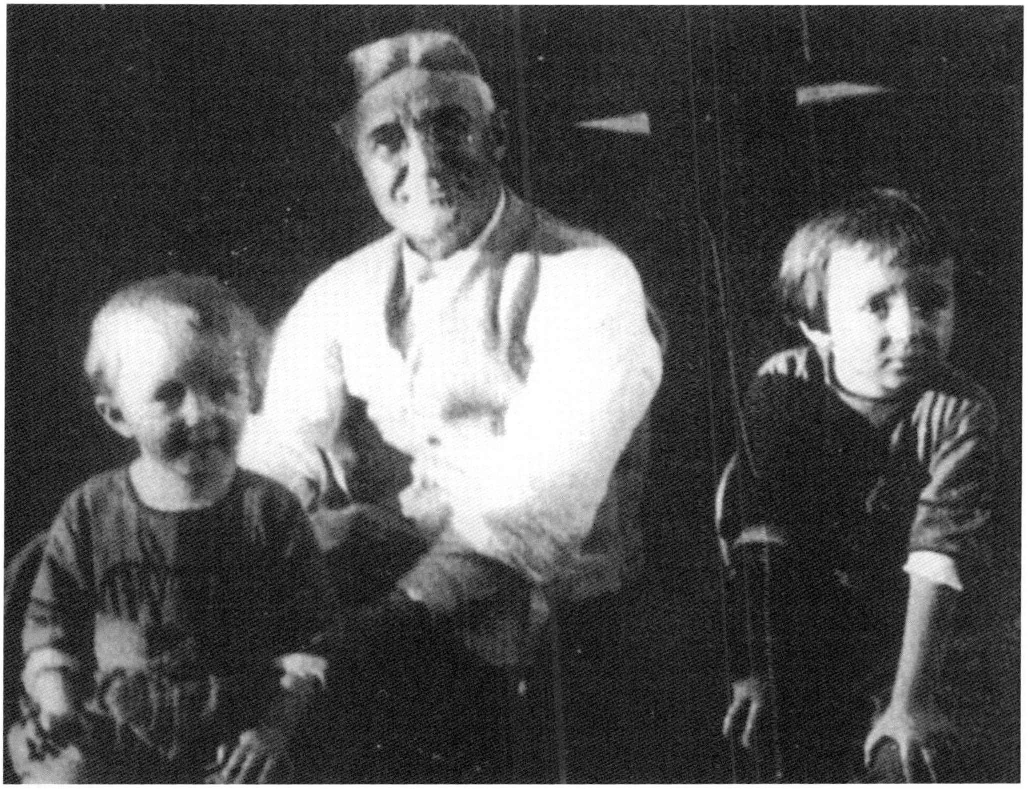

Walter E. Pierce

Walter Edgar Pierce was born in Texas in 1860, the son of Charles and Elizabeth Harding Pierce, who had moved to Texas from Rhode Island in 1854 to operate a sheep ranch. Walter never knew his father, who died shortly after Walter's birth. From a young age, Walter helped support the family with a variety of jobs. Largely self-educated, Walter was determined to move up in the world. As soon as he was able, he enrolled in a business college, the first step on a career path that eventually brought him to Boise.

By his mid-twenties, Walter had managed a hotel in Missouri, engaged in sheep ranching, and worked construction on the Kansas City & Southern Railroad. At age 26, he was a land agent in Morton County, Kansas, where he met Lindley H. Cox and John M. Haines. The three young men became partners in an exciting enterprise to build a Western city. After reviewing their options, the trio decided to move to Boise in 1890. Pierce, Cox, and Haines, doing business as W.E. Pierce & Company, quickly began developing and promoting their adopted town. The firm developed most of the neighborhoods in Boise's North End and platted subdivisions in the East End and along State Street. He also served as president of the Commercial Club (now the chamber of commerce); operated the Natatorium, Boise's natural hot-water resort; and organized an electric railway, the Boise & Interurban, which connected communities in Ada and Canyon Counties.

Pierce was also a family man. His first marriage ended in divorce, but when he married for a second time, he and his wife, Maude, became parents of two daughters, Elizabeth "Bette" and Margaret "Peggy." Even when devoting time to his family, Pierce was an unstoppable entrepreneur. He worked for years to bring a major modern hotel to town, eventually organizing the Boise Community Hotel Company to finance the construction of the Hotel Boise. By 1937, a *Statesman* reporter concluded that the city was a living monument to the vision and enterprise of W.E. Pierce. His legacy remains evident today in the existence of beloved neighborhoods like the North and East Ends and iconic landmarks like the Hoff Building (formerly the Hotel Boise) and the Idaho Building. (Courtesy of Maureen Ingram and Margaret Lundy.)

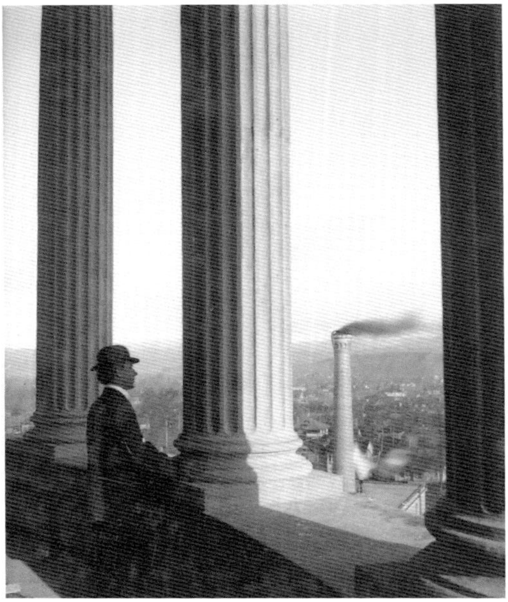

John Tourtellotte

The Idaho State Capitol is an icon for Boise and Idaho. This building and other notable Boise buildings were designed by John E. Tourtellotte, a founding partner of Boise's most prolific architectural firm, Tourtellotte & Hummel. A Connecticut native, Tourtellotte studied architectural drawing and began his career in 1885 at Cutting & Bishop, a Massachusetts firm. He worked there for four years before heading west to Pueblo, Colorado. Less than a year later, he arrived in Boise, where he worked as a contract architect. By 1894, Tourtellotte decided to concentrate on design, and by the turn of the century, Tourtellotte and his firm had designed dozens of structures—primarily homes, businesses, and churches—across southern Idaho and southeastern Oregon. (Courtesy of the Idaho State Historical Society.)

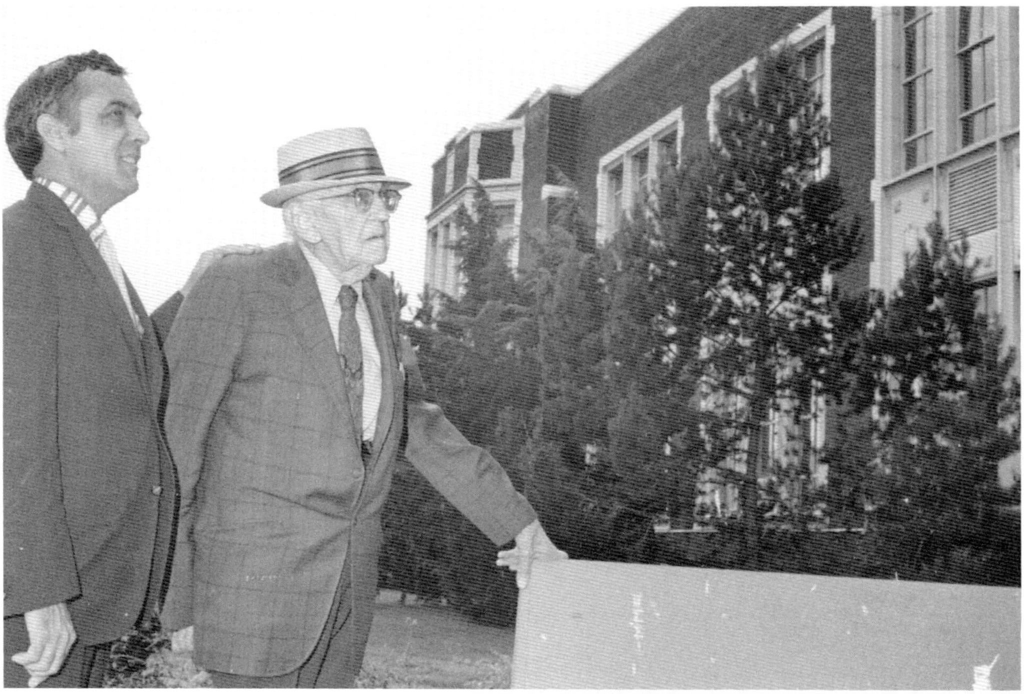

Charles Frederick Hummel

In 1903, John Tourtellotte partnered with Charles Frederick Hummel (right). Hummel was from Baden, Germany, and received his architectural training in Stuttgart, Germany. He worked in Switzerland as a civil engineer before immigrating to the United States in 1885. He moved to Boise in 1895. Tourtellotte moved to Portland in 1913, but kept an office in Boise. After Tourtellotte's death in Portland and Hummel's in Boise in 1939, the firm continued as Hummel Architects. (Courtesy of the Idaho State Historical Society.)

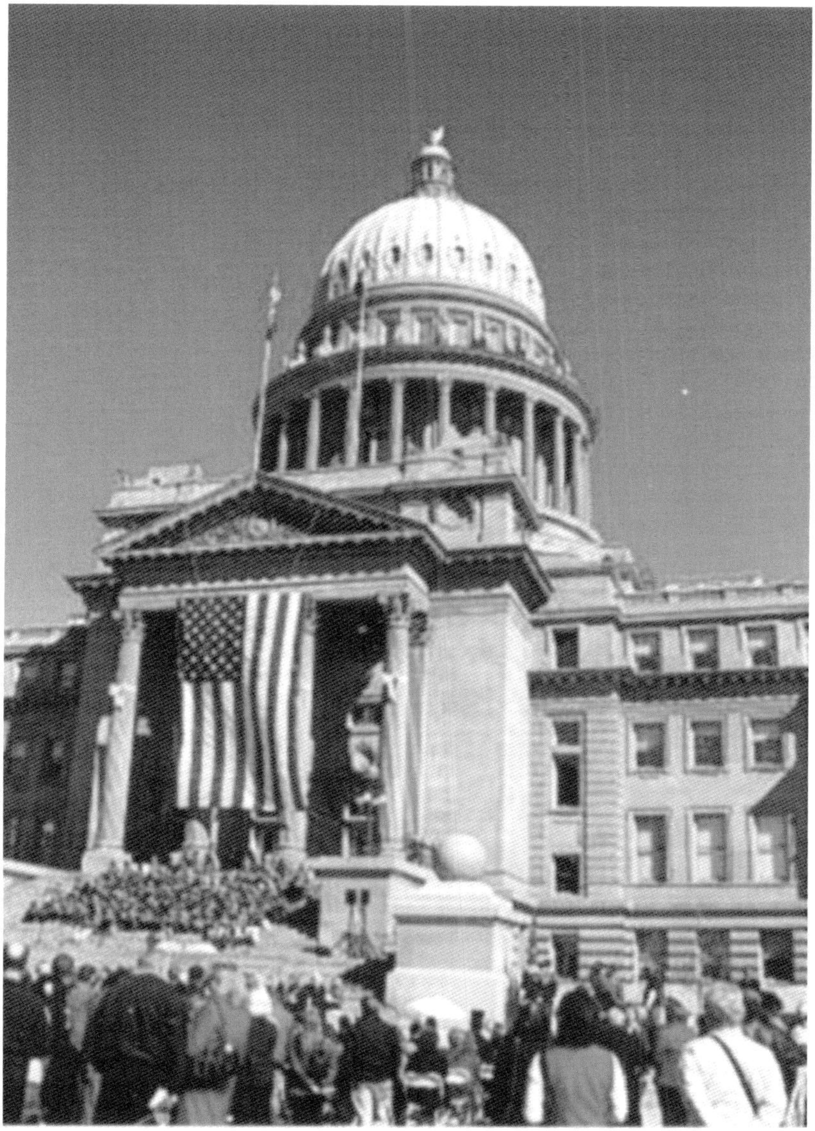

Idaho State Capitol

The capitol is one of the premier buildings designed by John E. Tourtellotte of Tourtellotte & Hummel. Construction on the central section of the building began in 1905 and expanded to the east and west in 1919. The building was renovated over three years starting in 2007 and rededicated in 2010. (Authors' collection.)

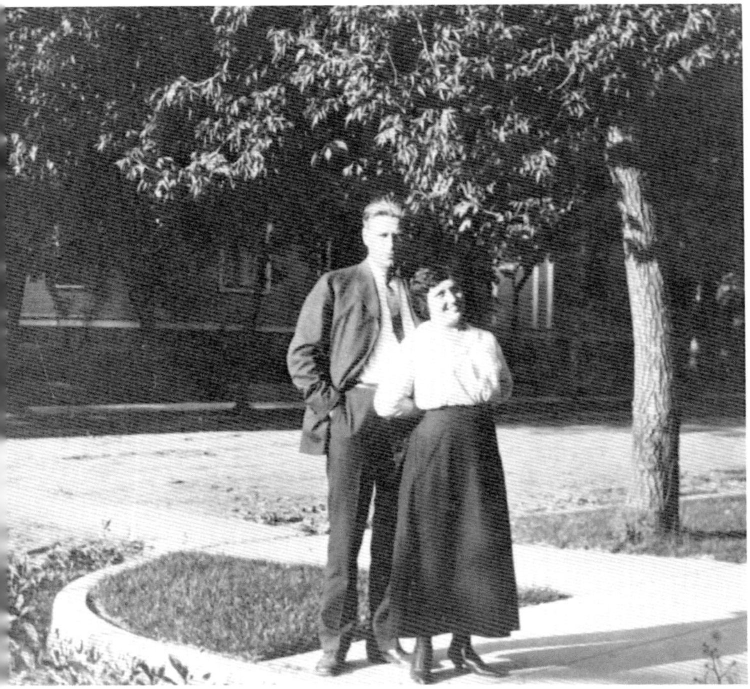

Ann Morrison

Harry Morrison and Ann Daly were married in December 1914. She became his constant companion and supporter during the early years of Morrison-Knudsen, earning the nickname "First Lady of Construction." When Ann died in 1957, Harry decided to create a memorial for her in the form of a beautiful park. The 153-acre park was donated to the City of Boise by the Harry W. Morrison Family Foundation and dedicated on June 7, 1959. Construction was completed in 10 months and cost more than $1.25 million. Ann Morrison Park is one of the largest parks in Boise, with sports fields, playgrounds, gardens, and a beautiful memorial area with a fountain and reflecting pond. (Courtesy of Mark Baltes.)

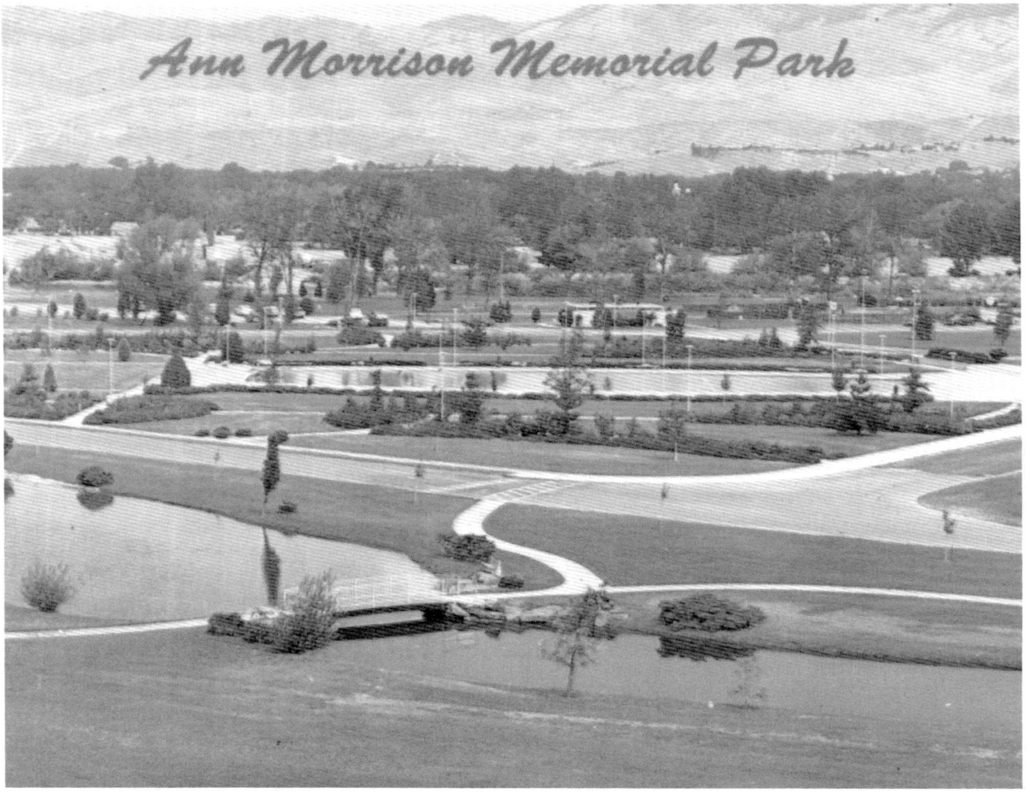

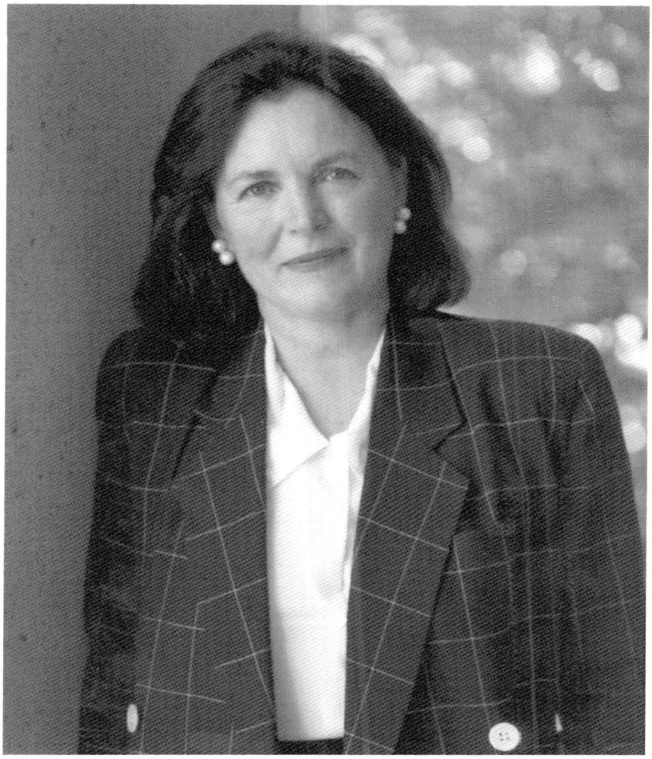

Adelia Garro Simplot

Visitors to Boise often stop on Grove Street at the Basque Museum and Cultural Center to learn about the rich history and culture of Basques in Idaho. The length of Grove Street between Sixth and Main is known as the "Basque Block," the only district like it in the United States. The block is decorated with Basque flags, and "Laburus," pinwheel symbols of Basque identity, are embedded in the street. The block is often alive with street dances, music, and celebrations of Basque culture. One woman, Adelia Garro Simplot, was critical to the preservation of buildings along the block. Her vision helped to promote and perpetuate Basque culture. Born in 1935 to Eustaquio Garroguerricaechevarri (Ed Garro) and Grace Ragsdale, Adelia is a first-generation Basque American. Her father immigrated to Boise in 1913 from Munitibar, in the province of Biscay. Her parents were married in 1933 and had four children including Adelia. Her father, a successful barber, had many Basque customers and Adelia and her siblings were raised with strong connections to their heritage. She started dancing lessons when she was 15 with Juanita Hormachea and had close ties to the Basque community through her relatives and dance. A good student and a hard worker, Adelia excelled at both school and work and enrolled in Idaho State College at Pocatello. She married Richard Simplot in 1953 and worked at the family-owned Simplot fertilizer plant as well as taking college courses. Her college career ended when she became pregnant with the first of her four children. In time, the young Simplot family moved back to Boise. Here Adelia became active in numerous community affairs, working for a local hospital auxiliary, as a charter member of the Idaho State Historical Museum and the Junior League, and as a director of the Boise Art Museum. She had an interest in preserving historic buildings in downtown Boise, and with Joan Carley, Mary Lesser, and Romaine Hon, co-founded the Idaho Historic Preservation Council. Her interest in her Basque heritage led her to purchase a historic Basque boarding house where a museum was established in 1985. Over time, the Basque Museum acquired a larger building next door to the old boarding house, expanding in 1993 and renamed the Basque Museum and Cultural Center, the cornerstone of the Basque Block. (Courtesy of the Basque Museum and Cultural Center.)

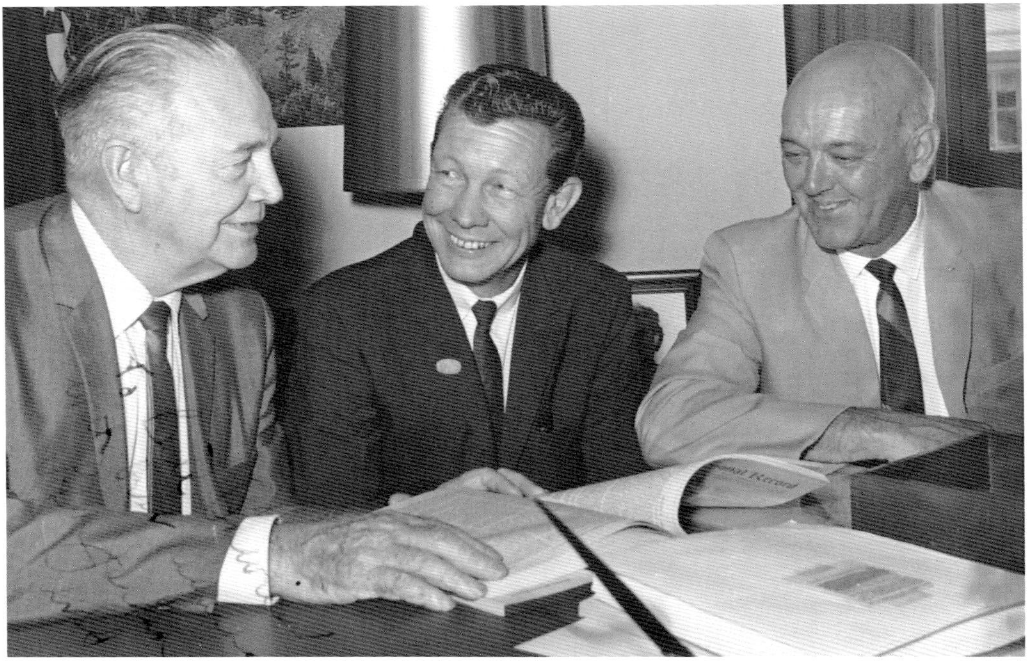

Bill Onweiler

The Boise River Greenbelt is a landmark in the City of Trees. Bill Onweiler, a Boise City councilman, was one of the visionaries behind it. In 1970, he produced a video with aerial footage of the Boise River and narrated it, describing his dream of what it could become. That dream became a reality 45 years later. The greenbelt (below) is a 23-mile trail linking over 850 acres of parks and natural areas bordering the river. Above, Onweiler sits between Len Jordan (left) and Sherm Perry. (Above, courtesy of Bill Onweiler Collection, Boise City Department of Arts and History; below, authors' collection.)

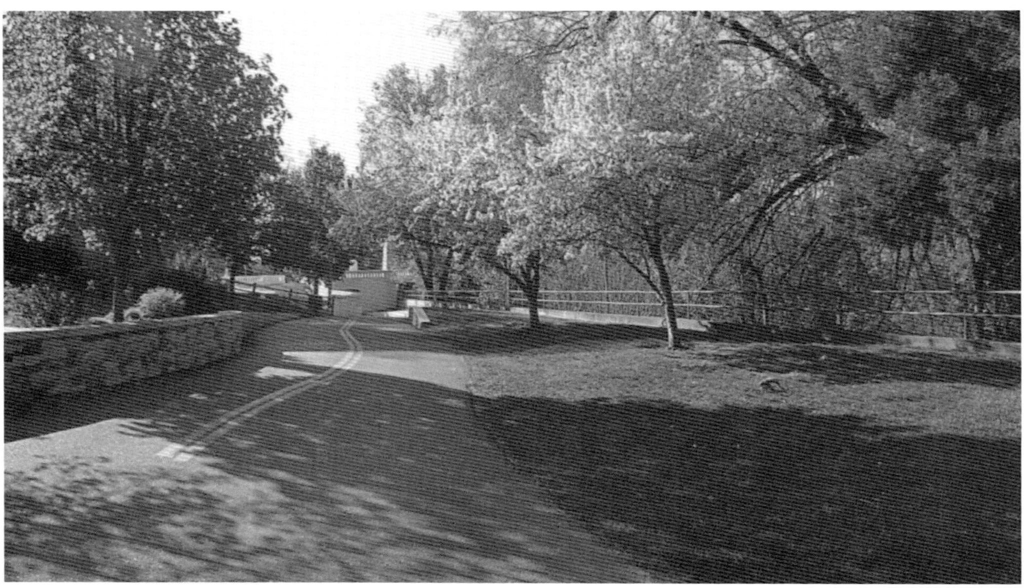

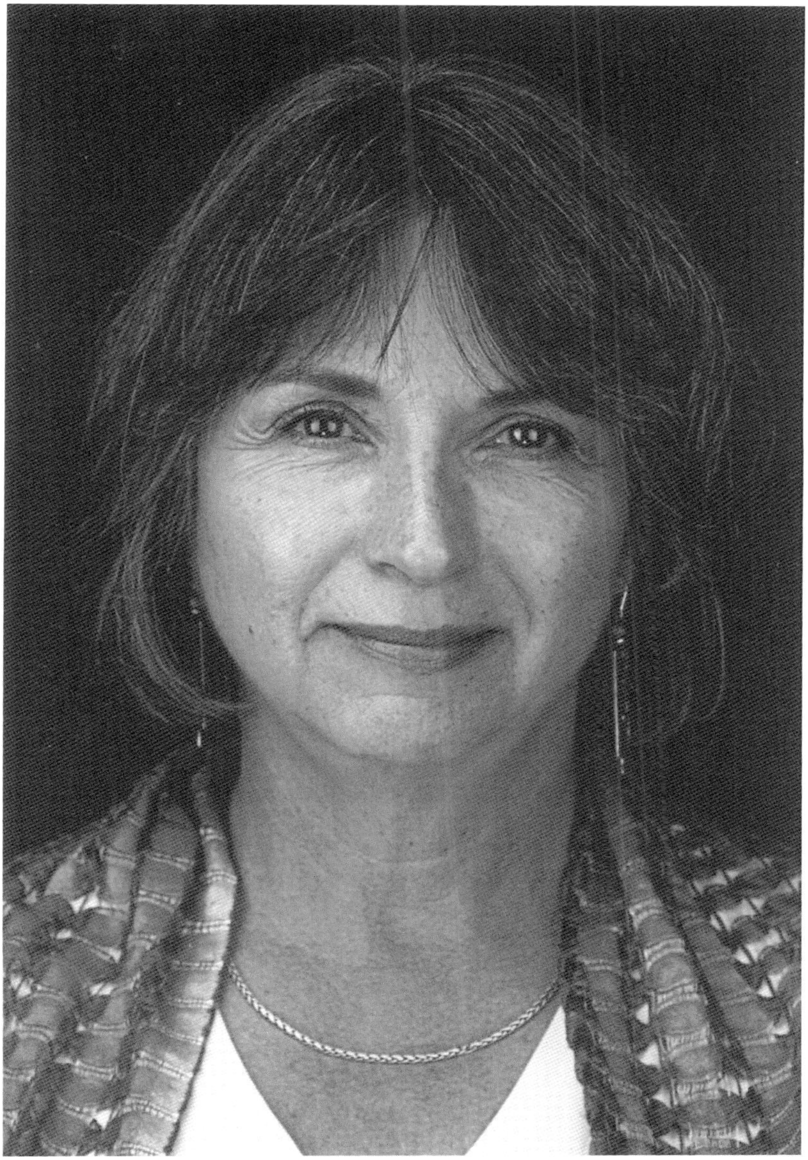

Terri Schorzman

The City of Boise established the Department of Arts and History in 2008, devoted to enhancing the community by providing leadership, advocacy, education, and support for arts and history. The department, led by Boise native Terri Schorzman, is dedicated to preserving the history of the city and inspiring appreciation for the past. Born in Boise, Schorzman left when her dad took a job in Colorado. She entered college there and received a bachelor's degree in history from Colorado State University, followed by a master's degree in American history from the University of California, Santa Barbara. After a stint as program director at the Smithsonian Institution's video history program, Schorzman and her husband, Steve, returned to Boise in 1995 to raise their two children. She was involved in several community and cultural organizations, and in 2008, was selected to head the new Department of Arts and History. (Courtesy of Boise City Department of Arts and History.)

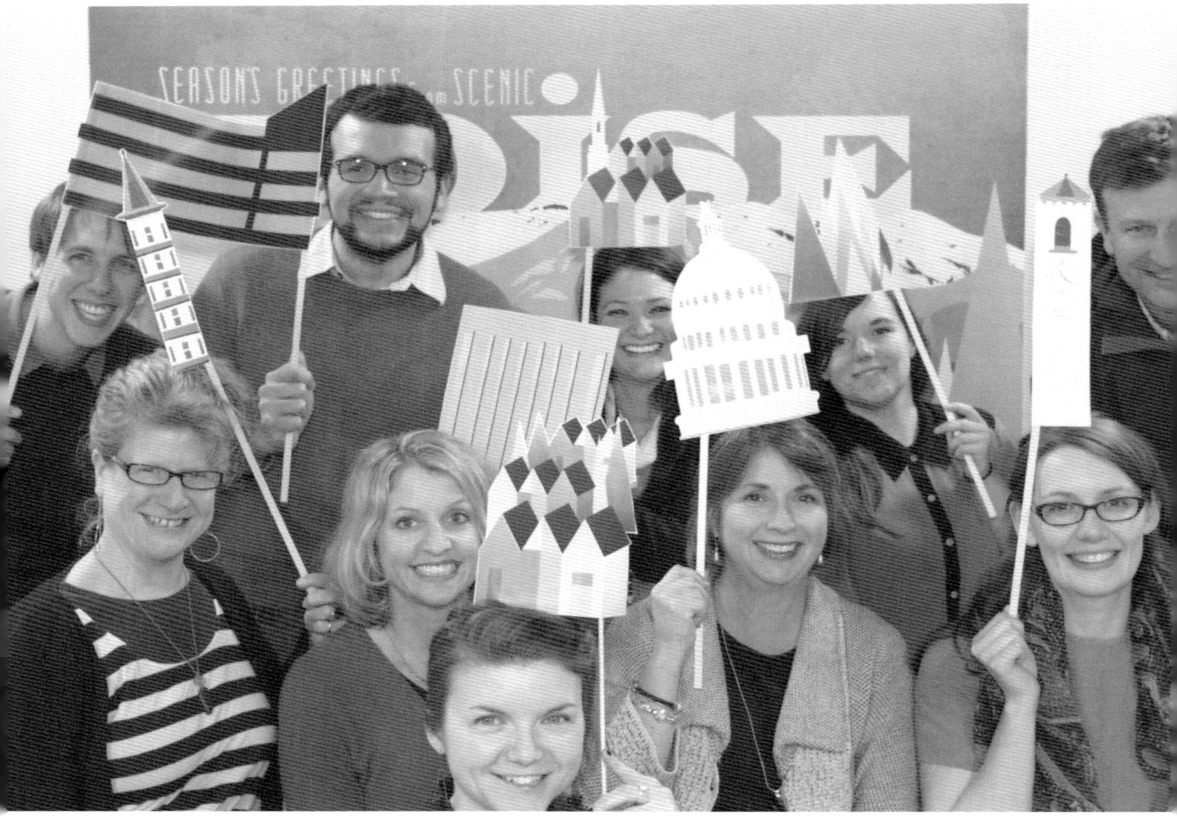

Boise City Department of Arts and History

The Boise City Department of Arts and History staff was the driving force behind the city's sesquicentennial celebration in 2013. Shown here are, from left to right, (seated) Karen Bubb, Amy Fackler, Rachel Reichert, Terri Schorzman and Brandi Burns; (standing) Anthony Parry, Ricardo Osuna, April Raine, Kaci Nicks, and Josh Olson. (Courtesy of the Boise City Department of Arts and History, photograph by Melanie Folwell.)

CHAPTER SEVEN

Mom & Pop and Then Some

Boise's entrepreneurs created numerous businesses, some with local significance and some that introduced Boise to the world. Businessman C.C. Anderson opened his first Golden Rule department store in 1896. By 1913, he had opened an additional seven stores throughout southwestern Idaho. In 1927, he opened Boise's largest department store, at Tenth and Idaho Streets. At the same time, a young man named Joe Albertson was attending college in the neighboring town of Caldwell. After two years, he left school to enter the grocery business, opening his first Idaho supermarket at Sixteenth and State Streets in 1939. The 100th Albertsons opened in Seattle in 1963, and over the next 30 years, the chain extended to almost every Western state. Other business leaders would bring national and international attention to Boise. Harry Morrison and Morris Knudsen started out as grading contractors in 1912, moving into the construction of irrigation systems. When the opportunity to bid on the construction of Hoover Dam came along, Morrison-Knudsen incorporated, and after reaching an agreement with several other companies, won the contract to build the dam in 1932. By the mid-1950s, M-K was one of the largest heavy-construction contractors in the world. At the turn of the 21st century, Boise became home to companies with national significance. Advances in technology brought a new type of entrepreneur to the city.

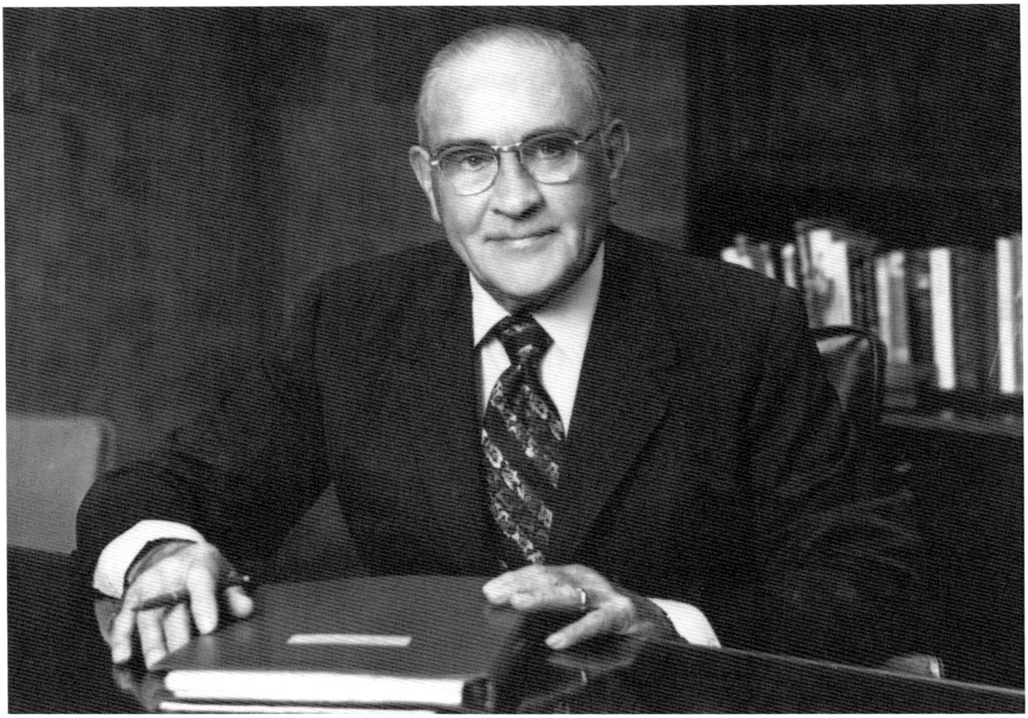

Joe Albertson

The Albertson family moved to Idaho from Oklahoma in 1909 when Joe (above) was three years old. He grew up in Caldwell, attending the College of Idaho, where he studied business and worked as a grocery clerk to help pay for college. In 1939, with an initial investment of $5,000 of his own money, and additional funds from family members, he founded the first Albertsons Food Center (below) on Sixteenth Street near downtown Boise. He pioneered the one-stop, self-service supermarket concept. From that first store in Boise, Albertsons grew into a network of hundreds of stores throughout the West. He and his wife, Kathryn, were also very generous, providing support to charities and schools. (Above, courtesy of the Idaho State Historical Society; below, courtesy of the J.A. and Kathryn Albertson Foundation.)

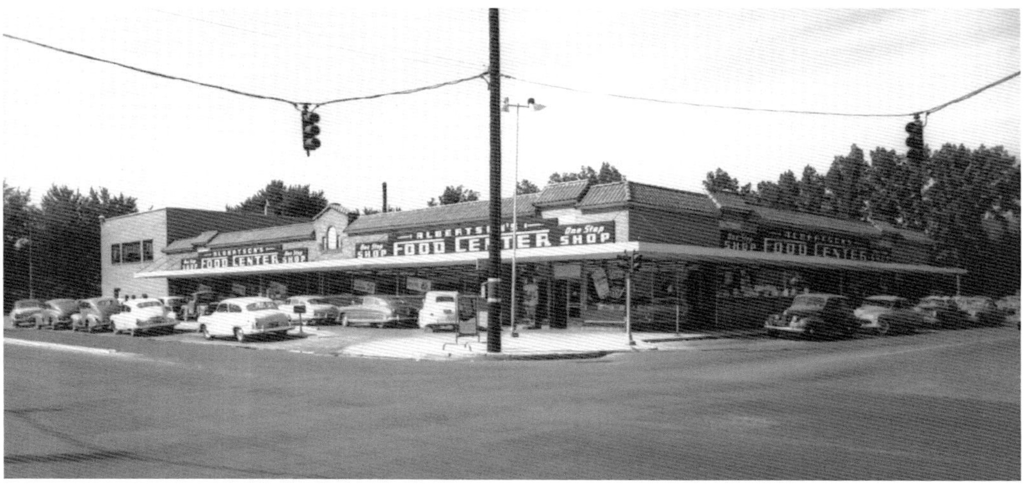

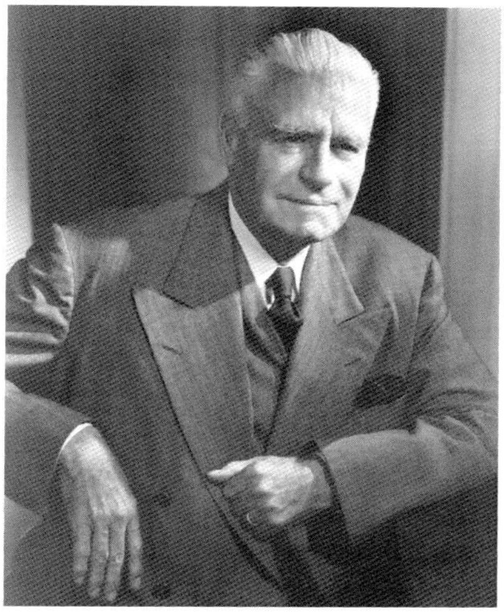

Harry W. Morrison

Morrison, born in Clinton, Illinois, in 1885, started working as a water boy for the Bates & Rogers Construction Company on a job for the Illinois Central Railroad at the age of 15. A few years later, when Bates & Rogers landed a contract for the Minidoka Project in Idaho, Morrison took another job and came out to Idaho to work. His experience on Minidoka led to employment on other reclamation projects, including the New York Canal and Diversion Dam. During that time, he met Morris Knudsen. The two became friends and then partners in 1912, forming the Morrison-Knudsen Company. In the mid-20th century, Morrison-Knudsen grew to become one of the largest construction firms in the United States, with projects around the globe. (Courtesy of the Idaho State Historical Society.)

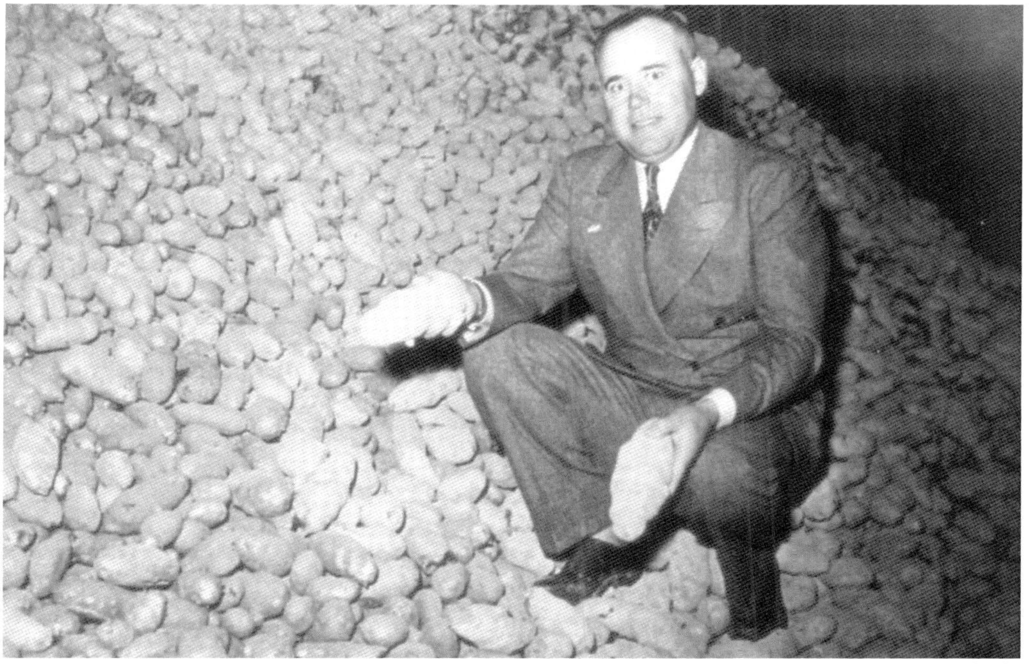

J.R. Simplot

Jack Richard Simplot was a shrewd businessman and colorful character. Known as "Mr. Spud," Simplot was born in the small farming town of Declo, Idaho. His was a true "rags-to-riches" story. After leaving home at 14, Simplot made his first fortune selling hogs. He then won a coin toss to win a new electric potato sorter and eventually parlayed that windfall into an estimated $3.6 billion fortune. He and the company he founded created the first successful frozen French fries and partnered with McDonald's to sell them worldwide. His corporate operations were in Boise, where he lived. Simplot bankrolled the startup costs for Micron Technology. J.R. Simplot, who never attended high school, donated millions to support higher education. In his later years, he was a familiar figure to Boiseans, faithfully attending football games at Bronco Stadium and traveling around town on a motorized cart. (Courtesy of the Idaho State Historical Society.)

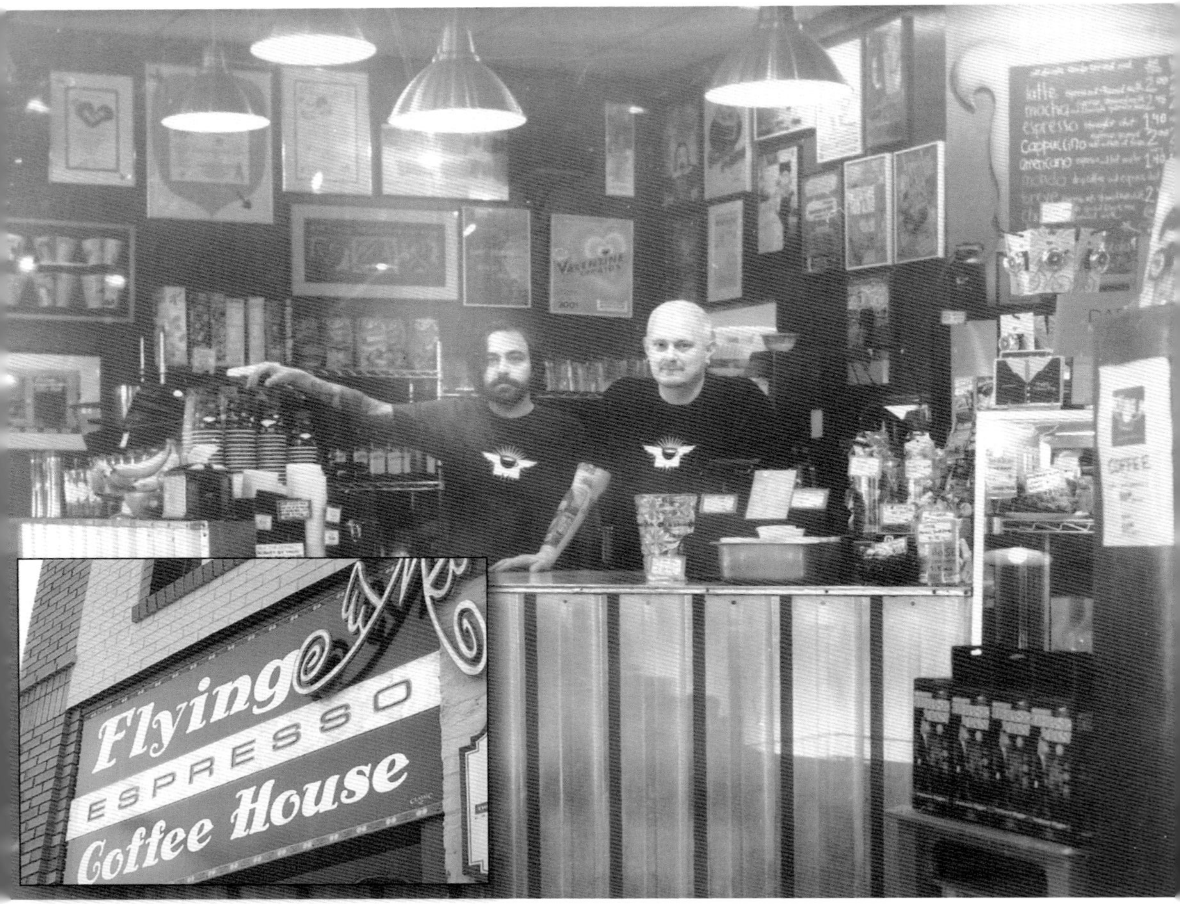

Kent Collins

"Unchained since 1992," the Flying M Coffee House has long been proud of its independence—not only is it not part of a regional or national chain, Lisa and Kevin Myers, the original owners, established a coffee-roasting company that provides the coffee filling cup after cup at the Flying M. The gift shop in the store includes a large section of locally produced artwork and serves as a gallery for an ever-changing exhibit of work by local artists. The Flying M has made its mark as a supporter of charitable causes, most notably, the Valentine for Aids silent art auction, which each year raises thousands of dollars for a local AIDS support program. In 2011, Kent Collins, who managed the coffeehouse for 12 years, became the sole owner. In this photograph, Collins (right) and Will Gillett stand at the counter. (Courtesy of Flying M; photograph by Melaine Folwell.)

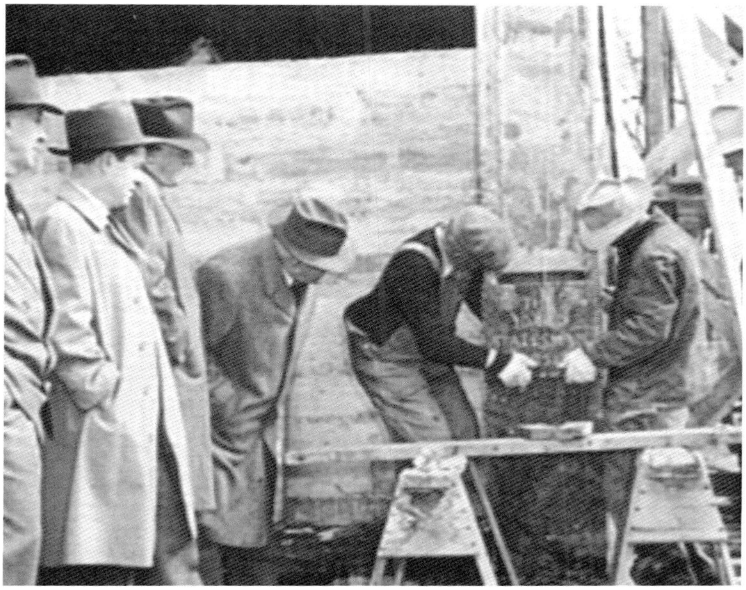

J.O. Jordan and J. Cecil Jordan

The Egyptian Theater, the Ada County Courthouse, and the Intermountain Gas Building were all constructed by the firm J.O. Jordan & Sons. J.O. Jordan arrived in Boise around 1901, working as a plasterer and then as a residential builder. His son John Cecil Jordan started school as an architecture student at the University of Washington following service in World War I. Cecil did not complete his degree, instead joining his father in business in 1920. Under Cecil's guidance, the company grew from residential construction to include commercial structures. One of its first large contracts was as general contractors for the Egyptian Theater (below) in 1927. From there, the family-owned company grew into a major construction firm that still exists today as Jordan-Wilcomb Construction Inc., believed to be Idaho's oldest operating construction firm. (Above, courtesy of Jordan-Wilcomb Construction Inc.; below, authors' collection.)

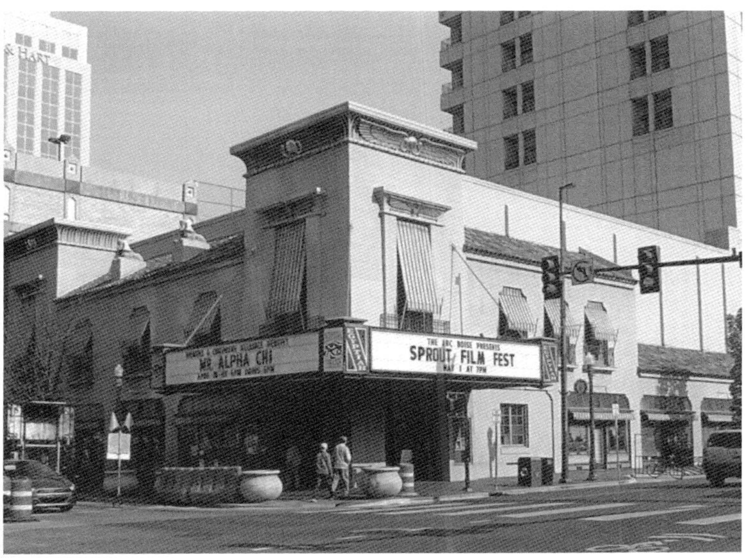

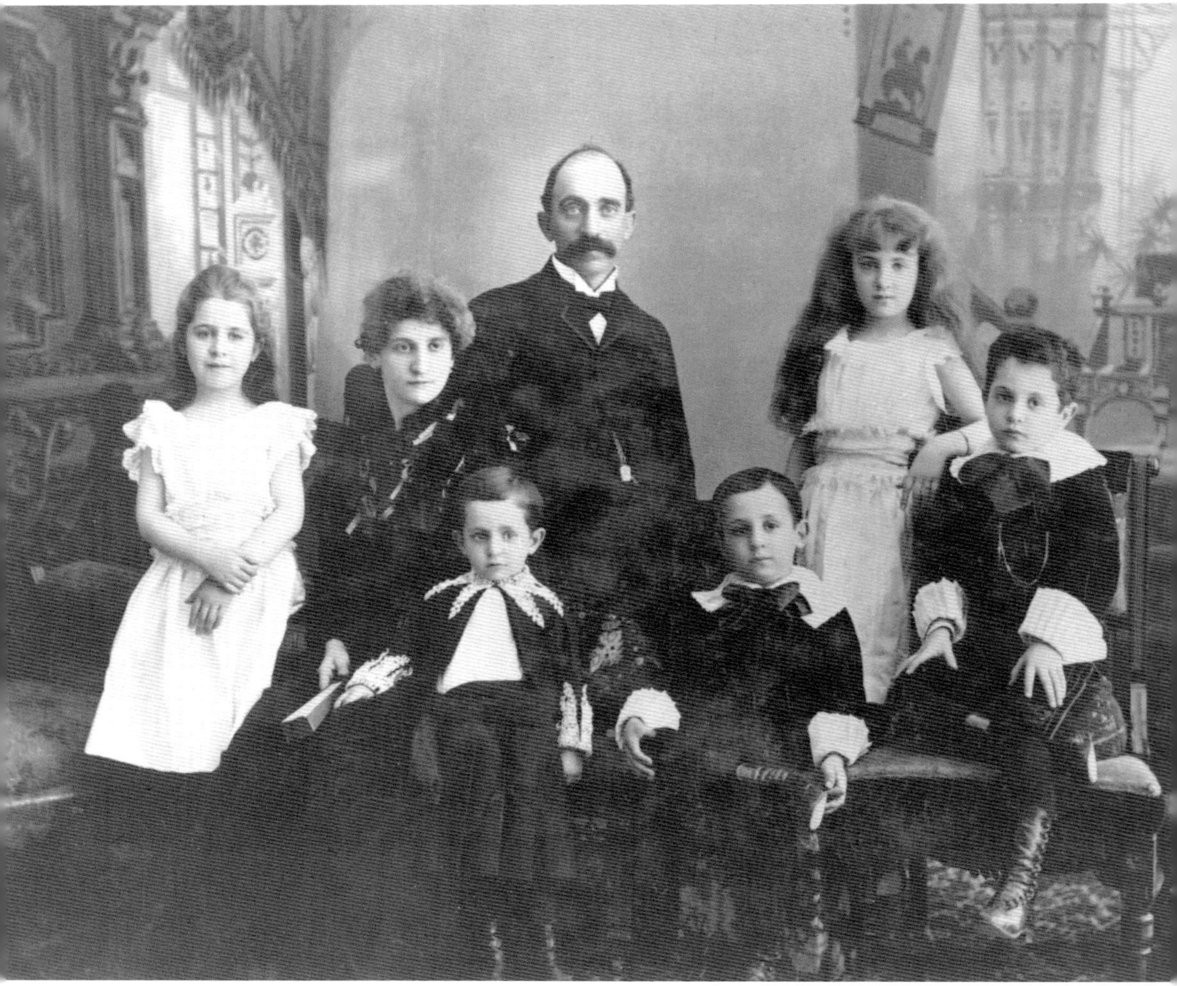

The Falk Brothers

Falk's Department Store was a well-known name in Boise and one of the longest-run businesses in town. The store was started in 1868 by three brothers from Germany, Nathan, David, and Sigmund. Called D. Falk & Company, the store supplied general merchandise. The store's name changed several times over the years, but the company remained continuously in operation as Falk's Idaho Department Store until 1986. Nathan and Rose Falk and their five children are pictured here. (Courtesy of the Idaho State Historical Society.)

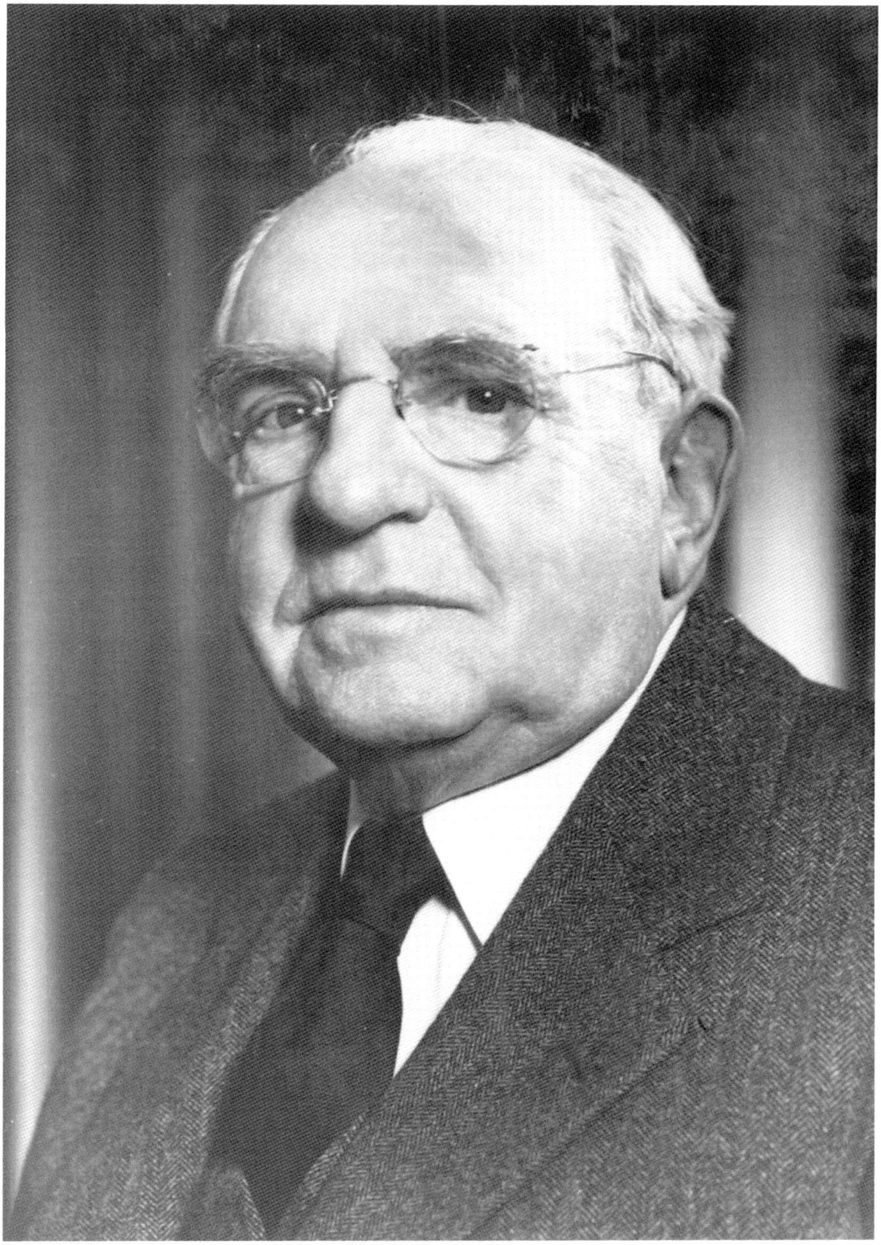

C.C. Anderson

When 23-year-old Christopher Columbus Anderson arrived in Boise in 1896, he opened a store that operated on a cash-only basis. His theory was that by accepting only cash but allowing full-refund returns, his store would create goodwill and thus guarantee success. The first store, called the Golden Rule Store, opened in Boise a few months after Anderson's arrival in 1896. By 1937, when Anderson merged his company with New York's Allied Stores, there were 34 locations operating as C.C. Anderson's Golden Rule Store in Idaho, Washington, Oregon, Colorado, and Utah. (Courtesy of the Idaho State Historical Society.)

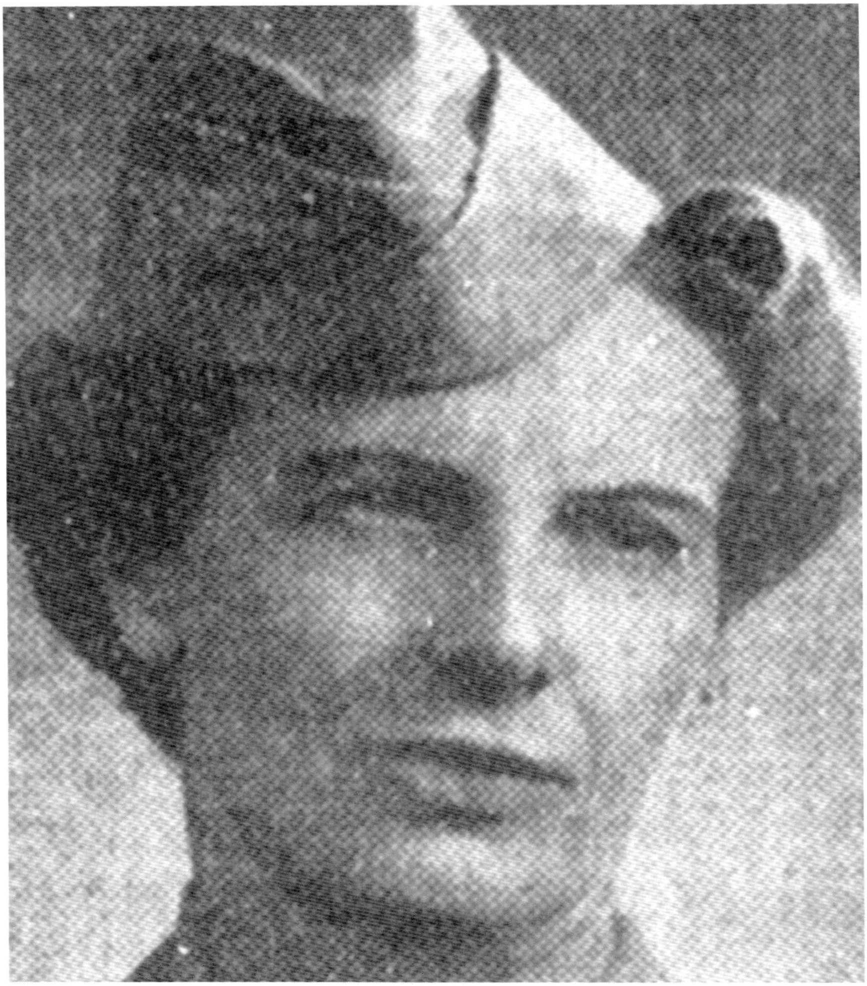

Maude L. Cosho

In 1932, after 11 years of marriage, Maude Cosho was left a widow with three young children when her husband was killed in a hunting accident. The tragedy occurred just as she finished serving her first term in the Idaho legislature and was running the Hotel Bristol, on the corner of Tenth and Grove Streets in downtown Boise. She almost lost the hotel, but Cosho turned things around and held on to it until she sold it in 1939. She served as the Boise City treasurer for two years, then ran successfully for the legislature two more times, serving in the House of Representatives in 1937 and 1939. Along the way, she became the first woman appointed to the House Appropriations Committee. She later ran unsuccessfully for lieutenant governor.

During World War II, she joined the Civil Air Patrol and then the Women's Army Corps, returning to Boise in 1946. By this time, she was in her late 40s and her children had grown, but she did not slow down. Named to the board of regents of the University of Idaho, she decided to pursue a master's degree in history, completing her thesis in 1951. Then, for a few years—in her late 50s by this time—she moved to Arizona and taught English to children of the Papago (now Tohono O'Odom) tribe. When she finally "retired" at age 70, Cosho returned to Boise, where she wrote a personal memoir for her family and a collection of biographies and information that she self-published as *An Idaho Hodgepodge* in 1981. Maude Cosho died later that year. (Courtesy of the Idaho State Historical Society.)

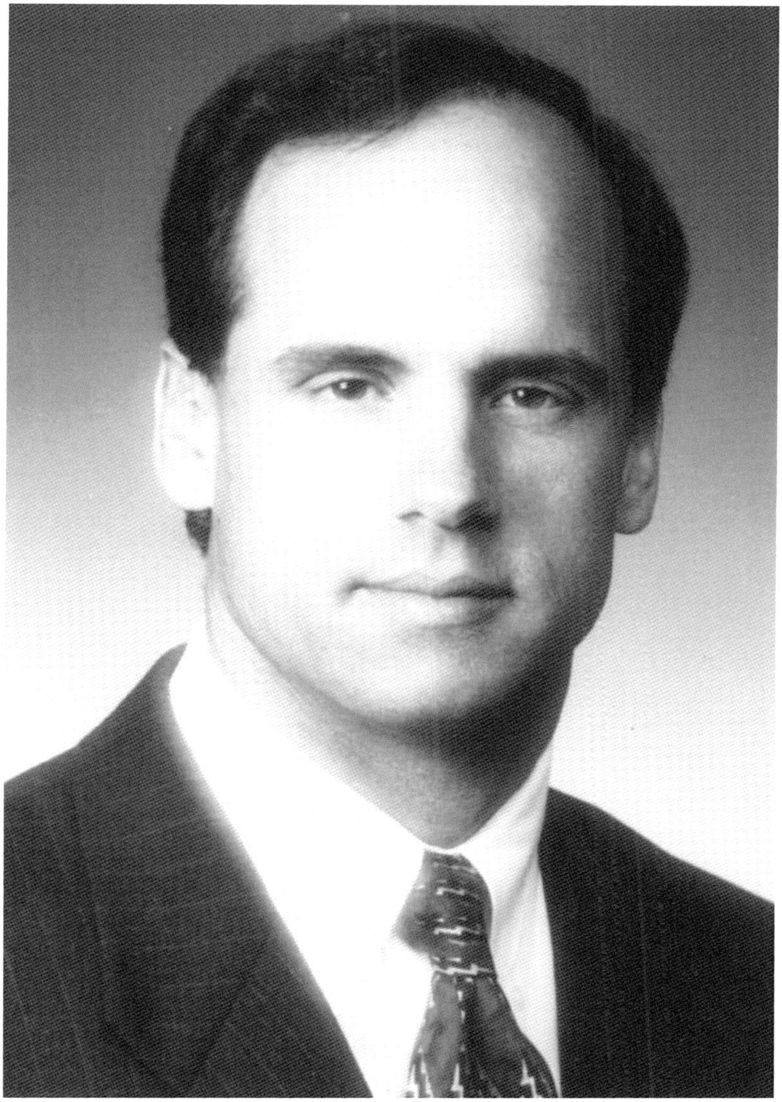

Steve Appleton

Steve Appleton arrived in Boise on a tennis scholarship to Boise State University. Not long after he graduated from BSU in 1982, he went to work for Micron, a new technology company. He started out on the manufacturing line, working the graveyard shift. His willingness to work long hours and study problems to help find solutions, along with his ability to get along with his coworkers, made him a standout employee. In 1994, at age 34, he became the CEO of what was by then a Fortune 500 company. As he achieved success, Appleton never forgot that he had graduated from Boise State University, and became one of the university's biggest supporters, spearheading large donations that resulted in the creation and expansion of programs providing training for workers in the high-tech industry. Following his tragic death in an airplane accident in February 2012, Boise State University chose to honor him with a monument on campus. In September 2014, the nine-foot statue by sculptor Benjamin Victor was placed on the east side of the Micron Business and Economics Building. (Courtesy of University Archives Collection, Boise State University Special Collections Department.)

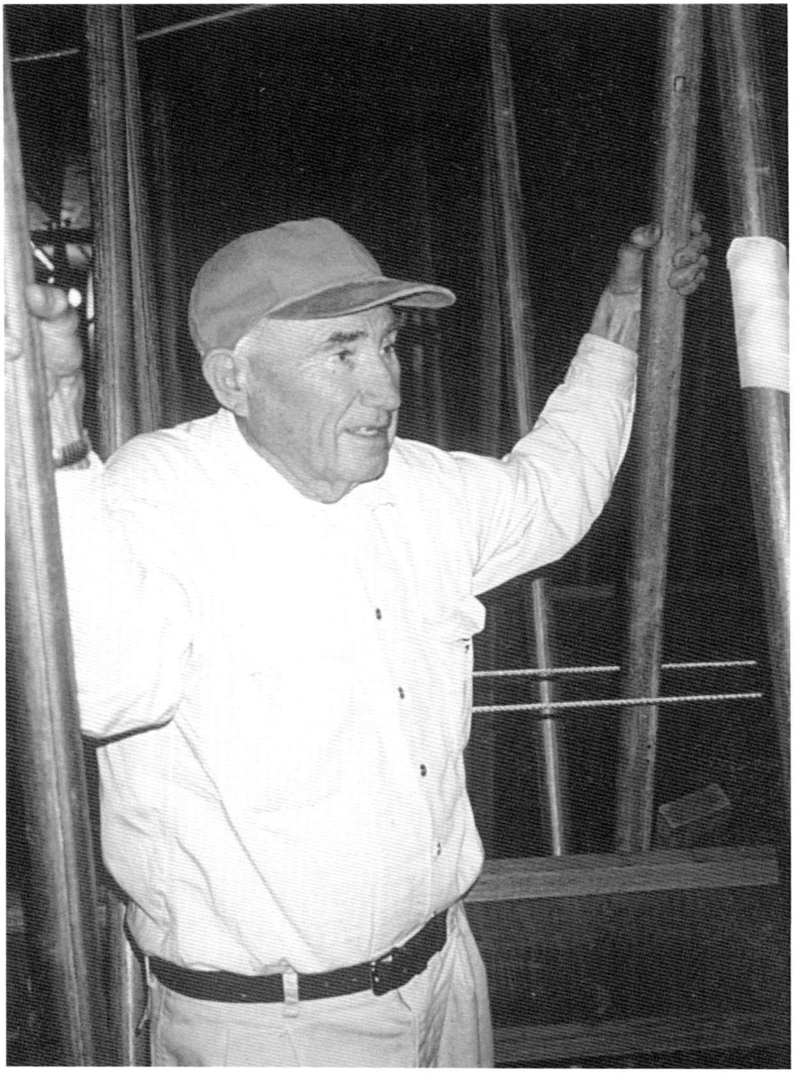

Art Troutner

Innovator, artist, architect, engineer, and businessman are all words that describe Art Troutner. Born Arthur Lowe Troutner in 1921 in the eastern Idaho farming community of Pingree, Troutner grew up on his family's 40-acre sugar-beet and potato farm. When he was 13, he was sent to Boise to live with his grandmother. He attended Boise High School and Boise Junior College. After a tour with the Army Air Corps as a crew chief for heavy bombers, he attended the University of Idaho architecture program, graduating in 1949. He never held an architect's license, but is credited with 60 architectural and engineering projects, including the circular Boise Little Theater and the University of Idaho's barrel-arched Kibbie Activity Center. He also designed homes scattered throughout Boise. His works feature Frank Lloyd Wright–inspired designs and represent the Mid-century Modern style. In 1960, he and Boise native Harold "Red" Thomas met and started Trus Joist Corporation to market and manufacture Troutner's lightweight wood and steel-composite Open-Web truss invention. Trus Joist was acquired in 2009 by Atlas Holding Company. The firm markets open-web trusses based on Art Troutner's designs. (Courtesy of David Nels Reese.)

CHAPTER EIGHT

Home Runs, Touchdowns, and Olympic Gold

Although Boise has no professional athletic teams, the city is familiar to sports fans across the country. Boise State University is home to Bronco Stadium, where the football team plays on the first blue AstroTurf field installed in a football stadium. In 2007, Boise State University gained a national reputation when the football team, pegged as the underdog at the Fiesta Bowl in Glendale, Arizona, beat Oklahoma in overtime. This made the Broncos and Boise famous throughout the country.

Football is not the only game in town. Boise's sporting history dates back to the 1860s, when some of the first baseball games were played here. Officially, horse racing began in 1875, when the Agricultural Park Association purchased land west of downtown and built a racetrack, stables, and seating for spectators. Today, racing continues at Les Bois Park. Polo became popular in the 1920s, when cavalry officers were still stationed at the Boise Barracks. Civilian and military teams competed, and Boise's polo teams became champions throughout the West. The Basques brought *pala* (racketball) and *pelota* (handball) to Boise. At one time, four *frontons* (courts) were located in the city. Today, only one remains, supported by the Boise Fronton Association, formed to preserve a century-old court and the sport. Boise is also known for the Idaho Women's Challenge, which provided female cyclists with a world-class challenge from 1984 to 2002. Besides team sports, individual athletes have brought recognition to the city, too. Herbert Lemp, Wayne Walker, Kristin Armstrong, and Gary Stevens are among those who contribute to Boise's thriving sports scene.

Herbert Lemp

Polo became a popular sport across the United States after it was adopted by Army cavalry units as a way to keep men and horses in shape and active. The first Army polo team was established at Fort Walla Walla, Washington, in 1892. Within a few years, the game had spread to other Army posts, including the Boise Barracks (formerly Fort Boise), where the first exhibition game was played by members of troops K and L of the 14th Cavalry in September 1909. By 1911, Herbert Lemp and several of his friends had formed a civilian team. For the next 40 years, Boiseans attended polo games, with the local lads playing teams from around the West.

Lemp, a talented and popular player, served as captain of the team from its formation until 1927. Under his leadership, the team was successful, hosting a number of regional tournaments. The players and their horses traveled to matches in other locations as well.

In March 1927, comedian Will Rogers, in the middle of a term as honorary mayor of Beverly Hills, came to Boise for a one-night appearance at the Pinney Theatre. A dedicated polo player, he found time to play a match while in town. The Boise team split into two squads for the event. Rogers was captain of one team, and Herbert Lemp headed the other. Rogers's team won. When Lemp was elected mayor of Boise a few weeks later, he invited the comedian back to Boise for a rematch—the two being the only "polo mayors" in the country. Sadly, before the game could be scheduled, and before he ever served a day as mayor, Herbert Lemp fell from his horse at a practice game. He died a few days later of his injuries, only a few hours after taking the oath of office in his hospital room. Over 1,000 people attended Lemp's funeral, and the procession extended from three miles outside of downtown to Morris Hill Cemetery on the Bench. (Courtesy of the Idaho State Historical Society.)

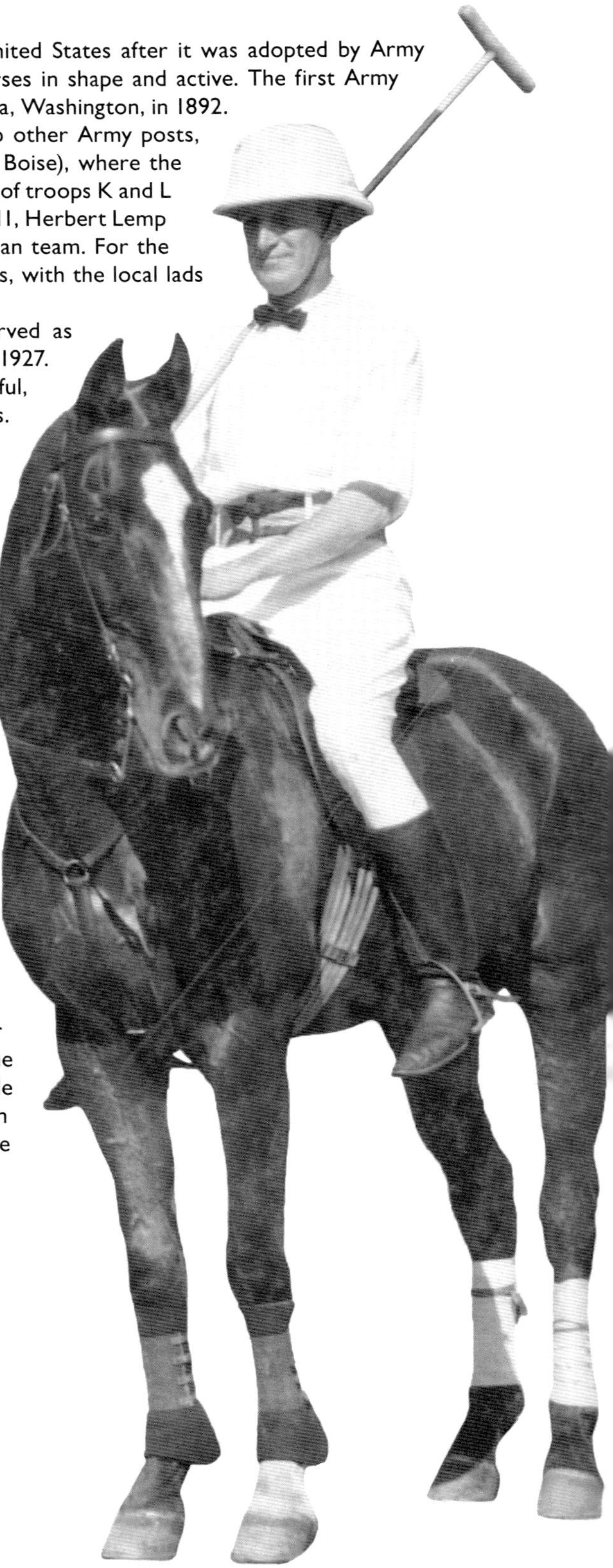

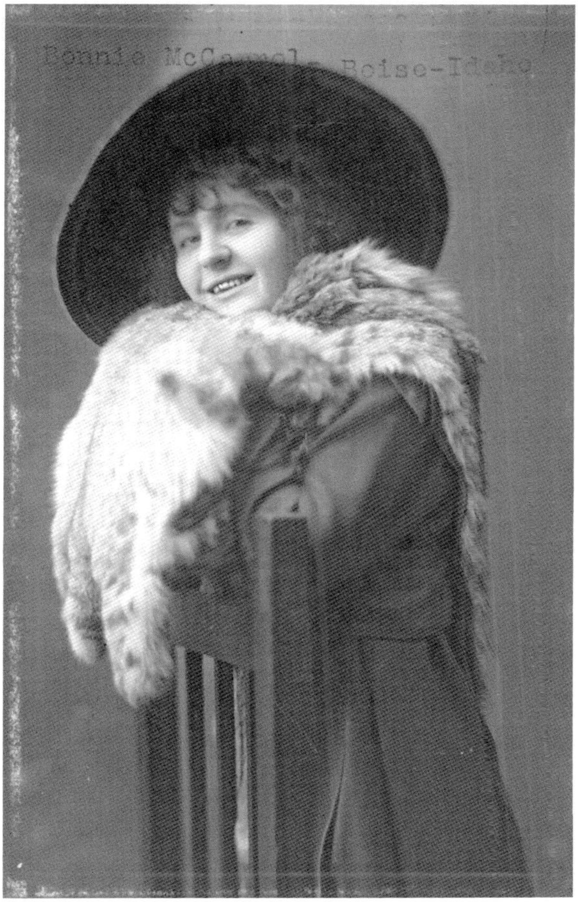

Bonnie McCarroll

On October 1, 1929, the *Idaho Statesman* announced the sad news: "Days of Riding End for Bonnie." Champion cowgirl Bonnie McCarroll had died of injuries sustained during an event at the Pendleton Round-Up. McCarroll was a member of an elite group of cowgirls who dazzled audiences of the early 20th century with feats of horsemanship and courage still talked about today. Mary Ellen "Bonnie" Treadwell was born a short distance from Boise in the small community known as Highland Valley. Growing up on her grandfather's large cattle ranch, she rode her first horse at age 10. At 14, she rode her first bronc, reminiscing later in her life that the horse began to "behave like a wild cat." Undeterred, she started to ride at local fairs in Boise and surrounding towns, eventually meeting Frank McCarroll, champion steer bulldogger, wrestler, and boxer. The "buckaroo boxer" and cowgirl were married in November 1914. A few years later, the couple began to travel the rodeo circuit. Bonnie made history in 1922 by winning the cowgirl bronc-riding championship at the two most prestigious rodeos in the nation at that time, Cheyenne Frontier Days and the first Madison Square Garden Rodeo. Slight of build and weighing between 95 and 112 pounds, she was a tough competitor. When she won the world championship at the Frontier Days, the judges unanimously agreed that "Mrs. McCarroll won on the merits of skill, horsewomanship, and nerve." She competed not only in the United States, but also in England, including rodeos at Wimbledon Stadium. During time off from the rodeo circuit, Bonnie and Frank made their home in Boise, where they planned to retire prior to her untimely death. After her accident, women's bronc riding was never again included in the Pendleton Round-Up; eventually, the incident led to the exclusion of women from the rodeo arena. (Courtesy of the Idaho State Historical Society.)

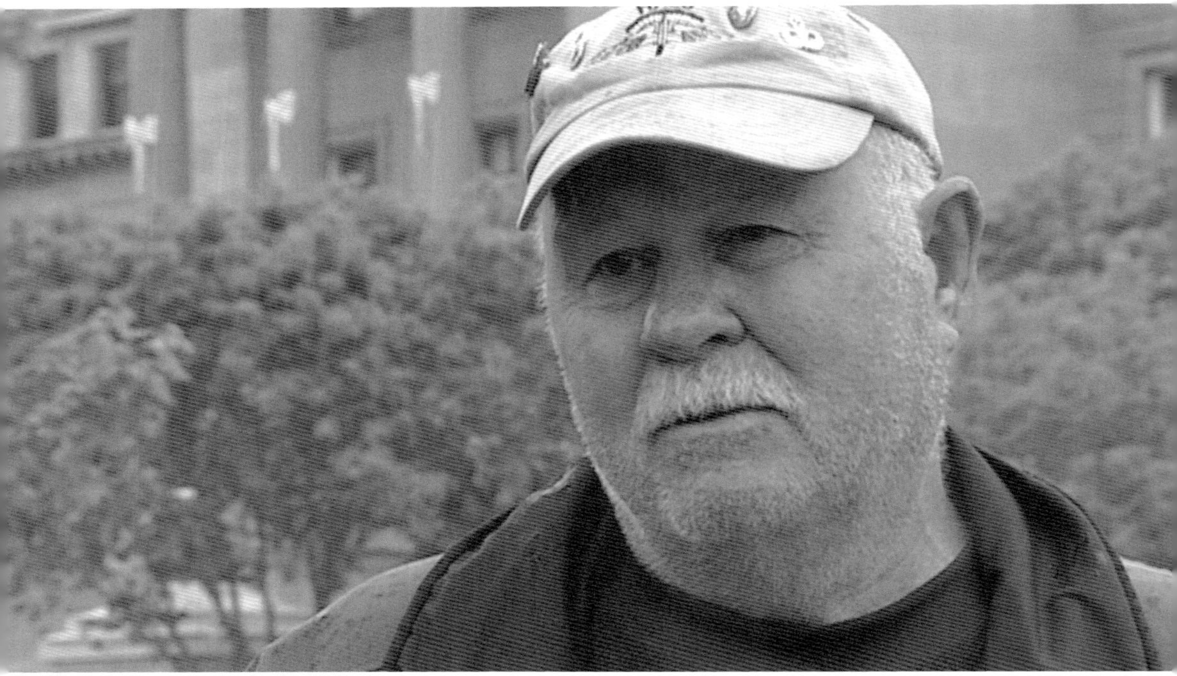

Jim Rabdau

In 1984, Jim Rabdau, a former Green Beret and cycling enthusiast, conceived a challenging bicycle road race for women. Rabdau believed that women could meet more strenuous challenges in competitive sports than were available to them at the time. He convinced Ore-Ida, a Boise-based frozen-food company, to sponsor the race, which it did until 1999.

From 1984 until 2002, Boise was home to the Idaho Women's Challenge, a women's cycling event that eventually attracted riders from 30 countries and gained a reputation for being one of the world's toughest courses. The race attracted more than 1,700 competitors, including a number of Olympic cyclists, and awarded more than $1 million in prizes. Later sponsors included PowerBar and Hewlett-Packard, but support sputtered in the shaky economy of the early 21st century, and efforts to find a sponsor in 2003 failed. The Idaho Women's Challenge inspired many young athletes and created an annual event that Boiseans who witnessed it will never forget. (Courtesy of Idaho Public Televsion.)

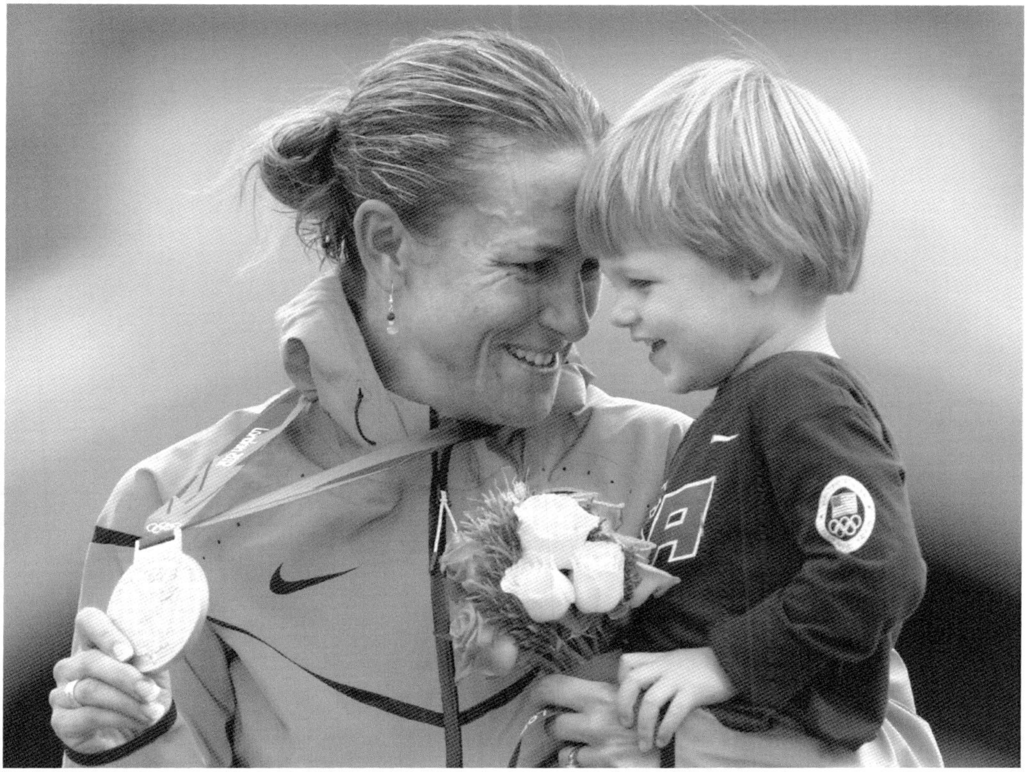

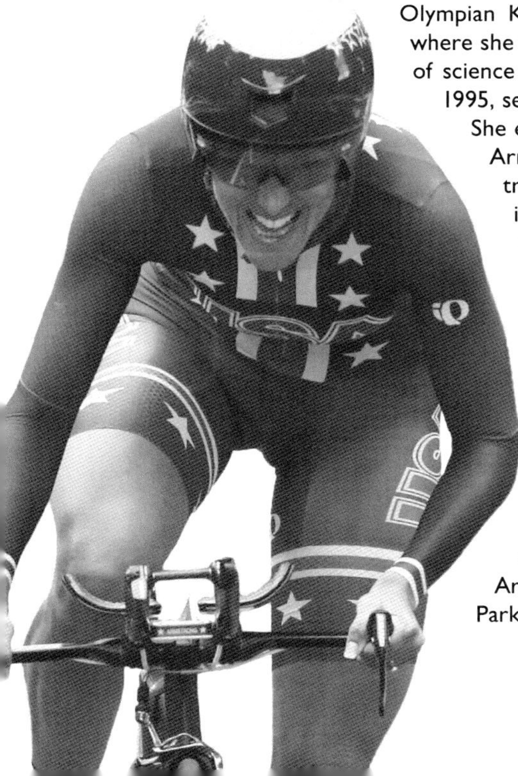

Kristin Armstrong Savola

Olympian Kristin Armstrong attended the University of Idaho, where she was active in intramural sports and earned a bachelor of science degree in sports physiology. She moved to Boise in 1995, serving as director of aquatics at the downtown YMCA. She experienced a renewed interest in competitive sports. Armstrong was training for the 2004 Olympics as a triathlete when she was diagnosed with osteoarthritis in 2001, which meant she could no longer run. She considered relinquishing her Olympic dream, but friends (including future husband Jim Savola) encouraged her to reconsider and concentrate on cycling, her strongest sport. Within a year, she won a spot on the HP Idaho Women's Challenge. Recruited by coach Jim Miller for the T-Mobile team, Armstrong attended the 2004 Olympics, riding to eighth place in the women's road race. She is the most successful female cyclist in US history, with two Olympic gold medals, three world titles, five national championships, and many other honors and awards. In 2014, the City of Boise dedicated the Kristin Armstrong Trail, a bike trail for children, at Boise Hills Park. (Courtesy of Kristin Armstrong Savola.)

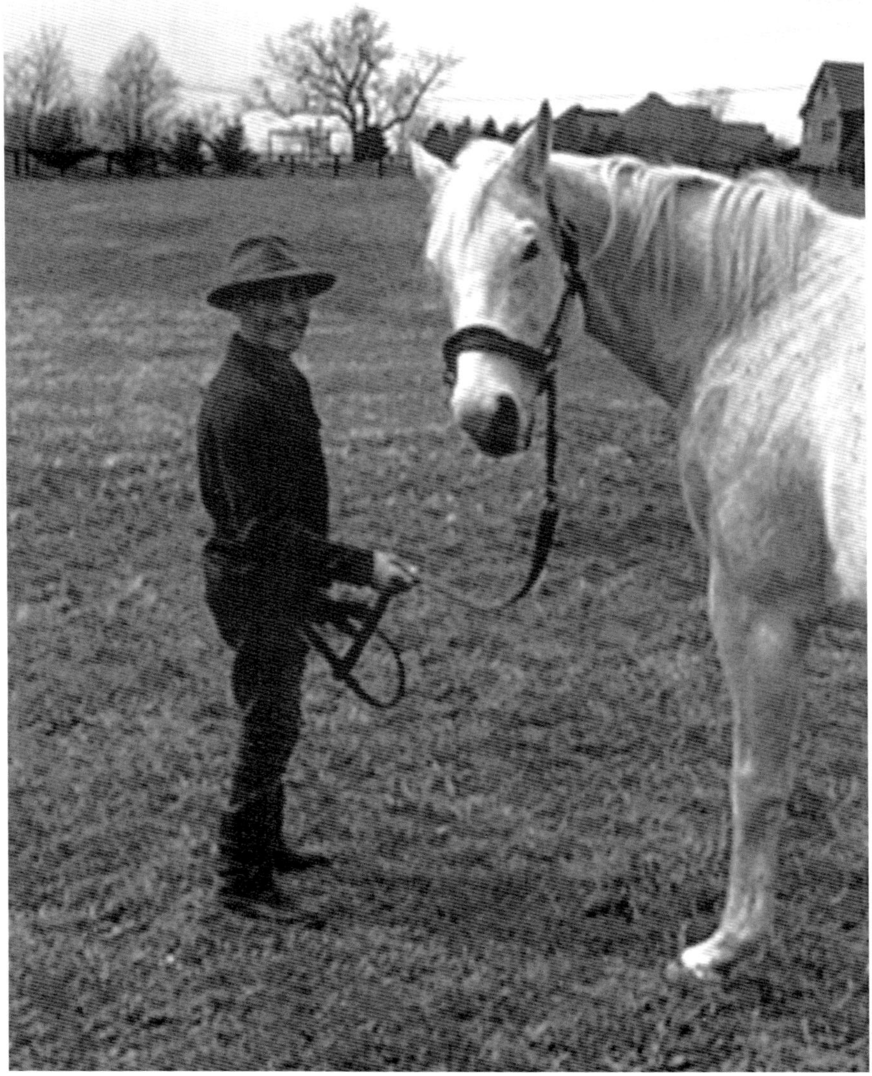

Gary Stevens
Stevens won his first race at age 16 in 1979 when he rode Lil Star, a horse his dad, Ron, had trained, at Boise's Les Bois Park. This was not only his first winning ride—it was his first race. Within a few years, Stevens had moved on to Washington and then to California. In 1988, he won his first Kentucky Derby. Since then, he has ridden to victory in an additional eight races on the Triple Crown circuit, along with other victories, including the Japan Cup, the Dubai International Cup, and the Canadian Stakes, which he won twice. He has won the Santa Anita Derby nine times. In 1993, he became the youngest jockey to achieve $100 million in winnings, and in 1997, Stevens was inducted into the National Racing Hall of Fame. He retired in 2005, but came out of retirement in 2013, winning the Preakness that year on Oxbow. In addition to his amazing racing career, Gary Stevens appeared in the Academy Award–nominated film *Seabiscuit*, and played a major role in the HBO series *Luck*. (Courtesy of Angie Stevens.)

Wayne Walker

Growing up in Boise, all Wayne Walker wanted to do was play sports. And he did, first for Boise High, then for the University of Idaho. He was a fourth-round draft choice of the Detroit Lions in 1958. Walker played 15 years for the team before retiring at the end of the 1972 season, stating, "One reason I have retired was that I felt my God-given abilities had taken me as far as they could. I never considered myself a superstar, just a good football player." Walker worked part-time as a sportscaster in Detroit during his off-season with the Lions. After retiring, he entered broadcasting full time, doing weekend sports on a local television station in Detroit before relocating to San Francisco, where he worked as sports director for KPIX-TV. When he left Boise, he knew he would return; in 1994, he moved back to his boyhood home. (Courtesy of University Archives, Boise State University Special Collections Department.)

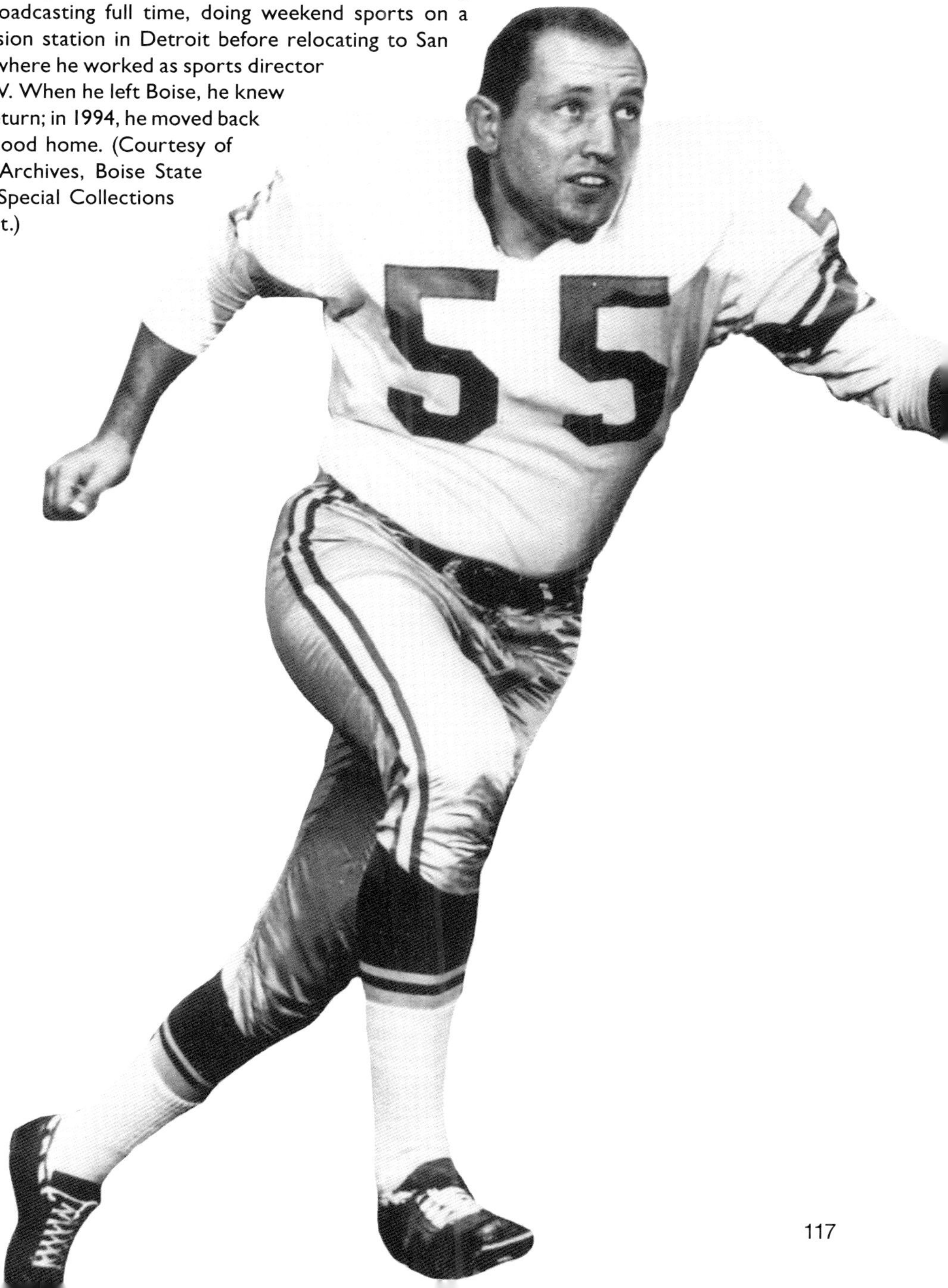

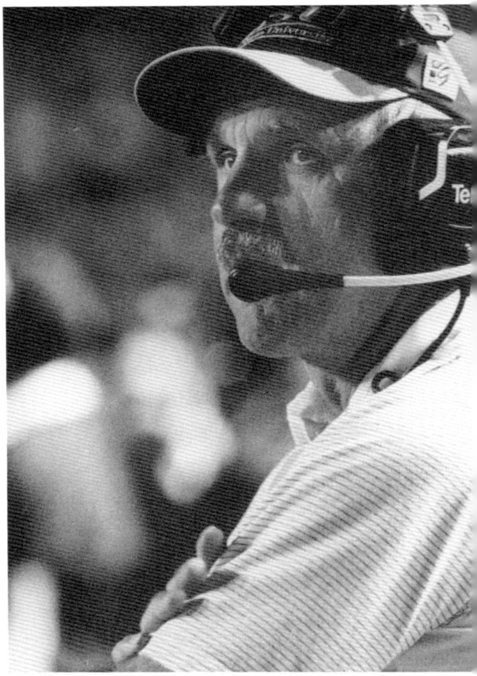

Ernest "Pokey" Allen

Credited with changing the face of the Boise State University football team, "Pokey" Allen was the head coach at BSU from 1993 until 1996. He grew up in Missoula, Montana, graduated from high school in 1962, then played quarterback for the University of Utah. After college, Allen played three seasons in the Canadian Football League. He started his coaching career in 1968 as an assistant coach at Simon Fraser University in British Columbia. Several assistant-coach jobs later, he was hired as head coach at Portland State University. In 1992, after his team defeated the Boise State Broncos, BSU hired Allen and his entire coaching staff. In 1994, they led the team to a 10-1 regular season record, a Big Sky championship, and the IAA national championship game against Youngstown State. Allen was also noted for his exuberant personality. Diagnosed with a rare form of cancer in late 1994, he faced the disease with courage and with one rule that he refused to break: Have fun—and don't let cancer get in your way. (Courtesy of University Archives, Boise State University Special Collections Department.)

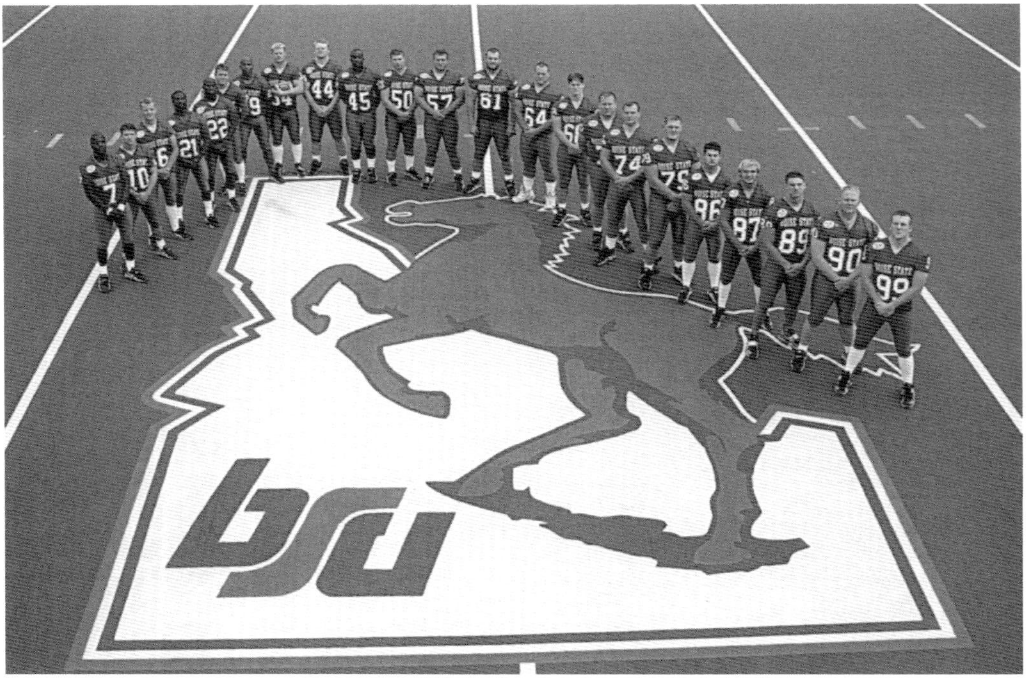

Boise State University

The blue turf of the Boise State Broncos is known by football players and fans nationwide. The unconventional playing surface was installed in 1986. (Courtesy of the Boise State University Library Special Collections Department.)

CHAPTER NINE

Out of the Ordinary

Every town has interesting people, buildings, and events that are hard to categorize but lend character to a community. Boise is universally known for its geothermal water and was the first city in the world to use it to heat businesses and residences. At one time, the city had a sizeable Chinese population, comprising large numbers of immigrants who followed the mining boom. A persistent urban myth claims there is a network of opium tunnels under the city streets. Boise has always been a city of celebrations, looking for any excuse to have a parade. The city has hosted Fourth of July parades and circus parades, complete with costumes, characters, and floats. Of these events, Hornika Brinika is perhaps the most unusual. Folklore, people, and events are all threads that make up the fabric of Boise's character.

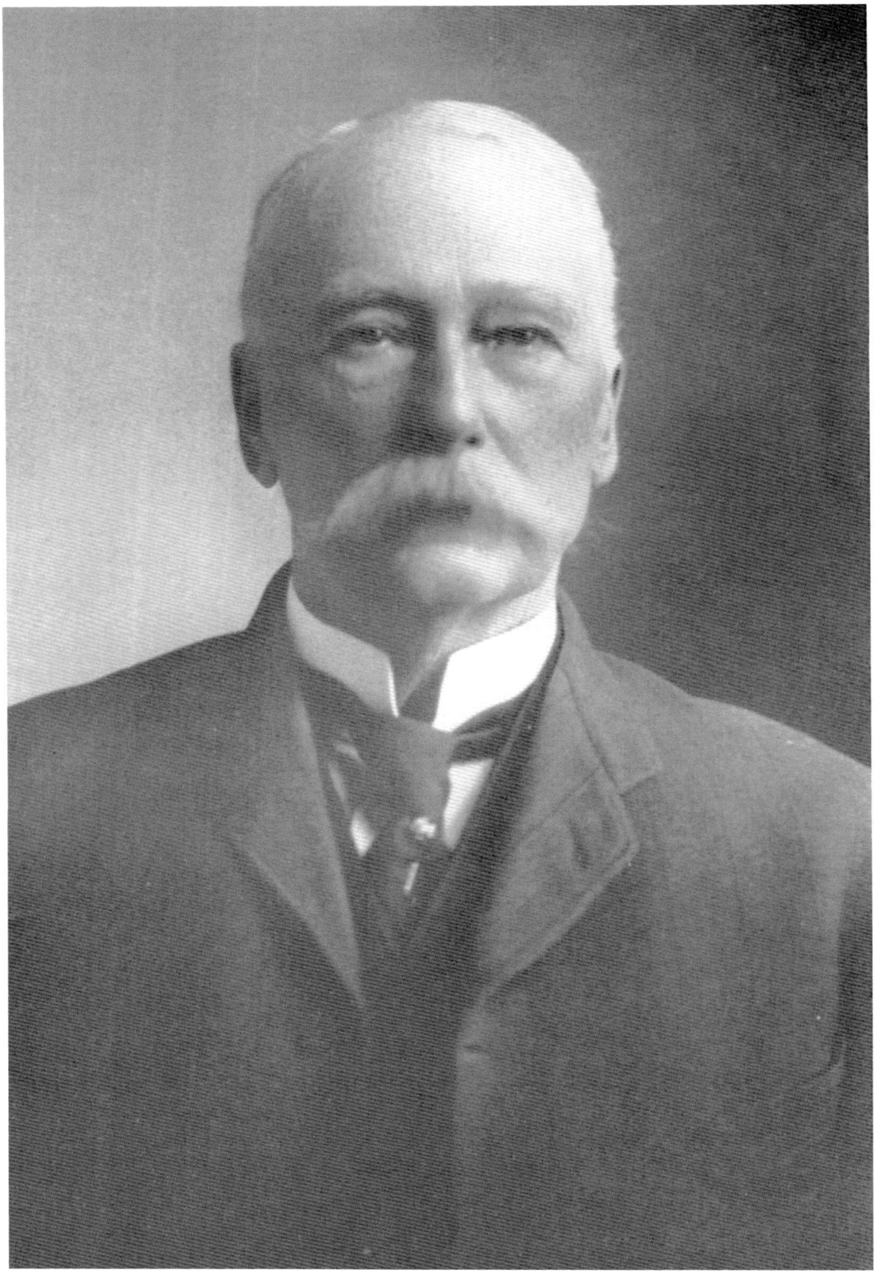

Hosea B. Eastman

Eastman was part of a group of businessmen who organized the Artesian Hot & Cold Water Company in 1891. Eastman and his brother Benjamin had interests in several hotels in Silver City and Ruby City, nearby mining towns in the 1860s. In 1877, the brothers bought the Overland Hotel in Boise and managed it until 1891. Eastman built the first water system in the city, the Boise Water Works, which later merged with the Artesian Hot & Cold Water Company. Investors included C.W. Moore, William Ridenbaugh, Nathan Falk, and Thomas Davis. (Authors' collection.)

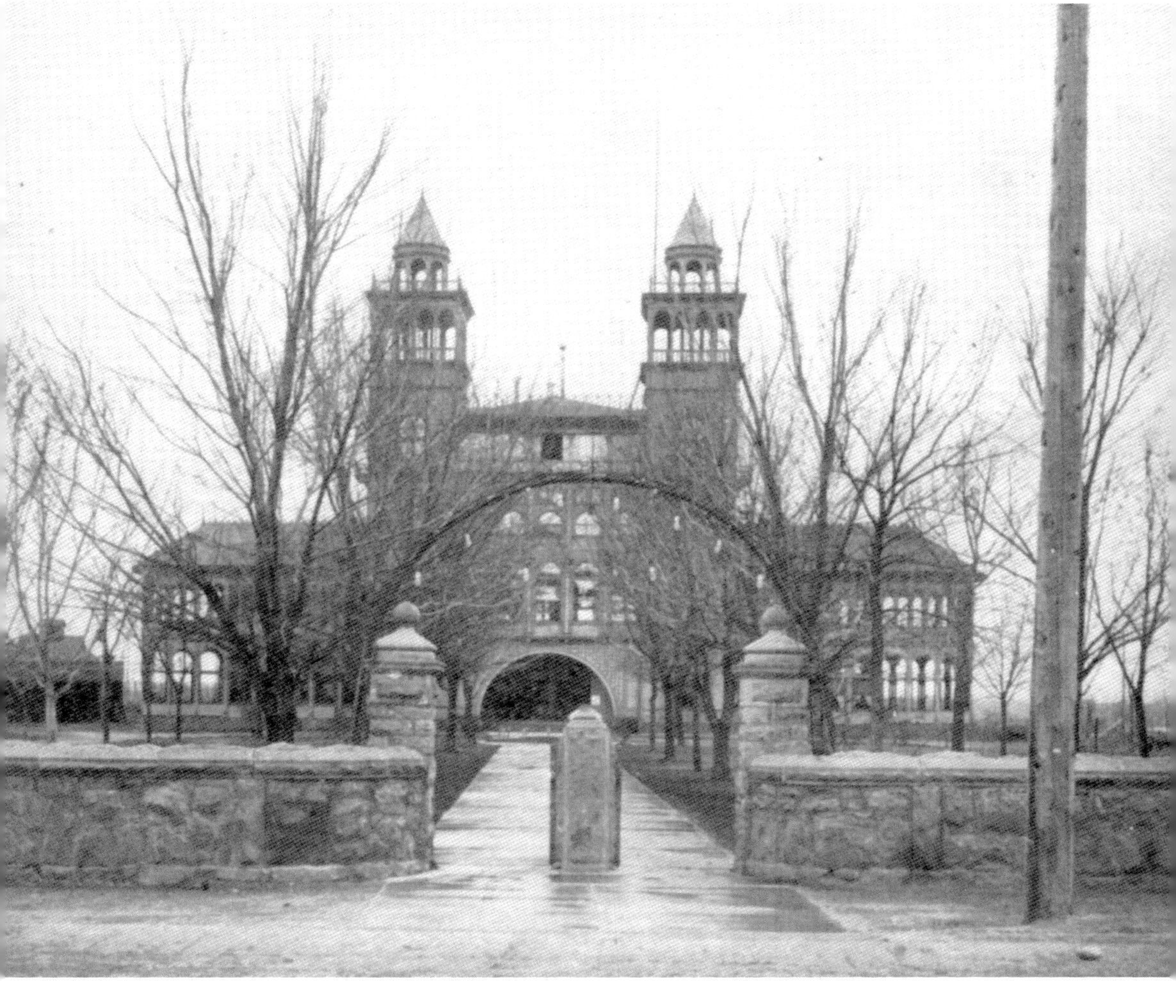

The Natatorium

The Artesian Hot & Cold Water Company drilled the first hot-water well in town, at the eastern edge of the city limits. The company laid hot-water pipes along Warm Springs Avenue. To use the hot water and attract customers, it opened the Natatorium at the end of the avenue in 1892. James Paulsen, an architect from Montana, designed the towering two-story building, which included Turkish baths, smoking rooms, and a pool that could be covered with a wooden floor for dances. Damaged by high winds in a summer storm, the building was razed in the 1930s. (Authors' collection.)

George Washington Stilts

In the 1890s, when Boise began to see itself as a modern city, the *Idaho Statesman* published lists of pioneers of the 1860s. Among the names was George Washington Stilts. Little is known about him before his arrival in Boise. He was established as a blacksmith in Boise by 1865, the same year he married Ellen Finnessy and settled down to life as a businessman.

Stilts was a prankster whose practical jokes and antics were frequently reported in the newspaper. Along with pranks, such as catching a neighbor's dog, shaving it, then painting it, or pretending to be deaf when called for jury duty, George Washington Stilts created two long-forgotten customs—the Third House, a mock legislature that met erratically during the legislative sessions of the territorial legislature, and Horniki Brinika, a fool's festival celebrated in conjunction with Independence Day. The Third House included some members of the actual legislature, along with less public-service-oriented citizens. The group elected the same officers as the territorial government and enacted legislation, usually parodying the laws of the current session. Horniki Brinika also made fun of political figures and community leaders. Dressed in costume, the "Horrible Hornies" were included in the official program for Independence Day, usually appearing at the end of the parade. When Stilts died in 1894, so did the traditions he created. Horniki Brinika came back in 1913, when several of the remaining pioneers of the 1860s insisted on reviving it for the 50th anniversary of Boise's founding, although no one knew the "official" spelling of the festival's name. Stilts's friends said he invented the moniker. No photograph is known to exist of Stilts. The sign for his business appears at left in this early photograph. (Courtesy of the Idaho State Historical Society.)

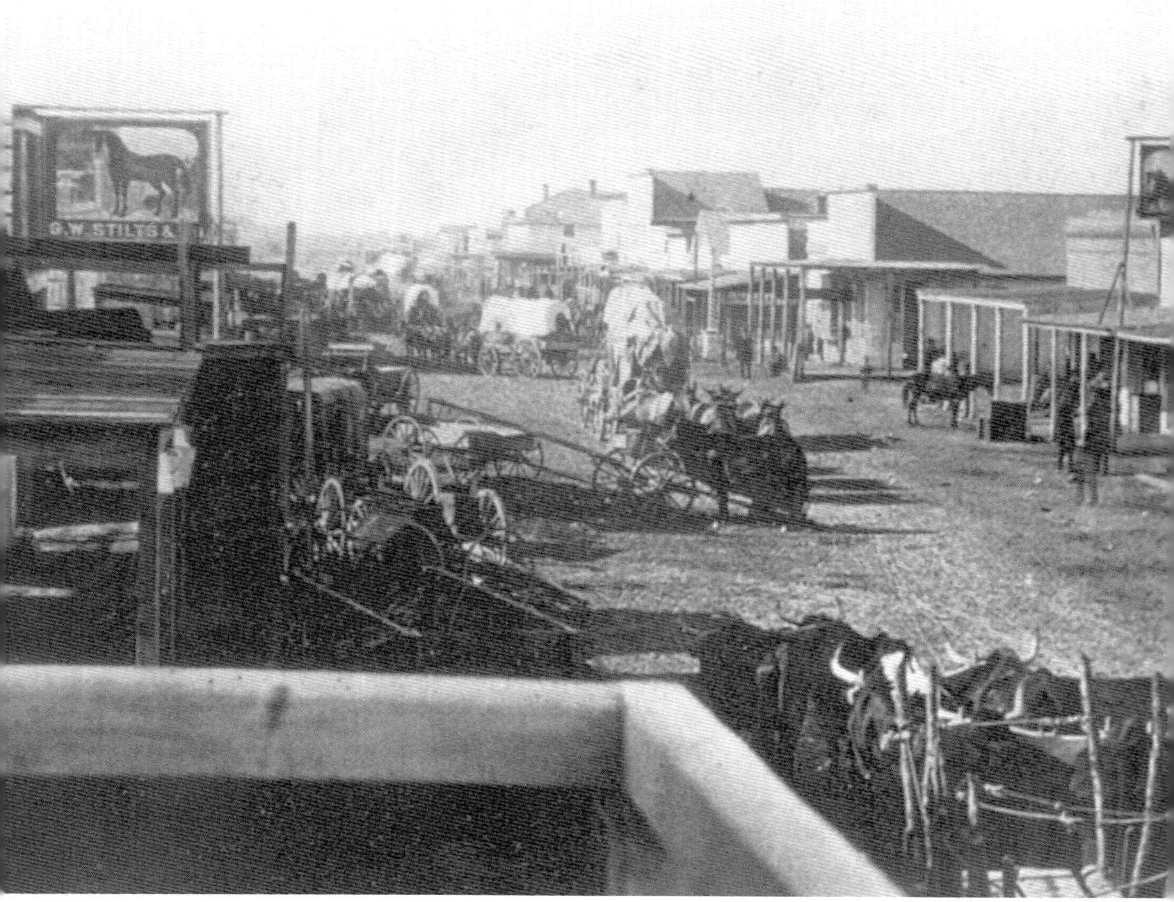

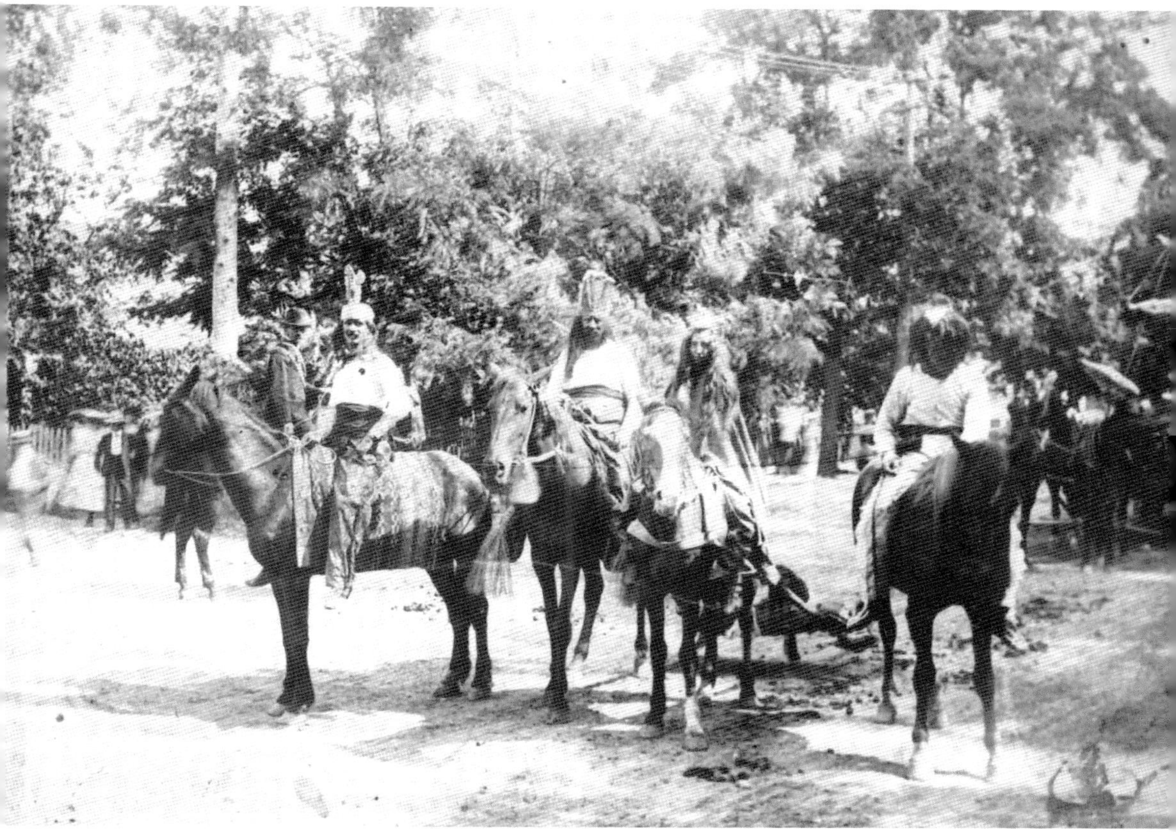

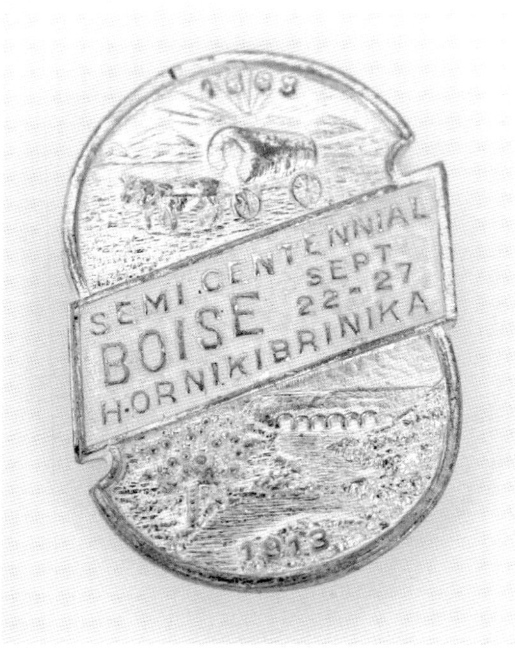

Horniki Brinika

Shown above is a group of "Horrible Hornies," participants in a Horniki Brinika event. Organized for the first time by prankster George W. Stilts for Independence Day in 1872, Horniki Brinika was a regular feature of the holiday in Boise until Stilts's death in 1894. Newspaper reports never provided a consistent spelling for the name. The event came back in 1913, when several of the remaining pioneers of the 1860s insisted on reviving it for the 50th anniversary of Boise's founding. Participants in the group wore pins like the one pictured at left. (Above, courtesy of the Idaho State Historical Society; left, courtesy Mark Baltes, photograph by Melanie Folwell.)

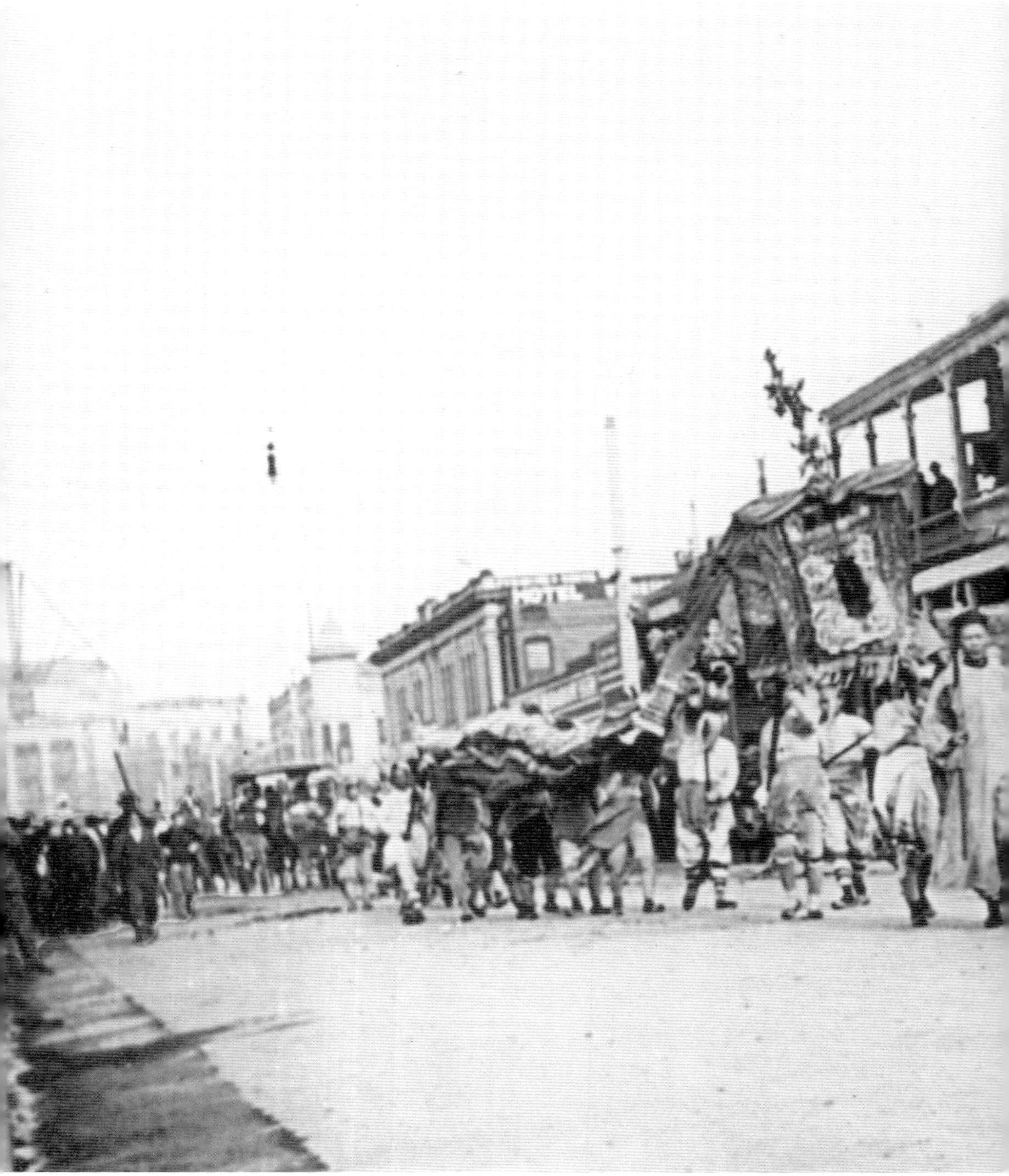

Chinese Tunnels

Although few Chinese remain in Boise, the story of Chinese tunnels in Boise's underground persists to this day. Legend of the tunnels took shape after the Idaho legislature passed a law in 1881 prohibiting smoking opium in public places. Legend has it that opium dens were moved underground, and the

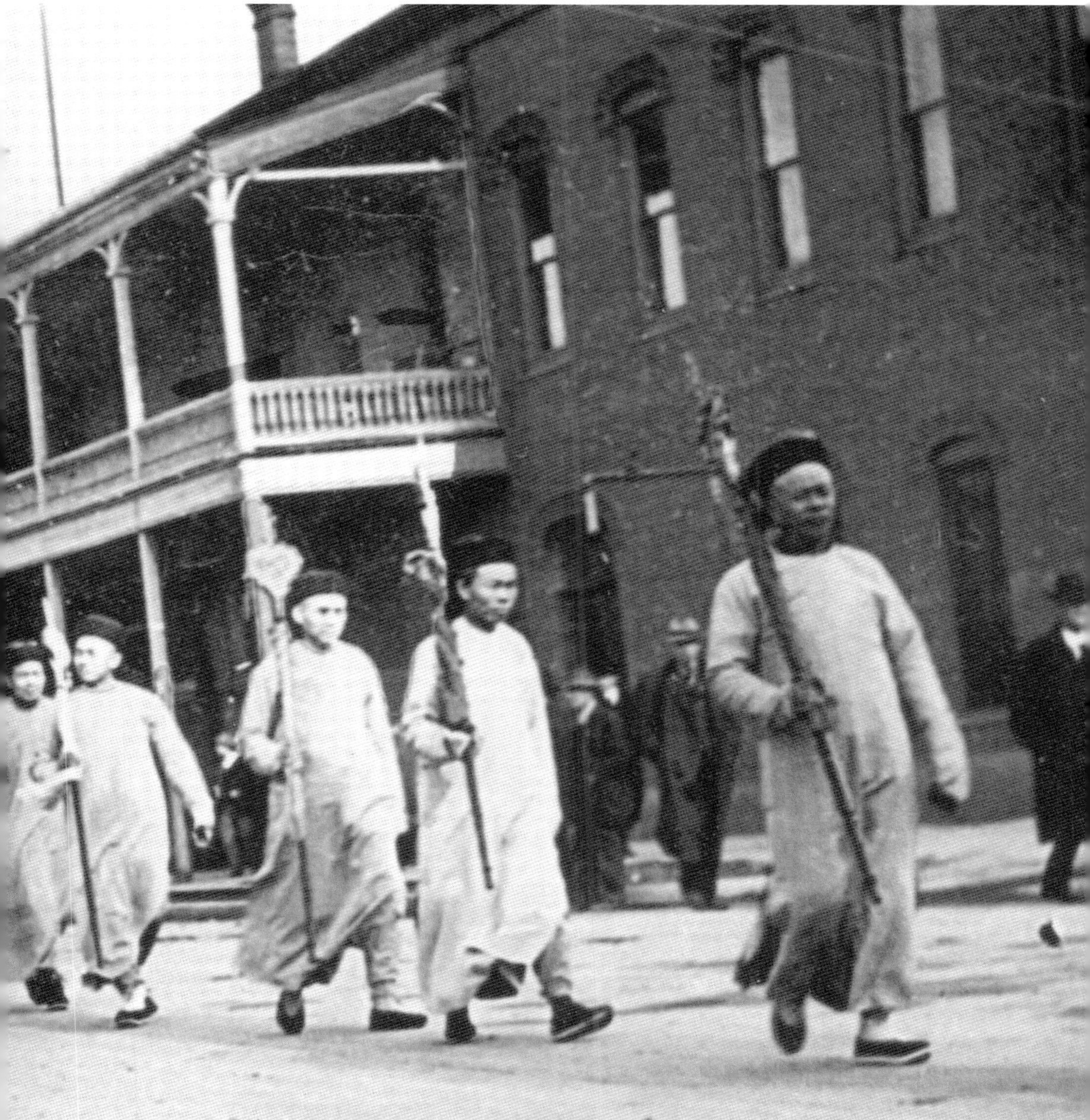

story of Chinese tunnels was born. Here, Chinese residents parade on Seventh Street around 1908. (Courtesy of the Idaho State Historical Society.)

BIBLIOGRAPHY

Arrington, Leonard J. *History of Idaho.* Moscow, ID: University of Idaho Press, 1994.

Hart, Arthur A. *The Boiseans: At Home.* Boise, ID: Historic Boise Inc., 1992.

Hummel, Charles Frederick, Tim Woodward, Jeanne Huff, Todd A. Shallat, and Otto Kitsinger. *Quintessential Boise: An Architectural Journey.* Boise, ID: Boise State University, College of Social Sciences and Public Affairs, 2010.

Idaho Centennial Commission, and Idaho Centennial Foundation. *Here We Have Idaho: People Make the Difference.* Boise, ID: Idaho Centennial Foundation Inc. by the Idaho Centennial Homecoming Committee, produced by *Boise* magazine (Idaho Annual Inc.), 1990.

Idaho Daily Statesman. Boise, ID. 1864–2002, online and microfilmed versions.

Memories: Joe Albertson. Boise, ID: Albertson's Inc., 1993.

Morrison, Velma V., and Kitty Delorey Fleischman. *The Bluebird Will Sing Tomorrow: Memoirs of Velma V. Morrison.* Boise, ID: Idaho Heritage Pub, 2003.

Penson-Ward, Betty. *Idaho Women in History: Big and Little Biographies and Other Gender Stories.* Boise, ID: Legendary Pub. Co., 1991.

Schwantes, Carlos A. *In Mountain Shadows: A History of Idaho.* Lincoln, NE: University of Nebraska Press, 1991.

Shallat, Todd A. *Ethnic Landmarks: Ten Historic Places That Define the City of Trees.* Boise, ID: Boise City Office of the Historian, 2007.

Sims, Robert C., and Hope A. Benedict. *Idaho's Governors: Historical Essays on Their Administrations.* Boise, ID: Boise State University College of Social Sciences and Public Affairs, 1992.

Wells, Merle W., and Arthur A. Hart. *Boise: An Illustrated History.* Woodland Hills, CA: Windsor Publications, 1982.

INDEX

Adams, Hortense, 31
Ah Fong, C.K., 57
Ailshie, Margaret Cobb, 34
Albertson, Joe, 102
Alexander, Moses, 28
Anderson, C.C., 107
Andrus, Cecil D., 48
Ann Morrison Park, 96
Appleton, Steve, 109
Armstrong, Kristin, 115
Bertram, John, 50
Bisterfeldt, Vern, 47
Boise City Arts and History Dept., 100
Borah, Mary "Mamie" McConnell, 46
Borah, William Edgar, 45
Bown, Joseph, 14
Bown House, 14
Buckner-Webb, Cherie, 63
Carley, Joan, 58
Cartee, Lafayette, 15
Chaffee, Eugene, 69
Christ Chapel, 17
Church, Bethine, 62
Church, Frank, 61
Cobb, Calvin, 33
Collins, Kent, 104
Collister, George, 39
Collister, Mary, 40
Columbian Club, 22
Columbia Theater, 76
Corlett, John, 38
Cosho, Maude, 108
Davis, Hester, 23
Davis, Julia, 11
Davis, Thomas, 11
Day, Samuel H. Jr., 53
Depot Motor Court, 42
Diamond Tooth Lil, 42
Dockery, Eva Hunt, 37
Doerr, Anthony, 85
Fackler, St. Michael, 16
Falk, Nathan, 106
Flying M, 104
Fong, Billy, 60
Foote, Mary Hallock, 72
Gillett, Will, 104
Green, Emma Edwards, 74
Hart, Arthur, 92
Hawley, James, 44
Hochstrasser, Gib, 84
Hogan, James, 32
Hormachea, Juanita, 54
Horniki Brinika, 123
Hummel, Charles Frederick, 94
Idaho Women's Challenge, 114
Jacobs, Cyrus, 12
Jausoro, Jimmy, 82
Jordan, J.O., 105
Jordan, J.C. "Cecil," 105
Julia Davis Park, 11
Kelly, Milton, 29
Kelly's Hot Springs, 29
Kempthorne, Dirk, 64
Klein, Edith Miller, 60
Lemp, Herman, 112
Lippincott, Lucille, 73
Lugenbeel, Pinckney, 10
McCarroll, Bonnie, 130
Mann, Cynthia, 70
Miller Helen, 67
Moore, C.W., 26
Morrison, Ann, 96
Morrison, Harry, 96, 103
Morrison, Velma, 79
Moulton, Elvina, 18
Nelson, Morlan "Morely," 51
Norman, Fred, 80
Oliver, Mamie, 68
Onweiler, Bill, 98
Penson-Ward, Betty, 37
Peterson, Dan, 89
Pierce, Walter E., 93
Pinney, James, 75
Preservation Idaho, 59
Rabdau, Jim, 114
Reed, Mary Maxine "Sally," 52
Revere, Paul, 87
Ridenbaugh, Mary Black, 20
Ridenbaugh, William, 21
Roach, William F. "Doc," 55
Schorzman, Terri, 114, 115
Shuler, Marilyn, 49
Simplot, Adelia Garro, 97
Simplot, J.R., 119
Sorrels, Rosalie, 86
Stevens, Gary, 116
Stigers, Curtis, 88
Stilts, George Washington, 122
Stringfellow, Nancy, 78
Swarthout, Jon, 83
The Book Shop, 78
Tourtellotte, John, 94
TrICA, 83
Troutner, Art, 128
Villeneuve, Nick, 77
Urquides, Jesus, 13
Ustick, Harlan P., 56
Walker, Wayne, 117
Wells, Merle, 66
West, John, 24
Wilson, Jean, 78
Wood, Fremont, 23
Zulaika, Juan, 82